Firms of Endearment

Firms of Endearment

How World-Class Companies Profit from
Passion and Purpose

Second Edition

Raj Sisodia
Jag Sheth
David Wolfe

Vice President, Publisher: Tim Moore
Associate Publisher and Director of Marketing: Amy Neidlinger
Executive Editor: Jeanne Glasser Levine
Development Editor: Natasha Torres
Operations Specialist: Jodi Kemper
Cover Designer: Chuti Prasertsith
Managing Editor: Kristy Hart
Project Editor: Elaine Wiley
Copy Editor: Bart Reed
Proofreader: Williams Woods Publishing
Indexer: Lisa Stumpf
Senior Compositor: Gloria Schurick
Manufacturing Buyer: Dan Uhrig

© 2014 by Rajendra S. Sisodia, Jagdish N. Sheth, and the Estate of David Wolfe
Published by Pearson Education
Upper Saddle River, New Jersey 07458

For information about buying this title in bulk quantities, or for special sales opportunities (which may include electronic versions; custom cover designs; and content particular to your business, training goals, marketing focus, or branding interests), please contact our corporate sales department at corpsales@pearsoned.com or (800) 382-3419.

For government sales inquiries, please contact governmentsales@pearsoned.com.

For questions about sales outside the U.S., please contact international@pearsoned.com.

Company and product names mentioned herein are the trademarks or registered trademarks of their respective owners.

Printed in the United States of America

6   16

ISBN-10: 0-13-338259-1
ISBN-13: 978-0-13-338259-4

Pearson Education LTD.
Pearson Education Australia PTY, Limited.
Pearson Education Singapore, Pte. Ltd.
Pearson Education Asia, Ltd.
Pearson Education Canada, Ltd.
Pearson Educación de Mexico, S.A. de C.V.
Pearson Education—Japan
Pearson Education Malaysia, Pte. Ltd.

Library of Congress Control Number: 2013954305

*We dedicate this book to the memory of our
dear friend David Wolfe—
a deep thinker, brilliant writer,
and wise and caring human being.
Our lives and those of countless others were
greatly enriched by his presence.*

—Raj Sisodia and Jag Sheth

Contents

Forewords x

Prologue   A Whole New World... xxi

Chapter 1   Building Business on Love and Care 1
            The Power of Love.. 4
            What Is a Firm of Endearment? 6
            FoE Stakeholders.. 11
            Identifying the Original Firms of Endearment 12
            Firms of Endearment vs. Good to Great Companies 15
            Selecting Companies for the Second Edition.................... 16
            The Unspoken Contract That FoEs Honor...................... 20
            The FoE Way... 22
            Endnotes 24

Chapter 2   New Age, New Rules, New Capitalism.......................27
            The Self-Actualization of Capitalism................................. 29
            Shareholders versus Stakeholders.. 34
            Emotionally Intelligent Management in FoEs.................. 38
            Finding the Will to Change 40
            Endnotes 44

Chapter 3   Dealing with Disorder 49
            The Communications Challenge............................ 52
            Endnotes 57

Chapter 4   Employees: From Resource to Source 59
            FoEs Put Meaning into the Work Experience 62
            The Partnership Advantage in Management-Union
            Relationships 65
            Building Trust 67
            The Joy of Work.. 69
            Training and Development Are Priorities in FoEs 75
            Recognition and Celebration Have High Priority
            in FoEs 77
            How FoEs View Part-Time Employees............................ 78
            Connecting Top to Bottom...................................... 79

The HR Department of the Future 80

Benefits That Flow to Shareholders from
Doing It Right 81

Endnotes 83

Chapter 5   Customers: Healing vs. Hucksterism 87

The New Marketing Paradigm 87

A New Consciousness 93

It's Not News: Committed Employees Yield
Committed Customers 96

How Not to Build Trust 99

FoEs Are Soulful 101

Endnotes 102

Chapter 6   Investors: Reaping What FoEs Sow 105

The Whole Foods Way to Shareholder Wealth 106

Who Are Today's Investors? 107

The Zen Way of Viewing the Pursuit of Profit 109

Bonding Investors, Employees, and Customers 112

Shareholder Returns 113

Conclusion 117

Endnotes 117

Chapter 7   Partners: Elegant Harmonies 119

Measures That Matter 122

Stakeholder Concinnity vs. Exploitation 126

Making Stakeholders Partners Increases Success
Potential 127

Collaboration Is More Profitable Than Exploitation 132

The Art of Ironic Management 134

Endnotes 139

Chapter 8   Society: The Ultimate Stakeholder 141

Business Values vs. Human Values 142

Pirate or Great Humanitarian? 144

FoEs and Society 146

Endnotes 161

Chapter 9   Culture: The Secret Ingredient 163

The Greatest Place to Work? 163

The Primacy of Culture 166

Unleashing Organizational Energy 169

Setting Organizational Vision: Seeing the
Larger Picture 169

Nurturing Organizational Values by Building
Endearing Cultures.. 178

FoE Cultural Characteristics............................... 179

Culture = DNA 186

Endnotes 187

Chapter 10   What We Have Learned 191

Distinguishing Traits of Firms of Endearment 191

Challenging Industry Dogma 192

Aligning Stakeholders' Interests............................ 193

Breaking Traditional Trade-Offs 196

A Long-Term Perspective 198

Organic Growth 199

Blending Work and Play...................................... 199

Rejecting Traditional Marketing Models.................. 201

Conclusion... 201

Endnotes 202

Chapter 11   The Other Side of Complexity 205

The Big Challenge of the Times: Transcending a
Zero Sum Mindset 211

FoE Management Requires Holistic Thinking 215

Getting to the "Other Side of Complexity"...................... 217

Conclusion... 220

Endnotes 222

Appendix A   Brief Company Profiles 223

U.S. Public Firms of Endearment.................................. 223

U.S. Private Firms of Endearment 235

Non-U.S. Companies... 247

Endnotes 252

Appendix B   Interview with Rick Frazier..257

Index..267

Forewords

Foreword to the First Edition

Television producer and writer Norman Lear once told me, "When I've been most effective, I've listened to my inner voice." Lear's inner voice gave him the courage to transform television's voice with his society-mocking domestic comedy *All in the Family*. Despite a string of impressive television successes, the raw texture of *All in the Family* made it a tough sell. But Lear was driven by a sense of mission on behalf of the entire country. His persistence paid off when CBS finally agreed to run the show.

Confident that one person can bring about big changes, Lear forced us to examine some of the most fetid prejudices that bubbled below the surface of society in the early 1970s. When *All in the Family* debuted, teeming throngs demanding civil rights for all and an end to the war in Vietnam swarmed in the nation's streets and on its college campuses. America's easy-going post–World War II composure was dissolving. Lear thought it was time that we tuned into our inner voices to hear what they had to say about how well we honored our claim to be a just society.

Firms of Endearment brings to mind Lear's respect for the counsel of his inner voice. Judging by recent headlines, corporate America has too few leaders who open their mental ears to their inner voices. Rather, they take cues for their behavior from the external world where pursuit of power over others is the daily priority. Sadly, such ambitions weigh on us with a pervasive presence that extends far beyond the world of business. We are regularly served up headlines calling attention to abuses of power in government, academe, clinical research centers, social service agencies, and religious organizations. We seem overrun these days with people in high positions who compromise their organizations and the general welfare with their propensities for self-aggrandizement, avarice, and other perversions of public and private trust.

Happily, *Firms of Endearment* gives us hope that we are not morally going to hell in a handbasket, a relentless stream of headlines about moral failures in high office notwithstanding. The men and women cited in this book, as exemplars of conscionable leadership, give us reason for optimism about the character of our future leaders in business and other sectors of society.

These executives operate by a guiding vision of service that takes into account all their primary stakeholders: customers, employees, suppliers and partners in the supply chain, the communities in which they operate, and, of course, their investors. Their companies follow a *stakeholder relationship management* business model rather than a traditional stockholder-biased business model. At all levels of operation, these companies exude the passion of their leaders for doing good while doing well. Following Polonius's advice to his son in *Hamlet*, these leaders are true to themselves. They evidence keen self-knowledge and project candor and maturity—three essential elements of integrity—in their interactions with others. In return, stakeholders in every category place uncommon trust in their companies and products. Beyond this, stakeholders develop a real affection for such companies. They literally *love* firms of endearment (FoEs).

It is not too much of a stretch to see that as FoEs proliferate—and they are doing that—the principles of leadership that guide their destinies will be adopted by organizations of every stripe. Indeed, the future well-being of this country could depend more than a little on executive leadership of the caliber and mindset described in this book.

With a title that stands for the empathetic concern of companies that wear their hearts on their sleeves, this book is about the pragmatic role of love in business. However, this is not new ground, as the authors note. Tim Sanders, then chief solutions officer of Yahoo!, lauded the idea of making love a strategic cornerstone of a company's operations in his 2002 book *Love Is the Killer App: How to Win Business and Influence Friends.* He wrote, "I don't think there is anything higher than Love…. Love is so expansive. I had such a difficult time coming up with a definition for Love in my book, but the way I define Love is the selfless promotion of the growth of the other." Three years later, Kevin Roberts, head of one of the world's largest ad agencies, Saatchi & Saatchi, wrote of brands transcending the mundane foundations of branding to reach a higher level of existence calling them "lovemarks." He put forth this idea in a book titled *Lovemarks: The Future Beyond Brands.*

Firms of Endearment is a paean to leaders driven by a strong sense of connectivity to their fellow beings. It celebrates leaders who leverage their humanness by inspiring others to join them in making the world a better place. A few years ago, Timberland CEO Jeffrey Swartz accepted a friend's invitation to spend a half a day in a teen halfway house. His friend promised him that his life would never be the same. After answering a troubled teen's question about what he did ("I'm responsible for the global execution of strategy"), he asked the teen what he did. "I work at getting well." Swartz said later that the teen's answer trumped his own answer.

Swartz's friend was right. His life changed that day. He left his office as a hard-driving executive striving to make Timberland the biggest and best in its category and returned as an inspired leader bent on enlisting his entire company in a campaign to "make the world a better place." That is literally how Jeff Swartz describes his company's mission today. Doubtless, some will charge Swartz with shortchanging his stockholders. However, the stock of this footwear and outdoor apparel company has risen more than 700 percent over the past ten years. It has better than doubled in the past three.

The effectiveness of FoE leadership testifies to something most of us have known for a long time but have generally not felt comfortable talking about it in our organizations: Praiseworthy leaders achieve greatness by inspiring love in others for their vision.

Judging by the stories in this book, Yahoo!'s Tom Sanders is absolutely right: Love is the killer app. Love helped turn FoE Southwest Airlines into the most successful airline in history—33 years of unbroken profitability. Appropriately, its stock symbol is LUV. Co-founder Herb Kelleher consciously developed a culture of love that ironically encompasses his employees' unions. FoE Commerce Bank's founder, Vernon Hill, adapted the "love is the killer app" idea to banking to make Commerce the fastest organically growing bank in America. The culture of love nurtured by FoE Costco co-founder Jim Sinegal protects shareholders against ill-taken management decisions based on the demands of Wall Street analysts who would have Costco pay employees less, pare back their benefits, and charge customers more.

It would be good enough that FoEs simply did well by their non-shareholder stakeholders while modestly rewarding their investors.

However, as the authors show, FoEs have generally rewarded their shareholders to an astonishing degree.

In the end, this book is about leadership and the culture that leaders of FoEs develop and nourish. When asked about their biggest competitive advantage, most CEOs of FoEs say it is their corporate culture. Southwest Airlines so much believes this that it has a 93-member Culture Committee. The committee's job is to ensure continuation of the culture that has made Southwest arguably the most successful airline in history. Committee membership includes employees from every level.

It is hard to imagine the executives we have recently seen led away from their companies in handcuffs spending much time thinking about their corporate cultures. True leaders focus less on their own self-interests than on the interests of the whole. They believe that the full well-being of one depends on the well-being of all. Leaders who focus on their own gains in running a company or other organization are not true leaders. They may be positioned as the head of a global enterprise, a branch of government, a congressional office, a major university, or a local parish, but they are leaders in name only. They command others only by virtue of their positions, not by the content of their character. They are so consumed with self-interest that they are blind to the well-being of others.

All that said, this book makes it easier to imagine that someday not far down the road everyone will demand of leaders in business, corporations, and every other type of organization the kind of impassioned pursuit of a broader purpose found in FoEs. As the authors of this remarkable book observe, two things have happened to make that so. The first is the Internet. As it entered the mainstream of society, it dissolved the information advantage organizations have traditionally had over their constituencies. The Internet has shifted the balance of information power to the masses. This has made it much harder to hide the misdeeds of morally deficient leaders and organizations.

The second event is the aging of the population. For the first time in history, people 40 and older are the adult majority. This is driving deep systemic changes in the moral foundations of culture. Higher levels of psychological maturity mean greater influence on society of what Erik Erikson called "generativity"—the disposition of older people to help incoming generations prepare for their time of stewardship of the common good.

Abraham Maslow spoke of people who operate at the higher reaches of maturity as being concerned about matters beyond their own skins. That sums up the disposition of FoEs. With clear-minded certainty about the correctness of their balance between the pursuit of purpose and profits, the leaders of FoEs involve their companies in matters beyond their immediate boundaries—generally with felicitous results for shareholders.

Warren Bennis
University Professor; Distinguished Professor of
Business Administration
University of Southern California

First Foreword to the Second Edition

I was one of the lucky few who had an opportunity to read the wonderful business book *Firms of Endearment* while it was still in manuscript form prior to publication. A good friend of mine, Kathy Dragon, was on an airplane several years ago and just happened to be seated next to David Wolfe, one of the co-authors of the book. David was excited about the book, and when he described its content he mentioned that Whole Foods Market was one of the companies they had profiled as a "firm of endearment." Kathy became excited when she heard this and told David about her close friendship with me, and that I would no doubt enjoy reading the book. David gave her a copy of the manuscript to pass on to me to read.

Such are the small coincidences that can change people's lives and alter our destinies. To say that I read *Firms of Endearment* would be a gross understatement—I devoured it. Of course I was very happy that Whole Foods was one of the 18 public companies they featured in the book, but that was only the beginning of the impact this book had on me. I was already quite familiar with Stakeholder Theory through my reading of Ed Freeman's original and brilliant work on the subject, but I was unaware that there were several other companies besides Whole Foods Market that were conducting their businesses in such similarly conscious ways. Up until that point, I had believed that Whole Foods was some kind of unusual odd duck that had created a unique business culture based on fulfilling our higher purposes as a business (besides just making a profit) and consciously creating value for all of our major interdependent stakeholders (customers, employees, suppliers, investors, communities, and the environment). I had thought we were virtually alone in the world and I was overjoyed to discover that there were other well-known businesses that thought and acted in much the same way.

After reading *Firms of Endearment*, I soon met with David and Raj. We discovered that we shared many ideas and had a commitment to "evangelize" our ideas to the larger world. We began a dialog discussing the ideas outlined in *Firms of Endearment*—ideas that I had been calling "Conscious Capitalism." We believed that these ideas deserved a much larger audience, and we began to plan our first Conscious Capitalism conference to bring together like-minded people into dialog.

With an initial modest gathering of about 20 people, we launched an initiative to spread the ideas of Conscious Capitalism throughout the world. Many much larger and hugely successful conferences have followed over the past six years. It was at one of these conferences in Boston that I was able to meet the third author of *Firms of Endearment*, the renowned marketing scholar Jag Sheth. Jag has been a prolific author of dozens of books, including the classic *The Theory of Buyer Behavior* and *Clients for Life*. For many years, Jag served as Raj's mentor, and in that role alone his contribution to the Conscious Capitalism movement has been immense.

Business is by far the greatest value creator in the world. As Raj and I state it in our book *Conscious Capitalism* (Harvard Business Review Publishing, 2013), "We believe that business is good because it creates value, it is ethical because it is based on voluntary exchange, it is noble because it can elevate our existence, and it is heroic because it lifts people out of poverty and creates prosperity." Business has such enormous potential to do good in the world. Much of the good is currently being done "unconsciously" simply by creating products and services that people value, providing jobs, and generating profits. However, business can also be done much more consciously, with higher purpose and optimal value creation for all of the major stakeholders while creating cultures that optimize human flourishing. As people, particularly leaders, become more conscious, we are able to create new types of entrepreneurial enterprises that will help solve our most serious problems and will evolve humanity upward to fulfill our unlimited potential as a species. *Firms of Endearment* is a very important and ground-breaking book because it points the way that all businesses should aspire to emulate and ultimately transcend. I am grateful to the authors for their landmark contribution to elevating business practice and thereby benefiting humanity.

John Mackey
Co-founder and Co-CEO of Whole Foods Market

Second Foreword to the Second Edition

This new edition of *Firms of Endearment* continues to break important new ground in understanding the power of capitalism to transform our world for the better. In the first edition the authors suggested that firms that pay attention to how they create value for stakeholders might perform better. They gave us an introductory quantitative analysis and a set of rich stories that made the analysis make some sense.

In this new edition they take a giant step forward. They give us a "proof of possibility," thereby grounding a new story of business in solid economic analysis and practical management thinking. The role of passion and purpose is not well understood in a world where the dominant story of business that we read everyday suggests that only money and profits count. Furthermore, this dominant story suggests that businesspeople are greedy and self-interested. We see this played out everyday in the press, in government responses to crises, and sometimes we see executives themselves making the same attributions.

It's time to stop this nonsense, and the authors give us a roadmap.

Every business always has and always will create value for customers, employees, communities, suppliers, and the financiers who put up the investment. Firms of endearment are those companies that realize this principle of stakeholder value creation and orient themselves around it. These are the companies we love to do business with. They are the brands we recommend to our friends, and if we are smart, they are the investments we have in our portfolios, 401(k) plans, and so on.

None of what this book says should be surprising. What is surprising is the resistance that can be encountered. Many narrow-minded economists, as well as many critics of business, just "know" that business is really about the money. They then make the logical error of inferring that the purpose of business is to make as much money as possible. That's like saying that because we need red blood cells to live, the purpose of life is to make red blood cells.

Our great companies, including the ones in this book, but in the past as well, are fueled by passion and by a sense of purpose. Great business leaders channel their employees' desires to be a part of something bigger than themselves and to be a part of making the world a better place for their children into the overall purpose of their business. Profit is an outcome. And, of course, there are no guarantees here. Sometimes companies do their best around a purpose and indeed fail, or they fail to keep that purpose in front of them, or conditions simply change.

The twenty-first century requires a new way of thinking about business. Thankfully that story is beginning to emerge with books like *Firms of Endearment*. It will repay close study, seeing how your company is both like and unlike the examples in the book. And, hopefully it will cause you to ask questions about your own purpose, both in terms of your company and your individual situations.

This is not the end of the new story of business, but it is a good beginning. Hopefully it will inspire others to "critique by creating something better." I urge you to see it not as the definitive word on how to run a business, but as a proof of possibility that creating value for stakeholders with purpose and passion is an idea that works and whose time has come. It offers hope that we can be the generation that makes business better and leaves a better world for our children.

R. Edward Freeman
University Professor; Elis and Signe Olsson Professor of
Business Administration
The Darden School, University of Virginia

Acknowledgments

We would like to acknowledge the valuable assistance of John Warden and Alex Romeo in helping conduct the financial analysis of the firms. We also appreciate the many conversations we had with Rick Frazier on how to evaluate companies using a stakeholder approach. His insights and suggestions have been invaluable. Jeff Cherry and Peter Derby have also been very helpful in this regard.

Many people have been great supporters of the original *Firms of Endearment*. Their insights and suggestions have been very valuable to us in making this revision. In particular, we would like to thank John Mackey, Kip Tindell, Shubhro Sen, Abilio Diniz, Fred Kofman, Ricardo Gil, Doug Rauch, Doug Levy, Rand Stagen, Vinit Taneja, Kiran Gulrajani, Dr. Manesh Shrikant, Harsh Mariwala, Debashis Chatterjee, Vineeta Salvi, Tony Buono, Alan Hoffman, Michael Gelb, Howard Behar, Youngsul Kwon, Michael Lee, Ashwini Malhotra, Sudhakar Ram, Ketan Mehta, Ashank Desai, R. Sundar, and Roy Spence.

Raj Sisodia acknowledges the work of his many students at Bentley University in evaluating numerous companies over the years using the criteria laid out in this book. He would also like to thank his daughter Maya for her editorial work on the book.

Jag would like to thank Joey Reiman and Suhas Apte for their enthusiasm and encouragement to revise the book. He would also like to thank Ishan Dey, Aarya Budhiraja, and Rohan Parekh for providing research support. Finally, he thanks his personal assistant, Nicole Smith, for her administrative support.

About the Authors

Raj Sisodia is the F.W. Olin Distinguished Professor of Global Business and Whole Foods Market Research Scholar in Conscious Capitalism at Babson College in Wellesley, MA. He is also co-founder and co-chairman of Conscious Capitalism, Inc. He has a Ph.D. in marketing from Columbia University. Raj is the co-author of *The New York Times* bestseller *Conscious Capitalism: Liberating the Heroic Spirit of Business* (Harvard Business Review Publishing, 2013). In 2003, he was cited as one of "50 Leading Marketing Thinkers" by the Chartered Institute of Marketing. He was named one of "Ten Outstanding Trailblazers of 2010" by Good Business International, and one of the "Top 100 Thought Leaders in Trustworthy Business Behavior" by Trust Across America for 2010 and 2011. Raj has published seven books and more than 100 academic articles. He has consulted with and taught executive programs for numerous companies, including AT&T, Nokia, LG, DPDHL, POSCO, Kraft Foods, Whole Foods Market, Tata, Siemens, Sprint, Volvo, IBM, Walmart, Rabobank, McDonalds, and Southern California Edison. He is on the Board of Directors of The Container Store and Mastek, Ltd., and is a trustee of Conscious Capitalism, Inc. For more details, see www.rajsisodia.com.

Jag Sheth is the Charles H. Kellstadt Professor of Marketing in the Gouizeta Business School at Emory University. He has published 26 books, more than 400 articles, and is nationally and internationally known for his scholarly contributions in consumer behavior, relationship marketing, competitive strategy, and geopolitical analysis. His book *The Rule of Three* (Free Press, 2002), coauthored with Raj Sisodia, has altered current notions on competition in business. This book has been translated into five languages and was the subject of a seven-part television series by CNBC Asia. Jag's list of consulting clients around the world is long and impressive, including AT&T, GE, Motorola, Whirlpool, and 3M, to name just a few. He is frequently quoted and interviewed by *The Wall Street Journal*, *The New York Times*, *Fortune*, *Financial Times*, and radio shows and television networks such as CNN, Lou Dobbs, and more. He is also on the Board of Directors of several public companies. In 2004, he was honored with the two highest awards bestowed by the American Marketing Association: the Richard D. Irwin Distinguished Marketing Educator Award and the Charles Coolidge Parlin Award. For more details, see www.jagsheth.net.

The late **David B. Wolfe** was an internationally recognized customer behavior expert in middle-age and older markets. He was the author of *Serving the Ageless Market* (McGraw-Hill, 1990) and *Ageless Marketing: Strategies for Connecting with the Hearts and Minds of the New Customer Majority* (Dearborn Publishing, 2003). David's consulting assignments took him to Asia, Africa, Europe, and throughout North America. He was widely published in publications in the U.S. and abroad. He also consulted to numerous Fortune 100 companies, including American Express, AT&T, Coca-Cola, General Motors, Hartford Insurance, Marriott, MetLife, Prudential Securities, and Textron.

Prologue

A Whole New World

The future is disorder. A door like this has opened up only five or six times since we got up on our hind legs. It's the best possible time to be alive, when almost everything you thought you knew is wrong.

The mathematician Valentine, in Tom Stoppard's play
Arcadia

This book reaches the public eye at the dawn of a new era in human history—perhaps more so than any previous era that inspired historians to give it a name signifying its import. Looking back hundreds of years—thousands of years, say some[1]—this new era may be unmatched in the scale of its effect on humankind. Numerous credible authors have testified in their writings that something this big is happening. Francis Fukuyama declared the end of a major cultural era in his famous and controversial essay "The End of History" (1989). A little later, *Science* magazine editor David Lindley foretold the demise of the Holy Grail of physics—the General Unified Theory—in *The End of Physics* (1993). The next year, British economist David Simpson claimed that macroeconomics had outlived its usefulness in *The End of Macro-Economics* (1994). Then, science writer John Horgan ticked off legions of scientists with his provocative book *The End of Science* (1997). That same year, Nobel Laureate chemist Ilya Prigogine told us in *The End of Uncertainty* (1997) of an imminent broad-reaching shift in scientific worldview that would make much of what stands as scientific truth today scientific myth tomorrow.

So many endings must mean so many new beginnings. Around the start of the 1990s, virtually no major field of human endeavor was spared from predictions of its ending—not literally, but certainly in terms of past conceptualizations of its nature. The world of business is no exception. It is experiencing far-reaching changes in our understanding of its fundamental purposes and how companies should operate. Indeed, looking at the magnitude of change in the business world, it is not overreaching to suggest that an historic *social transformation of capitalism* is underway.

Twenty or so years ago, just as the Internet was going mainstream, few could have credibly predicted the scale of this transformation. In this book, we provide some measure of that scale by profiling companies that have broadened their purpose beyond the creation of shareholder wealth to act as agents for the larger good. We view these companies not as outliers but as the vanguard of a new business mainstream.

We call this era of epochal change the "Age of Transcendence." The dictionary defines *transcendence* as a "state of excelling or surpassing or going beyond usual limits."[2] We're not the first to speak of a transcendent shift in the *zeitgeist* of contemporary society; Columbia University humanities professor Andrew Delbanco says, "The most striking feature of contemporary culture is the unslaked craving for transcendence."[3] This craving for transcendence could be playing a strong role in the erosion of the dominance of scientifically grounded certainty, which has characterized worldviews in western societies since the dawn of modern science. Subjective perspectives based on how people *feel* have gained greater acceptance in recent times.

Others have taken note of the rising subjectivity of worldviews. One is French philosopher Pierre Lévy, who has devoted his professional life to studying the cultural and cognitive impacts of digital technologies. He believes that the shift toward subjectivity may prove to be one of the most important considerations in business in this century.[4] Lévy also believes that Ayn Rand–style objectivism, firmly embraced by Milton Friedman and his protégés, is passing into history as feelings and intuition have risen in stature in the common mind. Malcolm Gladwell's bestselling book on intuition, *Blink,* is a testament to that, as is James Surowiecki's *The Wisdom of Crowds.*

The dramatic upsurge of interest in spirituality in the U.S. that has helped spawn stadium-sized "mega churches" is another indication that something big is happening in the bedrock of culture.

Numerous consumer surveys report that people are looking less to "things" and more to experiences to achieve satisfaction with their lives.[5] For many, the experiences they most covet transcend a world that is materialistically defined by science, and for that matter most of traditional business enterprise.

People who lead companies are not insulated from the influences of culture. After all, they drink from the same cultural waters as the customers they serve and the employees they lead. The executives we write about as exemplars in this book reflect in their managerial philosophies the changes in culture we've been talking about. They are champions of a new, humanistic vision of capitalism's role in society. It is a vision that transcends the narrower perspectives of most companies in the past, rising to embrace the common welfare in its concerns. Former Timberland CEO Jeffrey Swartz (whose company has been acquired by VF Corp.) unabashedly said that his company's primary mission was "Make the world a better place." But Swartz and the other executives we hold up as role models in this book are not starry-eyed do-gooders. They are resolute and highly successful business professionals who augment their human-centered company vision with sound management skills and an unswerving commitment to do good by all who are touched by their companies. We call their companies "firms of endearment" because they strive through their words and deeds to endear themselves to all their primary stakeholders—customers, employees, suppliers, communities, and shareholders—by aligning the interests of all in such a way that no stakeholder group gains *at the expense of* other stakeholder groups; rather, they all prosper together. These executives are driven as much by what they believe to be right (subjectively grounded morality) as by what others might more objectively claim to be right.

Ponder for a moment what the results of a Conference Board survey say about the moral outlook in executive suites across the country. Seven hundred executives were asked why their companies engaged in social or citizenship initiatives. Only 12 percent mentioned business strategy. Three percent mentioned customer attraction and retention, and one percent cited public expectations. The remaining 84 percent said they were driven by motivations such as improving society, company traditions, and their personal values.[6] We don't think members of this 84 percent all sat down and calculated in rational fashion the direct payoff of carrying out their duties according to high moral standards. More likely, we believe, most simply feel in their gut what they should be doing. This is how movements and revolutions unfold: as much from the heart as from the mind. What we write about in this book is a powerful movement if not altogether a revolution.

We are poised precariously at what physicists call a bifurcation point—an interregnum of normalcy between the poles of death and birth (or rebirth), when an old order faces its end and a new order struggles to emerge from its fetal state. At such times, the future becomes more uncertain than usual because events within the time and space boundaries of a bifurcation point have infinite possible outcomes. This is why Valentine declared, "The future is disorder" but challenges us to join efforts to bring forth a new order with the yeasty lure: "It's the best possible time to be alive when almost everything you thought you knew is wrong."

Humankind is entering a realm where no one has gone before. Its landscape is as unfamiliar to us as the world that we've known until now would be to a time traveler from the eighteenth century. Let's travel back in time to better appreciate the evolutionary nature of culture through brief reflections on the antecedent two cultural ages in U.S. history from which the Age of Transcendence is emerging.

The Age of Empowerment

We call the first cultural era in America the "Age of Empowerment." The signing of the Declaration of Independence and publication of Adam Smith's *An Inquiry into the Nature and Causes of the Wealth of Nations* in 1776 marked its beginning. That these two epochal events in human history occurred in the same year is an extraordinary historic coincidence. The former event was about a free society, the latter about free markets. Joined at the hip, democracy and capitalism marched into the future to bring forth a whole new world, one that would elevate the lot of the common man to heights never experienced or imagined before in human history.

For the first time in history, ordinary people were empowered by codified law to shape their own destinies. People born without social distinction could raise themselves from abject poverty to the highest public and private offices. A free market economy aided their efforts. Liberal education and laws that rewarded industry supported America's determination to become a great nation. As decades went on, millions of families rose out of subsistence existence. The aristocratic culture of Europe may have generated great philosophic thinking in the Age of Enlightenment, but common folk in America generated great material accomplishment in the Age of Empowerment. By the end of the Age of Empowerment, which we mark around 1880, America was connected coast-to-coast by telegraph lines, railroads, a single currency, and a national banking system that the Lincoln presidency had established. Another great accomplishment of the Lincoln administration was the establishment of the land grant college program that increasingly brought the benefits of higher education to the masses. The nation was primed for its next great cultural era.

The Age of Knowledge

The intellectual and economic liberation of the masses paved the way for the Age of Knowledge. Within a half-dozen years of 1880, Alexander Graham Bell invented the telephone, and Thomas Edison invented the phonograph, the first practical incandescent light bulb, and the first central electrical power system.

During the Age of Knowledge, the U.S. transitioned rapidly from an agrarian to an industrial society. Science exploded into daily life. The time from laboratory prototype to the marketplace came to be often measured in months instead of decades. Great scientific breakthroughs spawned great industries. And great industries created the modern consumer economy. Economic gains across society raised living standards to previously unimaginable heights. Childbirth and childhood deaths became rarities. Life expectancy in the U.S. shot up from 47 years at birth in 1900 to 76 years at birth by 1990.

Business management took a seeming leap forward in the early years of the twentieth century when Frederick Winslow Taylor introduced scientific discipline to the practice of management in *Scientific Management* (1911). Alfred P. Sloan invented the modern corporation after becoming president of General Motors in 1923. In 1921 John Watson, head of Johns Hopkins' psychology department and founder of the behaviorist school of psychology, joined the J. Walter Thompson advertising agency to establish the first consumer research center in the nation. Science now undergirded the full spectrum of business—from product design and organizational management, to consumer research and marketing.

Ever since Ransom E. Olds established the first assembly line (no, it wasn't Henry Ford; he just mechanized Olds' assembly line), the operating focus of business has been on constant improvements in productivity—getting more and more from less and less. For a long time, this served society well. Quality of life steadily rose while the cost of living steadily fell. The material wellbeing of ordinary people reached astonishing levels. Materialism became the bedrock of business, society, and culture.

In time, however, preoccupation with productivity and cost cutting to improve bottom lines began to take a toll on communities, workers, their families, and the environment. Scores of communities fell into economic disrepair as companies abandoned them for venues promising lower operating costs. Legions of families endured abject suffering as their breadwinners struggled to find new jobs. Life was sucked out of villages, towns, and center cities across the nation. Sprawling slums filled with the carcasses of abandoned factories became unwelcoming neighborhoods. Apologists justified business decisions that wreaked havoc on individuals and their families and neighborhoods by invoking the Darwinian "survival of the fittest" theme. The pro-business argument was simple: To reap the benefits of capitalism, society must tolerate the pain it sometimes causes people on the lower rungs of society.

But growing numbers are now wondering, "How much more pain do we have to live with?" Ordinary citizens increasingly view commerce as lacking a human heart. They feel that most companies see them as just numbers to be controlled, manipulated, and exploited. They know that to many companies they have little flesh-and-blood realness—that they have the same abstract quality as people on the ground have for pilots dropping bombs from 40,000 feet.

But the times they are a-changing, as Bob Dylan sang in the 1960s.

New Republic senior editor Gregg Easterbrook has observed, "A transition from material want to *meaning want* is in progress on an historically unprecedented scale—involving hundreds of millions of people—and may eventually be recognized as the principle cultural development of our age."[7] (Italics added.)

Welcome to the Age of Transcendence, the highest pinnacle that humanity has yet ascended to.

The Age of Transcendence

The point of tracing America's cultural evolution since its founding is to focus attention on the idea that free societies continuously progress through processes of cultural evolution, the equivalent of a person's evolutionary progress in what psychologists call "personality development." Societies, like people, are driven to strive for being more today than they were yesterday, and more tomorrow than they are today. Indeed, Steve McIntosh suggests that this is the very purpose of evolution:

> The evolutionary story of our origins has tremendous cultural power that transcends the boundaries of science; it shapes the view of who we are and why we are here. Yet many of the scientific luminaries responsible for educating the public about evolution tell us that it is an essentially random or accidental process with no larger meaning. However, as the scientific facts of evolution have increasingly come to light, these very facts demonstrate that the process of evolution is unmistakably progressive. As we come to see how evolution progresses, this reveals evolution's purpose—to grow toward ever-widening realizations of beauty, truth, and goodness.[8]

While scientific discovery and technological development have been the primary catalysts in the evolution of culture, recent demographic changes have played quite a large role in reshaping culture. Aging populations are altering the course of humankind. But this is not the first time demography has reset the directions of humankind.

Recent findings by anthropologists indicate a sudden increase in longevity 30,000 years ago that changed human culture dramatically. The longevity gains created a population explosion among grandparents. For the first time in human history, relatively large numbers of postmenopausal women were available to support their daughters and granddaughters and to begin refining domestic life. More grandfathers were available to instruct young males in "the old ways," thus strengthening generational continuity. Many anthropologists regard the "grandparent phenomenon" as a major turning point in the cultural evolution of humankind. Among other benefits, the sharp increase in the grandparent population led to a moderation of the aggressive behavior of youth. This reduced tribal warfare, freeing tribal attention and energy to move toward higher states of cultural development.[9]

Something similar could be happening today—that is, the rapid growth of an aging population is altering the *zeitgeist* of society, driving humankind toward higher states of cultural development. We can cite 1989 as the formal start of this new course because starting that year, most adults in the U.S. were 40 or older for the first time in history (the median age of adults now exceeds 45 across the American population and is more than 50 for Caucasians). Like an echo of the moderating influences brought about by an explosion in the grandparent population 30,000 years ago, the aging of the population in the vast majority of nations in the world today raises the prospects for a "kinder and gentler society"—to use Peggy Noonan's words in a campaign speech she wrote for George H. W. Bush in 1988.

But another development occurring around the time the new "mature adult" majority came into being has also played a major role in catalyzing quantum changes in the bedrock of culture. Also in 1989, British software engineer Tim Berners-Lee invented the World Wide Web. Within a few short years, the Internet went from being an arcane communications tool used mostly by an elite few to a mainstream artifact used by tens of millions. The World Wide Web shifted the balance of information power to the masses. It dramatically changed how people interact with each other, democratized information flow, and forced companies to operate with far greater transparency.

The Age of Transcendence bears similarities to what author Daniel Pink calls the "Conceptual Age" in his book *A Whole New Mind*. Pink defines the Conceptual Age as an "economy and a society built on the inventive, empathetic, big-picture capabilities of what's rising."[10] He describes the Conceptual Age as the successor to the Information Age. We define our term for the same era a bit differently. The Age of Transcendence signifies a cultural watershed in which the physical (materialistic) influences that dominated culture in the twentieth century ebb while metaphysical (experiential) influences become stronger. This is helping to drive a shift in the foundations of culture from an objective base to a subjective base: people are increasingly relying on their own counsel to decide their course of action. This trait is typically present among people in midlife and older who are generally less subject to the "herd" behavior that is so prevalent among youth. That shift acknowledges a long suppressed idea in a world largely guided by the Newtonian certainty that Ilya Prigogine says is scattering to the winds: *Ultimately, everything is personal.*

Pink wrote enthusiastically about society moving from the more rational perspectives commonly associated with the left brain to the more emotional, intuitive perspectives usually associated with the right brain. He argued that companies in the U.S. need to move more toward right brain values to work an advantage over companies abroad who want to build relationships with American consumers. As he sees it, this means that U.S. companies must connect with what he calls the six senses of the Conceptual Age in product design, marketing, and customer relations. These six senses are design, story, symphony, empathy, play, and meaning.[11] They all have deep roots in the brain's right hemisphere.

However, the issue of change in the foundations of culture is not as simple as a matter of left brain versus right brain. We see the marketplace generally favoring companies that integrate both right and left brain perspectives to yield what Austrian neurologist Wolf Singer calls "unitive thinking," which is a distinct third kind of thinking in Singer's mind that he claims is the ultimate source of creativity.

In the wake of René Descartes' formulation of the scientific method, the Western mind came to be dominated by "either/or" constructs that are largely moderated in the analytical left brain. That side of the brain tends to rank things hierarchically in categories. It routinely excludes from serious consideration what doesn't fall into a clearly defined category. To put this in a business context, in exclusionary left brain thinking, stakeholders are relegated to categories. Connections between stakeholders in differing categories are incidental and accidental. The picture is quite different among firms of endearment (FoEs). Their leaders think in unitive fashion, approaching their tasks with holistic vision in which all players in the game of commerce are interconnected and significant.

Welcome, again, to the Age of Transcendence. Settle down, get comfortable, and read on. There are many new rules to learn, because *almost everything you thought you knew could be wrong.* We are going to be in this age for quite a while—probably for the rest of your life, and longer.

Overview of Chapters

Here is a preview of the journey you have just embarked on:

- In Chapter 1, "Building Business on Love and Care," we introduce the firms of endearment business philosophy and summarize its astonishing performance in today's challenging business environment.

- Chapter 2, "New Age, New Rules, New Capitalism," discusses the new rules for business in the Age of Transcendence and offers the unconventional idea that an increasing number of companies are behaving in ways that mirror the increasing influence of self-actualization needs and processes that derive from our aging society.

- Chapter 3, "Dealing with Disorder," discusses how and why the social transformation of capitalism that is underway is happening.

- We now start looking at how FoEs manage their relationships with each stakeholder group. In Chapter 4, "Employees: From

Resource to Source," we look at how these companies deal with their employees, creating happy and productive work environments in which employees are highly motivated, valued, and well rewarded.

- Chapter 5, "Customers: Healing vs. Hucksterism," addresses customer relationships, describing the new marketing paradigm that is emerging in the Age of Transcendence. This includes honoring the legal as well as the unspoken emotional contract that companies have with their customers—and, indeed, with all stakeholders.

- In Chapter 6, "Investors: Reaping What FoEs Sow," we show how companies can and must relate to their investors in financial as well as emotional terms.

- Chapter 7, "Partners: Elegant Harmonies," addresses business partners, including suppliers, distributors, retailers, and others. As companies outsource more and more value creation, business partners are becoming increasingly crucial to success. This chapter shows how FoEs manage these vital relationships in a symbiotic and mutually beneficial way.

- Chapter 8, "Society: The Ultimate Stakeholder," deals with how FoEs relate to the world at large, including the communities within which they operate, competitors, governments at all levels, and nongovernmental organizations. We view society as the ultimate stakeholder because it subsumes each of the other stakeholders within it. The key message here is that FoEs are enthusiastically welcomed into the communities where they operate, and view governments as partners in value creation rather than adversaries.

- Chapter 9, "Culture: The Secret Ingredient," addresses issues of leadership and corporate culture.

- Chapter 10, "What We Have Learned," summarizes what we have learned about the FoE way of doing business.

- Chapter 11, "The Other Side of Complexity," concludes the book with a vision of the "simplicity on the other side of complexity" that describes the FoE management philosophy.

- Appendix A, "Brief Company Profiles," provides thumbnail sketches of each FoE featured in the book, highlighting what makes the company unique and what we can learn from it.

- Appendix B features an interview with Rick Frazier, Founding Partner of Concinnity Advisors, LP. This interview elaborates on the empirical basis for selecting the publicly traded U.S. companies in our analysis.

Endnotes

1. *Washington Post* Reporter Joel Garreau asserts in his book *Radical Evolution: The Promise and Peril of Enhancing Our Minds, Our Bodies—and What it Means to Be Human*, Doubleday, 2004, pg. 3: "(The) gulf between what engineers are actually creating today and what ordinary readers might find believable is significant. It is the first challenge to making sense of this world unfolding before us, in which we face the biggest change in tens of thousands of years in what it means to be human."

2. http://www.wordreference.com/.

3. Andrew Delbanco, *The Real American Dream: A Mediation on Hope,* Harvard University Press, 1999, pg. 113.

4. Pierre Lévy, *Collective Intelligence,* Perseus Book Group, 2000, p. 4.

5. Marita Wesely-Clough, trends expert at Hallmark Cards, Inc., says, "Watch for people of all ages to scale down and simplify, to insure they have time to invest in what matters—friends, family, giving back, their legacy. Boomers approaching retirement will lead this trend." (http://retailindustry.about.com/od/retail_trends/a/bl_trends2005.htm). This is a common refrain among consumer trend watchers, including the Yankelovich Monitor, which issued a report in 2002 stating that consumers were striving to simplify their lives by relying less on "stuff" to make them happy (David B. Wolfe with Robert Snyder, *Ageless Marketing: Strategies for Reaching the*

Hearts and Minds of the New Customer Majority, Dearborn Trade publishing, 2004, pg. 20.)

6. Sophia A. Muirhead, Charles J. Bennett, Ronald E. Berenbeim, Amy Kao, and David Vidal, *Corporate Citizenship in the New Century: Accountability, Transparency and Global Stakeholder Engagement*, R-1314-02-RR, New York: Conference Board, 2002.

7. Gregg Easterbrook, *The Progress Paradox: How Life Gets Better While People Feel Worse,* Random House, 2003, pg. 317.

8. Steve McIntosh, *Evolution's Purpose: An Integral Interpretation of the Scientific Story of Our Origins*, Select Books, 2012; quote drawn from http://www.stevemcintosh.com/books/evolutions-purpose/.

9. Lee Bowman, "The dawn of grandparents proved positive for humans," *Seattle Post-Intelligencer,* July 6, 2004. (http://seattlepi. nwsource.com/national/180825_wisdom06.html).

10. Daniel H. Pink, *A Whole New Mind: Moving from the Information Age to the Conceptual Age*, Riverhead Books division of Penguin, New York, 2005.

11. *Design:* paying attention to aesthetics when carrying out any task. *Story:* conveyance of information to consumers, employees, and others through storytelling techniques. *Symphony:* the ability to put together pieces to create a holistic picture; synthesis is a good synonym. *Empathy:* identifying with and understanding another person's circumstances, feelings, and motives. *Play:* putting fun into every activity to enhance both pleasure and creativity. *Meaning:* Extending the value of an activity beyond the moment and self.

1

Building Business on Love and Care

This book is not about corporate social responsibility. It is about enlightened business management.

This book owes much to the ideas of R. Edward Freeman, who in 1984 made a strong case for a stakeholder-based business model in his book *Strategic Management: A Stakeholder Approach* (Pittman Publishing). As management professor Ronald W. Clement wrote in an article examining stakeholder management theory, "Freeman was the first management writer to so clearly identify the strategic importance of groups and individuals beyond not only the firm's stockholders, but also its employees, customers, and suppliers. Indeed, he saw such widely disparate groups as local community organizations, environmentalists, consumer advocates, governments, special interest groups, and even competitors and the media as legitimate stakeholders."[1]

Firms of Endearment had its origins in discussions among the authors about writing a book on the topic of how marketing has lost its way, consuming ever-more resources but delivering less in terms of customer satisfaction, loyalty, and especially trust. Our initial working title was *In Search of Marketing Excellence.* However, as we continued exploring the topic and identifying companies that spent less on marketing than their industry peers but achieved far more, we uncovered a more holistic truth: that customers are best served by companies that create superior value and have close relationships with *all* their stakeholders—employees, suppliers, the communities in which they operate, and, of course, their stockholders. This realization led us to the work of R. Edward Freeman, who among other distinctions, heads the Center for Applied Ethics at University of Virginia's Darden School of Business.

Since the publication of Freeman's seminal book on stakeholder-based business models, a flood of articles and books have examined and argued for and against the stakeholder approach to business management. In this book, we present evidence that supports Freeman's ideas about the interconnected and interdependent nature of stakeholders.

This book is a clarion call for companies—indeed, organizations of every stripe—to reorganize and become vehicles of service to every stakeholder group. We offer a substantial volume of case-based evidence that companies that hew to a stakeholder relationship management (SRM) business model develop a distinctive and lasting competitive advantage and outperform their peers along multiple dimensions, including financial.

We believe that SRM business models will increasingly be seen as the most efficacious way to achieve *sustained* superior business performance. To understand why, we need to reflect on the profound changes taking place in the cultural bedrock of U.S. society as well as in every other developed nation. The aging of developed societies is a major factor in these changes. With the majority of adults now 45 and older, the worldviews, values, and needs of the young no longer have the influence on society they once did. The worldviews and values associated with midlife and beyond have become more influential on culture than ever. Surveys by consumer trend watchers such as the Yankelovich Monitor bear this out. Myra Stark of the global ad agency Saatchi & Saatchi stated the following in an essay titled "The State of the U.S. Consumer 2002:"

> In the face of threats to our safety, our way of life and our economic stability, Americans have pulled back from many of the things that seemed to matter in the '90s—materialism, career, the celebrity culture, the affluent attitude—and are rethinking how they want to live and work. Daniel Pink, author of *Free Agent Nation,* calls this new seriousness "the flight to meaning." "In turbulent times," he says, "people get serious about finding meaning."[2]

The meaning of life—and the meaning of one's own life in particular—is a perennial issue in midlife and beyond whose influence on society as a whole was less pronounced when the young were the majority. But with the adult majority now consisting of people over the age of 45, the search for meaning has a major influence on the ethos of society at large, including on corporate cultures everywhere.

It is common for people nearing or beyond the career-building and family-raising years to ask, "What am I going to do with the rest of my life?" This self-query arises from a sense that one should be doing more than serving just one's self; one should begin thinking about serving the larger collective "self." We discovered many business leaders who have asked themselves a similar question: "How are we going to make this company an instrument of service to society even as we fulfill our obligation to build shareholder wealth?"

As we said in the Prologue, we are in the early stages of a new era that we call the Age of Transcendence. Numerous consumer surveys reveal that people are increasingly looking for higher meaning in their lives than simply adding to the store of things they own. This is a signature trait of people in midlife and older who are not battling basic survival issues, either materially or emotionally. The search for meaning is changing expectations in the marketplace and in the workplace. Indeed, *we believe it is changing the very soul of capitalism*.

Many have long regarded capitalism as an economic concept without a soul; it is all about business and markets. However, as we see it, the edifice of capitalism is undergoing its farthest-reaching transformation since Adam Smith published *The Wealth of Nations* in 1776. The nature of the transformation can be summed up in one short statement: Companies are increasingly motivated by and being held accountable for humanistic as well as economic performance.

A *humanistic company* is run in such a way that its stakeholders—customers, employees, suppliers, business partners, society, and many investors—develop an emotional connection with it, an affectionate regard not unlike the way many people feel about their favorite athletic teams. Humanistic companies—or *firms of endearment*—seek to maximize their value to society as a whole, not just to their shareholders. They are the ultimate value creators: They create emotional, spiritual, social, cultural, intellectual, ecological, and, of course, financial value. People who interact with such companies feel safe, secure, and fulfilled in their dealings. They enjoy working with or for the company, buying from it, investing in it, and having it as a neighbor.

Numerous companies are successful and admirable in many ways but lack a strong emotive dimension. We argue that for the best prospects of success in the future, companies will need to combine an emotive dimension with operational efficacy. Some have called the emotive dimension the "soul of a company." Companies without a soul face a doubtful future.

Of course, millions of customers routinely buy from companies to which they feel no emotional attachment. Customers can be loyal in *behavior* to a company without being loyal in *attitude*. Attitudinal loyalty comes from emotional attachment. It is attitudinal loyalty that matters most in sustaining the long term survival and success of a business, especially in today's rapidly evolving marketplace.

The social transformation of capitalism is being driven by cultural changes of tectonic proportions that corporations, governments, and business schools ignore at their peril. This book examines the nature of this transformation, why it is happening now, and what it will take for companies to succeed in this new environment. Companies that do not understand capitalism's evolving identity—what many are now calling "Conscious Capitalism"—could have a short life expectancy because the forces driving this makeover are essentially unstoppable. They have become part of who we are in these times. Every company has the choice of going with the flow of these forces and being lifted to new heights or being drawn under by the churning rip tides of historic change.

The Power of Love

Most Wall Street analysts and corporate bean counters haven't caught on to the idea that there is much profit to be gained by bringing love into business operations. However, they and any others whose eyes roll at hearing the words *love* and *management* joined together would do well to read James Autry's *Love and Profit*. First published in 1991, the book followed Autry's retirement as chief executive officer of Meredith Corporation Magazine Group. Meredith publishes *Better Homes & Garden, Ladies Home Journal,* and *Country Life,* among other titles. *Town and Country* editor-in-chief Pamela Fiori called *Love and Profit* "the most enlightening book about management written in the last twenty-five years."[3] *Love and Profit* is a book of poetry about business with inspired prose between poems.

How can a book of poetry be considered the "most enlightening book about management in the last twenty-five years?" Easy. Autry focuses on strategically crucial dimensions of human behavior that relatively few companies acknowledge in their policies and operations. Most business leaders think in terms of numbers and profit. *Love* and *profit* is an alien conjunction of words that is quantitatively murky. What's the payoff? Well, as that sage of sages Albert Einstein said, "Not everything that can be counted counts, and not everything that counts can be counted." It is attention to the *immeasurable* qualitative dimensions of life that gives FoE companies their crucial competitive differences from their competitors.

In his book *A Whole New Mind*, Daniel Pink in effect endorses Einstein's counsel on the limitations of measuring what counts. He posits that America's continued economic vitality depends on "...supplement(ing) well-developed high-tech abilities with abilities that are high concept and high touch"[4] (echoes of John Naisbitt's *Megatrends* from a quarter century ago). Pink elaborates:

> High concept involves the ability to create artistic and emotional beauty, to detect patterns and opportunities, to craft a satisfying narrative, and to combine seemingly unrelated ideas into novel invention. High touch involves the ability to empathize, to understand the subtleties of human interaction, to find joy in one's self and to elicit it in others, and to stretch beyond the quotidian, in pursuit of purpose and meaning.[5]

Pink's words capture the essence of the cultural foundations of FoE companies. However, the prevailing view still is that business survival is mostly a numbers game. But according to Pink, we are in a new era in which company survival and growth will depend less on *quantitative* factors and more on *qualitative* factors. Perhaps the most powerful qualitative factor present in the culture of FoEs we've examined is love—a deep, tender, ineffable feeling of affection[6] that runs from company to stakeholder and back again to the company.

James Autry wrote in *Love and Profit*, "Good management is largely a matter of love." He elaborates:

Management is, in fact, a sacred trust in which the well-being of other people is put in your care during most of their working hours. It is a trust placed upon you first by those who put you in the job, but more important than that, it is a trust placed upon you *after you get the job* by those whom you are to manage.[7]

Tim Sanders, former Chief Solutions Officer of Yahoo!, sings from the same sheet of music in his book, *Love Is the Killer App: How to Win Business and Influence Friends*:

I don't think there is anything higher than Love.... Love is so expansive. I had such a difficult time coming up with a definition for Love in my book, but the way I define Love is the selfless promotion of the growth of the other.[8]

Kevin Roberts, CEO of one of the world's largest ad agencies, Saatchi & Saatchi, proposes in his book *Lovemarks: The Future Beyond Brands* that love should be the foundation of all marketing:

At Saatchi & Saatchi our pursuit of Love and what it could mean for business has been focused and intense. Human beings need Love. Without it they die. Love is about responding, about delicate, intuitive sensing. Love is always two-way. When it is not, it cannot live up to the name Love. Love cannot be commanded or demanded. It can only be given.[9]

Copyrights, trademarks, servicemarks, and now lovemarks, says Roberts. That's how the strongest brands will institutionalize their uncopyable distinction from competing brands. This is more than a sea change. It is a planetary change. A cosmic change. It is as far removed from marketing theory of the past as instant messaging is from Victorian-era letter writing.

What Is a Firm of Endearment?

Consider the words *affection, love, joy, authenticity, empathy, compassion, soulfulness,* and other terms of endearment. Until recently, such words had no place in business. That is changing. Today, a growing number of companies comfortably embrace such terms. That is why we coined the phrase "firms of endearment," or FoE. Quite simply, an FoE is a company that *endears* itself to stakeholders by bringing the interests of all stakeholder groups into strategic alignment. No stakeholder group benefits at the expense of any other stakeholder group, and each prospers as the others do. These companies meet the functional and psychological needs of their stakeholders in ways that delight them and engender affection for and loyalty to the company.

During the 1990s, the phrase "share of wallet" became popular among marketers. It became the primary focus of the marketing approach called customer relationship management (CRM). However, the term signified an emotionally barren, largely impersonal and quantitative view of customers. For the vast majority of companies, CRM was more about better targeting and deeper exploitation of customers through data management than about empathetically attending to their needs. Instead of customer relationship management, it would have been more accurate to call it customer *data* management.

FoEs have bought into a different idea; they strive for *share of heart*. Earn a place in the customer's heart and she will gladly offer you a bigger share of her wallet. Do the same for an employee and the employee will give back with a quantum leap in productivity and work quality. *Emotionally* bond with your suppliers and reap the benefits of superior offerings and responsiveness. Give communities in which you operate reasons to feel pride in your presence, and enjoy a fertile source of customers and employees. (Of course, the phrase "share of heart" suggests that there is a fixed amount of love and care to be divided among claimants. In reality, there is no such limit, as the expression "Love is not a pie" suggests.)

And what about shareholders? Except perhaps among day traders and other short-term speculators, most shareholders probably enjoy feeling good about the companies in which they invest. They want good returns, but they also take delight in investing in companies they truly admire. Most do not want support companies that are morally deficient. Of no little importance, institutional investors such as university endowment funds and pension funds have grown increasingly conscious of the moral character of companies they invest in; witness the rapidly growing trend toward sustainable, responsible, and impact investing.

Unfortunately, the vast majority of companies today cannot be described as firms of endearment. Many have enjoyed success in the past, but find themselves increasingly vulnerable and criticized from all sides. Such companies are under growing pressure today, while their FoE competitors stand tall with all their stakeholder groups while acquitting themselves with distinction in investment markets. The message of this book is clear and simple: Provided that sound management is in place (no amount of moral correctness can save a badly managed company), *endearing companies tend to be enduring companies*.

FoEs share a distinctive set of core values, policies, and operating attributes. Here is a sampling:

- They subscribe to a purpose for being that is different from and goes beyond making money.
- They actively *align* the interests of all stakeholder groups, not just balance them. Instead of trading off the interests of one group versus those of another (for example, higher wages for employees versus higher profits for investors or lower prices for customers), they craft business models in which the objectives of each stakeholder can be met simultaneously and are in fact strengthened by other stakeholders. The key to this "concinnity" is that the activities of FoEs are executed within a system that allows for the active alignment of stakeholder interests. For example Whole Foods Market captures this idea in its formal "Declaration of Interdependence," which acknowledges the idea that stakeholder groups constitute a family whose members depend on one another.
- Their executive salaries are relatively modest. In a typical year, Costco co-founder and former CEO Jim Senegal's salary was $350,000, accompanied by a bonus of $200,000. By contrast, the average CEO of a comparable public company received $14.2 million in total compensation in 2012.

- They operate at the executive level with an open door policy. For example, when Honda has a big problem, it implements *waigaya*—temporary suspension of social protocols based on rank, thus making it possible for workers on the lowest rungs to personally present a proposed solution to the highest executives involved. Harley-Davidson has a similar policy, except less ceremonial: Any employee on any day has access to the highest offices in the company.

- Their employee compensation and benefits are significantly greater than the standard for the company's category. For example, Trader Joe's pay and benefits in the first year for full-time employees are double the U.S. average for retail employees.

- They devote considerably more time than their competitors to employee training. For example, The Container Store's first-year employees get an average of 263 hours of training versus the retail industry's average of eight hours.

- Their employee turnover is far lower than the industry average. For example, Southwest Airlines' employee turnover is half that of other major airlines.

- They empower employees to make sure customers leave every transaction experience fully satisfied. For example, a Wegmans Food Markets employee once sent a chef to a customer's home to overcome a customer's mistake and cook the Thanksgiving meal. (Yes, Wegmans employs chefs, some from five-star restaurants.)

- They make a conscious effort to hire people who are passionate about the company and its products. For example, Patagonia tries to only hire people who are passionate about nature. Whole Foods Market tries to draw as many employees as possible from the ranks of "foodies."

- They consciously humanize the company experience for customers and employees, as well as creating a nurturing work environment. For example, Google provides free gourmet meals around the clock for all employees.

- They project a genuine passion for customers, and emotionally connect with them at a deep level. By earning a larger share of customers' hearts, they earn a larger share of customers' wallets. Nordstrom, for example, is legendary for its commitment to outstanding customer service.

- Their marketing costs are far lower than those of their industry peers, while customer satisfaction and retention are far higher. For example, Jordan's Furniture spends less than one-third the industry norm on marketing and advertising, while generating industry-leading sales per square foot that are more than five times the industry norm. Google has built one of the world's most valuable brands without any advertising.

- They view their suppliers as true partners and collaborate with them to move both their companies forward. They help suppliers reach higher levels of productivity, quality, and profitability. Suppliers, in turn, function as true partners, not as beleaguered indentured servants. For example, Honda is said to "marry suppliers for life." Once a supplier has gained admittance to the Honda family of suppliers, the company does everything it can to help the supplier improve quality and become more profitable.

- They honor the spirit of laws rather than merely following the letter of the law. They apply uniformly high operating standards across the world, regardless of local requirements that may be considerably less stringent. For example, IKEA's policy is that if strict laws concerning chemicals and other substances are imposed in a country where it does business, all suppliers in all countries must conform to such laws.

- They consider their corporate culture to be their greatest asset and primary source of competitive advantage. For example, Southwest Airlines has an elected "Culture Committee" charged with sustaining and strengthening the company's unique culture.

- Their cultures are resistant to short-term, incidental pressures, but also prove able to quickly adapt when needed. As a result, they are typically the innovators and breakers of conventional rules within their industries. Stonyfield Yogurt shuns traditional advertising, for example, relying instead on creative social media campaigns.

While financial data surely is important in analyzing a company's strength and past performance, qualitative indicators are even more important in assessing a company's future prospects. In fact, we would go so far as to say that in many instances, qualitative factors may be more revealing in drawing the picture of a company's future performance than quantitative factors.

FoE Stakeholders

This book is organized around the five major stakeholders of modern corporations. As a memory tool, we have listed them in Table 1.1 in a way that creates the acronym "SPICE."

Table 1.1 The five major stakeholders of modern corporations

Stakeholder	Definition
Society	Local and broader communities as well as governments and other societal institutions, especially non-governmental organizations (NGOs); we also include the environment as part of this stakeholder
Partners	Upstream partners such as suppliers, horizontal partners, and downstream partners such as retailers
Investors	Individual and institutional shareholders as well as lenders
Customers	Individual and organizational customers
Employees	Current, future, and past employees and their families

As Figure 1.1 shows, each stakeholder is linked to all of the others. As in any good recipe, the individual ingredients come together to form something completely new; the whole is greater than the sum of the parts.

Figure 1.1 The SPICE stakeholder model

Each of these relationships is an essential piece of the puzzle, and each must be managed in the following ways:

- There is a two-way flow of value between both parties to the relationship.
- The interests of all parties are aligned.

This is the essence of great management. It is what all corporations should strive for. It is the way to maximize the returns to society of all the investments that flow into every organization. It is the *Firms of Endearment* way.

Identifying the Original Firms of Endearment

Most studies of corporate exceptionalism (or "greatness," to use Jim Collins' term) start with financial performance and work backward to identify the causes or covariates. We started with humanistic performance—meeting the needs of stakeholders other than share-holders—and worked forward.

We described the process for identifying firms for the first edition of this book as "organic and analog." We were interested in identifying a representative sample of firms that met our humanistic criteria. We did not simply conduct a statistical analysis of a plethora of companies in search of those whose financial performance supported the FoE hypothesis that companies can do well while doing good. Also, we did not want to exclude private companies from our analysis, as we believe that some of the best-managed companies from a stakeholder perspective are privately owned.

What we did was ask people, "Tell us about some companies you love. Not just like, but *love.*" This process generated hundreds of candidate companies, many that are household names and many that we had never heard of. We then put them through a screening process that assessed the quantitative and qualitative performance of each company for each of the SPICE stakeholders. We also probed for vulnerabilities, asking questions such as the following: Would most people say that the world is a better place because this company exists? How extensive a track record have they built? Do they have intensely loyal customers? How well do they treat their part-time employees? How high is their employee turnover? Do they have a reputation for squeezing their suppliers? Do communities welcome them or oppose them when they try to enter or expand? Do they have a record of environmental violations? Do they follow uniformly high standards of conduct worldwide? How have they responded to industry downturns or crises of confidence?

We picked the most promising 60 or so of the companies that bubbled up through our exploratory research and assigned teams of MBA students to research them. We directed the teams to conduct secondary and primary research (through interviews with executives, employees, customers, and others) on the companies, covering all major stakeholder groups: customers, employees, suppliers, communities, governments, and investors. When each project was completed by its assigned team, the results were assessed by the other research teams to gauge the extent to which a company qualified as a company loved by its stakeholders (that is, was qualified to be called a firm of endearment). The projects were completed over a two-year period. Some companies were investigated multiple times. In the end, we picked 28 companies, of which 18 were publicly traded.

We understood, of course, that none of these companies is perfect; each has areas in which it is relatively weak or somewhat vulnerable. Generally, these weaknesses are confined to one or at most two stakeholder groups. On the whole, however, we judged these companies to be quite exemplary in significant ways. Once we had selected the 28 companies we felt best manifested a high standard of humanistic performance, we then conducted a detailed comparative analysis of the firms from an investor viewpoint. Our hypothesis at this stage was that these companies probably performed better than the "average" company, but generally not by a huge amount. After all, they pay their employees exceptionally well, do not squeeze their suppliers, deliver great products and experiences at fair prices to customers, are conscious of their environmental impact, and spend significant resources in the community—surely, all this should lead to a reduction in profits and thus the stock price. As we are constantly reminded, there is no free lunch, certainly not in the corporate world.

Imagine our surprise, then, when we completed our investor analysis. These widely loved companies (those that are publicly traded) outperformed the S&P 500 by huge margins, over ten-, five-, and three-year time horizons. In fact, **the public FoEs returned 1,026 percent for investors over the ten years ending June 30, 2006, compared to 122 percent for the S&P 500; that's more than an 8-to-1 ratio!**

If this is not a "feel good" story, we don't know what is. In fact, it is far more than a feel good story—it is a deeply inspirational one. Apparently, these companies have figured out that not only can you have your cake and eat it too, you can also give some to your friends, donate some to a soup kitchen, and help support the local culinary school. How is it that these companies can be so generous to everyone who costs them money (customers, employees, suppliers, communities) and still deliver superior (some would say spectacular) returns to investors? **The answer to that important question is what this book is all about.**

Firms of Endearment vs. Good to Great Companies

We were interested in one more comparison. Jim Collins' best-selling book *Good to Great* identified 11 companies that it described as going from "good" to "great" by virtue of their having delivered superior returns to investors over an extended period of time (the companies had each delivered cumulative returns at least three times greater than the market over a 15-year period). We compared our set of publicly traded FoEs with the 11 *Good to Great* companies. This is what we discovered:

- Over a ten-year horizon, the 13 FoEs outperformed the *Good to Great* companies 1,026 percent to 331 percent (a 3-to-1 ratio).

- Over five years, the 17 FoEs outperformed the *Good to Great* companies 128 percent to 77 percent (a 1.7-to-1 ratio).

- Over three years, the 18 FoEs performed on par with the *Good to Great* companies: 73 percent to 75 percent.

Note that none of the *Good to Great* companies made our cut, though one (Gillette, which was acquired by Procter & Gamble) did come close. We also have a semantic disagreement with that book when it comes to defining "great." To us, a great company is one that spreads joy and fulfillment and makes the world a better place because it exists, not simply a company that outperforms the market by a certain percentage over a certain period of time. By our criteria, then, a company such as Altria (formerly Philip Morris and one of the companies in *Good to Great*) cannot be considered "great" even though it may have performed handsomely for investors. With a broader, society-level accounting, Altria's value is considerably diminished, perhaps even rendered negative.

Great companies sustain their superior performance over time for investors, but equally important in our view, for their employees, customers, suppliers, and society in general. We are confident that the companies you will read about in this book will stand the test of time. If you are looking for a meaningful and deeply satisfying career, take a look at the opportunities these companies offer. If you are a potential customer, compare their offerings to others. If you run a business, consider partnering with them. If you represent a community, try to attract them to your neighborhood. If you are a business professor, get this affirming message out to your students. We don't think you will be disappointed.

Selecting Companies for the Second Edition

The first edition of *Firms of Endearment* utilized what we acknowledged was a somewhat subjective process for identifying companies that we believe to be good representatives of this way of being. This time around, we wanted to bring greater rigor to the selection process. We also wanted to widen our lens to include more companies outside of the retail and consumer products sectors, as well as more international companies. Our search for how we could accomplish this came full circle, leading us back to friends who have been with us on this journey from the beginning, including Rick Frazier, Jeff Cherry, and Peter Derby. Inspired by the vision and the stories in the book, Rick, Jeff, and Peter began work on an investment research process soon after the book was published in 2007. After investing a great deal of time, energy, and money over the past six years, they have produced what it is arguably the most comprehensive data-driven process for identifying U.S. companies that are guided by a multi-stakeholder operating system. (Appendix B includes additional information on the research process as part of an interview we conducted with Rick Frazier, Founding Partner at Concinnity Advisors, LP.)

As a first step, we asked Concinnity Advisors, LP to provide us with a list of companies that have consistently scored well enough with all stakeholders to be considered investment candidates *each* of the last five years. We believe it is important for companies to demonstrate consistency and stability over time in their approach to stakeholders. This yielded a set of 64 publicly traded U.S. companies. We also selectively looked at some companies that had made the cut four out of the last five years, especially if they had made it for the most recent four.

Next, we applied additional qualitative screens to the shortlisted companies. First, we looked at purpose. A company received a high score on this if it has a well-articulated and authentically lived purpose that goes beyond profit maximization. Companies received lower scores if the purpose was unarticulated but still lived, or if the purpose was articulated but not clearly manifested. Companies that did not have an articulated higher purpose and did not manifest one were rejected based on this criterion.

We used a similar approach to look at the company's leadership. The company received a high score if it has a purpose-driven, service-minded, and reasonably paid CEO. Companies with autocratic and excessively highly paid leaders were rejected based on this criterion. Lastly, we looked for evidence that the companies had cultures that were rooted in trust, caring, and authenticity. Companies with overtly competitive, fear-based, and non-collaborative cultures were rejected.

This combined quantitative and qualitative approach yielded a set of 28 U.S. publicly traded companies that we deem to be firms of endearment.

Of course, an important caveat applies to all of these companies. Just as there are no perfect human beings, there are no perfect companies. Every one of the companies can be criticized by some for a perceived deficiency in certain areas. But all things considered, we feel very confident in the set of companies we've identified, and anticipate that their strong caring cultures will enable them to continue to operate in this manner for a long time to come. It is also important to point out that our stakeholder data on these companies spans the years 2008–2012. That provides a long enough time span for us to be able to assert with some confidence that these companies are likely to continue operating in this way into the future. But it does not guarantee that all of these companies did operate with a stakeholder orientation prior to 2008, though we do believe that was the case for most of them.

Although we used case studies and some personal interviews to qualitatively screen the U.S. public companies that had been identified through Concinnity Advisors' scoring system, we had to rely entirely on the case study approach in order to identify a set of privately owned firms of endearment. This is because we did not have access to a similar database for private companies. In addition, the universe of private companies is much larger than that of public companies, making the challenge of identifying a small set of such companies even greater. Our approach was to identify a set of companies that appear to embody these virtues, without claiming that they are the only such companies or even that they are the *best* such companies. We have included 29 such companies in our list. In most cases, we have direct experience with these exemplary firms, and can attest to their deep commitment to the principles underlying this way of doing business and being in the world.

We followed a similar process to identify a set of 15 non-U.S. companies, which includes 13 publicly traded companies and two private ones. Our goal here was to point to a diverse set of companies from multiple geographies that all share a commitment to this philosophy of business. The list includes companies from Japan, South Korea, India, Denmark, France, Spain, Sweden, and Mexico.

Table 1.2 lists all the companies that are included in these various categories.

Table 1.2 The FoE companies

US Public Companies	US Private Companies	Non-US Companies
3M	Barry-Wehmiller	BMW (Germany)
Adobe Systems	Bon Appetit Management	Cipla (India)
Amazon.com	Co.°	fabIndia (India - private)
Autodesk	Clif Bar	FEMSA (Mexico)
Boston Beer Company	Driscoll's	Gemalto (France)
CarMax	GSD&M Idea City	Honda (Japan)
Chipotle	Honest Tea°	IKEA (Sweden - private)
Chubb	IDEO	Inditex (Spain)
Cognizant	Interstate Batteries	Mahindra & Mahindra
Colgate-Palmolive	Jordan's Furniture°	(India)
Costco	L.L. Bean	Marico (India)
FedEx	Method	Novo Nordisk (Denmark)
Google	Millennium Oncology°	POSCO (South Korea)
Harley-Davidson	New Balance	TCS (India)
IBM	Patagonia	Toyota (Japan)
J.M. Smucker	Prana	Unilever (UK)
Marriott International	REI	
MasterCard Worldwide	SAS Institute	
Nordstrom	SC Johnson	
Panera	Stonyfield Yogurt°	
Qualcomm	TDIndustries	
Schlumberger	The Container Store	
Southwest Airlines	The Motley Fool	
Starbucks	Timberland°	
T. Rowe Price	TOMS	
United Parcel Service	Trader Joe's°	
Walt Disney	Union Square Hospitality	
Whole Foods Market	Group	
	USAA	
	Wegmans	
	WL Gore	

° These companies are stand-alone subsidiaries of other companies, and operate essentially as private companies.

Finally, it is important to point out that all of these companies are at different points in their evolution toward becoming firms of endearment. Some of them have been on this path from the beginning, which in several cases was more than 100 years ago. Others have only recently discovered this approach to business and are now consciously moving toward it. A third subset of companies were born this way, lost their bearings for a while after becoming publicly traded, and at some point reconnected with their roots, rediscovered their soul, and became firms of endearment or conscious companies once again.

Appendix A provides thumbnail sketches of all the companies included in the preceding table. Examples of practices from many of them are included throughout the book.

As Table 1.3 indicates, firms of endearment have significantly outperformed the market over all time frames, ranging from three years to 15 years. They have also greatly outperformed the companies cited in the book *Good to Great* over the last 10 and 15 years.

Table 1.3 Financial performance

Cumulative Performance	15 Years	10 Years	5 Years	3 Years
US FoEs	1681.11%	409.66%	151.34%	83.37%
International FoEs	1180.17%	512.04%	153.83%	47.00%
Good to Great Companies	262.91%	175.80%	158.45%	221.81%
S&P 500	117.64%	107.03%	60.87%	57.00%

The Unspoken Contract That FoEs Honor

In an earlier career, one of us (Wolfe) owned a company that managed communities with mandatory membership homeowner associations. One day a disturbing fact hit us between the eyes: Our most technically proficient community managers were not always as successful in getting management contracts renewed as managers with less well-developed technical skills. We conducted a survey of association boards of directors in hopes of solving this mystery. The survey team came back with a startling insight: We had *two* contracts with every board—a *legal* contract and an *emotional* contract. The survey team told us, "You can be completely faithful to the legal contract but it's not likely to be renewed if you haven't satisfied the emotional contract. On the other hand, if you satisfy the emotional contract, the boards will cut you some slack on the legal contract."

From customers and employees to suppliers, partners, shareholders, and the community, the full spectrum of a company's stakeholders is bound up with a company via these two contracts:

- **Legal contract**—This contract is mostly explicit and is based on *quantitative* performance criteria established by jurisprudence as well as representations by a company and its agents in writing, oral communications, and actions.

- **Emotional contract**—This contract is mostly implicit or unspoken and is based on *qualitative* performance criteria established by stakeholders in the form of expectations that reflect their moral and ethical values and their experiential desires—what they want to experience, and what they want to avoid experiencing.

Former MIT Sloan School of Management professor Edgar H. Schein writing about the explicit or legal contract and the implicit or emotional contract (which he called the "psychological contract") suggested that unless the terms of the psychological contract are intuitively understood by all, long-term relationships are not possible and friction is likely in the short term.[10]

Quite likely one of the most common causes of corporate mortality is breaches of the emotional contract. When the emotional contract is egregiously breached, customers stop buying, worker productivity ebbs, suppliers become less responsive, partners bail out, shareholders put in sell orders, and community support evaporates.

Companies spend vast sums fortifying and defending themselves against legal challenges by various stakeholders, while apparently not realizing that the roots of a claim might lie in a breach of the emotional contract. People don't sue people or organizations for whom they feel affection—or as Kevin Roberts would say, "that they love."

Toro, the giant lawn mower and snow blower maker, discovered that by delivering better on the emotional contract it could decrease personal injury litigation. Toro's leadership once believed personal injury litigation was inevitable given the nature of its products. But in the mid-1990s, that belief was abandoned. Company representatives began making personal contact with injured customers. They apologetically extended the company's sympathy and suggested that if an immediate settlement could not be arranged, arbitration might be better and less of a hassle than going to court. The company used nonthreatening paralegals, experienced settlement counselors, and mediators familiar with Toro's preference for early case resolution. By mid-2005, Toro estimated that it had saved $100 million in litigation costs since it kicked off its nonaggressive and emotionally sensitive approach to avoiding litigation in 1994. It had not been in court for a single personal injury case—a truly amazing record for a company that builds dangerous equipment that falls into countless careless hands every weekend of the year.[11]

Amul Dairy Products, one of the best-known brands in India, is a widely loved company that understands the unspoken contract it has with customers. Dr. Varghese Kurien, Chairman of the National Cooperative Dairy Federation of India, observed at Amul's 50th anniversary celebration, "If Amul has become a successful brand... then it is because we have honored our contract with consumers for close to 50 years. If we had failed to do so, then Amul would have been consigned to the dustbin of history, along with thousands of other brands."

FoEs understand that their business operations are shaped by both spoken and unspoken contracts. Like partners in a successful marriage, they know that failure to honor the emotional contract with a customer means the end of customer loyalty.

The FoE Way

FoEs take an expansive worldview. Instead of seeing the world in narrow, constricted terms, they see its infinite positive possibilities. They believe deeply in the possibility of a rising tide that raises all boats. Faced with a competitive threat, they don't look to cut prices and costs and employees, but to add greater value.

FoEs are bathed in the glow of timeless wisdom. Their "softness" in a hard world comes not because they are weak or lack courage, but from their leaders' knowledge of self, psychological maturity, and magnanimity of the soul. These companies are forceful and resolute in standing up for their principles. FoE leaders have the courage to defend and act decisively on their convictions: Jeff Bezos at Amazon, Jim Sinegal at Costco, Jim Goodnight at SAS Institute, Sergey Brin and Larry Page at Google, Barry and Eliot Tatelman at Jordan's Furniture, Jim and Anne Davis at New Balance, Herb Kelleher at Southwest, Jeff Swartz at Timberland, John Mackey and Walter Robb at Whole Foods, Kip Tindell at The Container Store, Ron Shaich at Panera, Bob Chapman at Barry-Wehmiller, Danny Meyer at Union Square Hospitality Group, Yusuf Hamied at Cipla, Terri Kelly at W.L. Gore—the list goes on and on. These FoE leaders have built extraordinary, industry-transforming companies despite carping from some Wall Street critics who reflexively view their "capitalism with a human face" as a threat to shareholders' interests. The view that competitive advantage can be gained through a business model whereby all stakeholders add value and benefit from gains in value simply runs counter to the views of many analysts. Such critics are fundamentally myopic; they tend to view any stakeholders other than stockholders as net drainers of value, rather than a broader and deeper set of resources that can be leveraged to create even greater value than a company could otherwise create when it treats them merely as a means to the ultimate end of maximizing shareholder returns.

To be best prepared for doing business in the twenty-first century, business executives, especially those of companies that are leaders in their categories, would do well to ask themselves the ultimate existential question: "What are we here for?" They should ponder such nontraditional (in business) propositions as, "We are not here just to enrich investors; we have no culturally legitimized license to corrupt minds, bodies, and the environment; we cannot justify under the rubric of capitalism actions that are intended to tempt, seduce, and mislead customers into doing what can harm them; we have no right under any legitimate credo to dehumanize employees or to squeeze the financial life out of suppliers with unreasonable demands." As leaders of FoEs do, companies of every type and size should consciously shape their cultures around the idea that we are here to help others live their lives with greater satisfaction, to spread joy and well-being, to elevate and educate, and to help employees and customers fulfill their natural potential. As leaders in companies—and other institutions of public purpose—is it too much to accept as one's mandate the obligation to listen and to see, to open eyes and minds, to help people focus on what matters most? These sentiments are captured in our own words, but they are the sentiments of the leadership in every truly great business.

If FoEs can be described by any one characteristic, it is that they possess a humanistic soul. It is from the depths of this soul that their determination to render uncommon service to all stakeholders flows. These companies are imbued with the joy of service—to the community, to society, to the environment, to customers, to colleagues. The leaders of these great companies, as we define "greatness," intuitively recognize the inherent need that most people above subsistence level have to serve others. These companies—their leaders, their people—have the courage to buck hallowed traditions in capitalistic theory. They are succeeding, indeed thriving, against long odds in the face of often ill-conceived, onerous regulations and unscrupulous competitors. They are holding on to their humanity in the face of overwhelming short-term pressures. We should rejoice in their success, and spread their message of caring for their fellow beings and their bottomless optimism far and wide. We have written this book to do precisely that.

Endnotes

1. Ronald W. Clement, "The lessons from stakeholder theory for U.S. business leaders," *Business Horizons*, (2005) 48, pp. 255–264.

2. http://www.saatchikevin.com/workingit/myra_stark_report2002.html, 2002.

3. James A. Autry, *Love and Profit: The Art of Caring Leadership*, Avon Books, New York, 1991, back matter.

4. Daniel H. Pink, *A Whole New Mind: Moving from the Information Age to the Conceptual Age*, Riverhead Books, 2005, pg. 51.

5. Ibid.

6. http://www.thefreedictionary.com/love.

7. Autry *op cit*, pg. 19.

8. Tim Sanders, *Love Is the Killer App: How to Win Business and Influence Friends*, Crown Business, 2002.

9. Kevin Roberts, *Lovemarks: The Future Beyond Brands*, PowerHouse Books, New York, 2004, pg. 49.

10. Edgar H. Schein, *Organizational Psychology*, Englewood Cliffs, NJ, Prentice Hall.

11. Ashby Jones, "House Calls," *Corporate Counsel*, Oct. 1, 2004.

2

New Age, New Rules, New Capitalism

A darkening shadow hangs over the business landscape, cast by a daunting mass of customers, workers, investors, suppliers, and other stakeholders. Tolerance for executive mischief has run out, exhausted by the likes of Enron, Tyco, WorldCom, Adelphia Cable, and other multibillion-dollar corporate scandals.

"The business of America is business" was a statement made by President Calvin Coolidge in the 1920s. If this is true (and we are not sure it was ever really the case; we would rather say that the well-being of the nation and its people is the business of America—business being one very important tool for facilitating that), then recent trends about the public perception of business should be a matter of great concern. For the institution of business has rarely been held in such low esteem as it is currently. As *The New York Times* put it, "the majority of the public... believes that executives are bent on destroying the environment, cooking the books and lining their own pockets."[1]

Multiple polls confirm this grim new reality, one that cannot be overcome by any amount of slick public relations campaigns:

- Gallup has found that Americans' confidence in big business has declined steadily, from about 34 percent in 1975 to a historic low of 16 percent in 2009, rebounding to 19 percent in 2011.[2]

- A 2011 Harris Poll found that 88 percent of Americans think big companies have too much influence on government.[3]

- A 2011 survey by GFK Custom Research North America found that 64 percent of American consumers are finding it harder to trust corporations today compared to a few years ago;

55 percent say it will be harder for corporations to gain their trust in the future.[4]

- According to the 2011 U.S. Yankelovich Monitor, 79 percent of Americans agree that "business is too concerned with profits and not [concerned] enough with public responsibility:" 67 percent believe that "if the opportunity arises, most businesses will take advantage of the public if they feel they are not likely to be found out."[5] When Yankelovich asked Americans to rate their trust in major companies on a 0-to-10 scale in 2004, only four percent gave a response of 9 or 10.[6]

It's tempting to blame moral bankruptcy in the executive suite on a few bad apples rising to the top of the corporate barrel. But we must look beyond the C-level to fully plumb the problem. Ethical lapses at the top usually reflect a morally impoverished corporate culture in which money matters more than anything else. Boards (and investors, too) ought to pay closer attention to corporate cultures, for to paraphrase Winston Churchill, "We shape our culture and thereafter it shapes us."[7] A company's culture is a window on the executive soul.

For better or worse, the moral character of mainstream culture also influences executive behavior. In acting out their lives, people generally mirror the cultures in which they live. This holds true whether we're talking about a fad-conscious teen or a Lamborghini-driving Fortune 500 CEO. An ethos of acquisitiveness and competitive striving deeply imbedded in American culture encourages people to bend the rules to serve their ambitions. It can also create what people at Apple Computer came to term a "reality distortion field" around powerful, charismatic leaders—a refusal to acknowledge reality as it exists and to take responsibility for the consequences of one's actions.[8]

We may not be able to legislate morality, as politicians often say, but it would serve us all well to think about how we might shape our culture so that in Churchillian fashion more of us—and the companies we're associated with—could be reshaped for the better. Does our culture value the right things, we might ask ourselves? Do we hold corporations to high-enough standards, or do we cynically expect and accept deviant behavior in some of society's most powerful institutions as par for the course? What will it take to create a cultural environment that encourages more executives to balance personal ambitions with societal imperatives, and to eventually bring the two into alignment?

Answers to these questions are gradually being revealed in the social transformation of capitalism, which is a parallel event to the maturation of society due to aging populations.

The Self-Actualization of Capitalism

John Perry, former White House speechwriter and award-winning editor of several newspapers, views the roiling waves of change sweeping over us as major *realignments* in science, technology, medicine, education, the arts, religion, economies, demographics, social systems, governments, and institutions, both private and public, the world over. The list is not exhaustive. Perry goes on to say that he believes we are in the midst of a society-wide moral renaissance:

> Most compelling of all, fundamental beliefs and value systems are realigning. On balance, most of those realignments are for the good. This is, accept it or not, actually becoming a better world—and at no previous time in modern history has that statement been possible.[9]

Despite the daily feed of large-font headlines calling our attention to serious mischief in every institutional category, the evidence of a moral renaissance courses through contemporary literature. With more than 32 million hardcover copies sold and translated into more than 50 languages, pastor Rick Warren's *The Purpose Driven Life*, a book about a higher purpose in life than indulging one's worldly self, has become one of the best-selling nonfiction books in history.[10] Its success indicates people are hungrier than ever for a durable sense of meaning in their lives. This is a defining characteristic of the Age of Transcendence.

In the business book category, recent "morality" titles include Mihaly Csikszentmihalyi's *Good Business: Leadership, Flow and the Making of Meaning*; William Greider's *The Soul of Capitalism: Opening Paths to a Moral Economy*; Richard Barrett's *Liberating the*

Corporate Soul: Building a Visionary Organization; and Marc Benioff and Karen Southwick's *Compassionate Capitalism: How Corporations Can Make Doing Good an Integral Part of Doing Well*. Benioff and Southwick speculate about how the world would change for the better if every company donated a mere one percent of its sales, one percent of its employees' time, and one percent of its stock to better the communities in which it operates.[11]

Business has yet to broadly come to terms with the ebbing influence of materialistic values on what people want from life, which is the inevitable result of an aging society. This is an unprecedented shift that is changing the calculus of supply and demand in large ways.

Psychoanalyst Eric Fromm would say that we are transitioning from a *having* society to a *being* society. "Having" societies are steeped in self-centeredness and materialism. "Being" societies have an others-centered focus, and are deeply vested in high-ground moral values.[12]

For a full century, the consumer economy has been grounded in a materialistic *having* focus. That focus is now being diffused by rising desires for a sense of meaning that cannot be drawn from material things. Consumers may still want a given product, but along with that product many want a high-road experience that connects with their more mature *being* focus. For example, shoppers at FoE Whole Foods Market gladly pay substantially more than they would pay for eggs at Kroger's just for the good feeling that they are doing right by purchasing eggs from free-range hens.

Obviously, material appetites are not disappearing from society. Materialistic values and behavior are a fact of life. Young people in particular will always have hearty materialistic appetites. They express their identities and give evidence of their accomplishments and potential through the material things they acquire. But mainstream culture increasingly reflects the *being* focus that emerges at upper levels of psychological maturity as the thrill of accumulating "things" ebbs.

It is hard to overstate the significance of a softening of consumer interest in "things" to consumer-based businesses. In the U.S., the pre-middle-age adult population—the most having-focused demographic segment—is shrinking in some five-year cohorts while growing at less than a snail's pace in others. Abroad, the pre-middle-age adult population is shrinking in every developed nation. No consumer-based company can afford to not assess the effects of ebbing *having* desires on consumer behavior. To prosper, companies will increasingly need to learn how *being* customers are different from *having* customers. The shift toward a *being* ethos changes not only what people buy, but also how products should be designed both esthetically and functionally. It also changes how products should be presented to the marketplace: more as meaning-laden experiences and less as throw away trinkets

Psychologist Erik Erikson's term *generativity* is closely related to what Fromm meant by a *being* focus. Generativity is a disposition to help the next generation come into its own successfully. The surfacing of a spirit of generativity in a person's psyche moderates the ego—the source of materialistic appetites—so that psychic energy can be rerouted to help fulfill the needs of others. FoEs are a collective representation of the shift toward others-centeredness that higher levels of maturity lead to on an individual basis.

Members of today's middle age population (which we define here as encompassing ages 40–60 because those are arithmetically the middle adult years of the 80-year life expectancy of a newly minted adult) form a critical demographic mass that is turning the ethos of generativity into one of the most powerful forces in society. This mass, made up mostly of aging boomers, is reshaping the moral foundations of society. Few companies are immune to its influences. Generativity is a rising influence in business life, though in terms broader than Erikson conceived of. It is better known in business as *sustainability*, which the internationally constituted Bruntland Commission defined as "meeting the needs of the present generation without compromising the ability of future generations to meet their own needs."[13]

The emergence of a disposition for generativity marks a person's first step toward what American psychologist Abraham Maslow termed *self-actualization*, by his reckoning the pinnacle of psychological maturation.[14] He saw self-actualization as the end game of human development. It is about discovering the *real self* by transcending the *social self* that dominates the first half of life. Although not everyone reaches full self-actualization—Maslow said few do—most people get far enough along in the journey to develop a *being* focused worldview. Some of the key psychological characteristics of self-actualization are[15]

- Superior perception of reality (*more authentic, less influenced by idealizations*).
- Increased acceptance of self, of others, of nature.
- Increase in problem-centering (*removing self from the equation; not interested in being a hero*).
- Greater freshness of appreciation, and richness of emotional reaction.
- Increased identification with the human species.
- More democratic character structure (*genuine sense of equality, fairness*).
- Greatly increased creativity.
- Changes in value system. (*Values shift from materialistic, narcissistic influences to others-centered influences.*)

We posit that rising expectations for corporate social consciousness reflect the growing influence of generativity on societies the world over. A number of European nations now require annual reports on a company's "triple bottom line"—its performance relative to people, the planet, and profits. U.S. companies are voluntarily doing so in increasing numbers. According to the Governance & Accountability Institute, approximately 53 percent of the S&P 500 Index companies now issue annual corporate social responsibility reports.[16] It seems not far in the future when all publicly traded companies will have to issue some variation of such reports either because of law or investor and social pressure.

But for now, the issue of corporate social responsibility remains clouded by tradition. In 1970, Nobel Laureate economist Milton Friedman famously proclaimed in a *New York Times Magazine* article, "There is one and only one social responsibility of business—to use its resources and engage in activities designed to increase its profits so long as it stays within the rules of the game."[17] Many still swear by Friedman's proclamation. However, a recent *McKinsey Quarterly* global survey revealed that four out of five executives believe the role of corporations goes beyond simply meeting obligations to shareholders. Only one in six agrees with Milton Friedman's famous dictum. Even GE's charismatic former head, Jack Welch, long seen as a staunch advocate of a shareholder-dominated worldview, has put forth a more nuanced view: "On the face of it, shareholder value is the dumbest idea in the world. Shareholder value is a result, not a strategy... your main constituencies are your employees, your customers and your products."[18]

While one swallow does not a spring make, Welch's statement is a harbinger of the biggest ideological change in capitalism since Adam Smith wrote *The Wealth of Nations*. Capitalism is acquiring a more human face than seemed possible to most observers just one generation ago. Former Harvard business scholar Ira Jackson says we're at the starting line of an "entirely new stage of capitalism" that he calls "capitalism with a conscience."[19] Paul Hawken, co-founder of the gardening supply outfit Smith & Hawken, sees a paradigm shift toward *natural capitalism.* This brand of capitalism is based on environmental integrity and the needs of people rather than on the contrived needs of companies (narrowly defined as maximizing profits). Two of the authors of this book (Raj Sisodia and David Wolfe) became involved after the publication of the first edition of *Firms of Endearment* in helping launch a global movement called "Conscious Capitalism."[20]

Midlife is a private period of transcendence—that is, a time of rising above the material world in a search for deeper meaning in one's life than acquiring more "stuff." Daniel Pink, writing for the Yahoo! Trend Desk noted, "Liberated by prosperity but not fulfilled by it, Americans are slowly refocusing their lives away from the material and toward the meaningful. As Nobel-prize winning economist Robert William Fogel has written, prosperity has 'made it possible to extend the quest for self-realization from a minute fraction of the population to almost the whole of it.'"[21]

This midlife disposition toward self-realization or self-actualization is not new to the human experience. Vedic literature from ancient India going back thousands of years speaks of the time in life when a person should break his connections with the world to rise to higher levels of being. To do this he must submerge the ego. This frees him to better focus on others—family, community, and the species. While the values of people in midlife have not changed in thousands of years, the proportion of adults experiencing these values has dramatically changed. Middle age and older people are now the culture-shaping majority. For the first time in history, most adults are in the years when self-actualization needs begin influencing behavior in significant ways.

The growing influence of self-actualization on mainstream culture is reshaping the way business is done. Indeed, it might be said that we are experiencing the beginning moments of *the self-actualization of capitalism*. More and more, companies are submerging their corporate egos, as it were, to focus more intensely on others—on their stakeholders, from customers and employees to suppliers, shareholders, and society at-large.

Jeff Immelt, successor CEO to Jack Welch at General Electric, signifies the accelerating movement toward companies striving to do good while doing well. In late 2004, he told 200 of his top executives that GE needed to do four things to remain a leader. Three of the four were laudable but predictable: execution, growth, and hiring great people. But at the top of the list was virtue. This is a momentous shift. In the business world, when GE talks, other companies listen. Immelt put it succinctly: "To be a great company today, you have to be a good company." He elaborated:

> "The reason people come to work for GE is that they want to be about something that is bigger than themselves. People want to work hard, they want to get promoted, and they want to get stock options. But they also want to work for a company that makes a difference, a company that's doing great things in the world.... Good leaders give back. The era we live in belongs to people who believe in themselves but are focused on the needs of others.... The world's changed. Businesses today aren't admired. Size is not respected. There's a bigger gulf today between haves and have-nots than ever before. It's up to us to use our platform to be a good citizen. Because not only is it a nice thing to do, it's a business imperative."[22]

Shareholders versus Stakeholders

As we noted in the Prologue, University of Virginia business school professor R. Edward Freeman is credited with being the first to fully articulate the idea of a stakeholder relationship management

(SRM) business model. In his groundbreaking 1984 book *Strategic Management: A Stakeholder Approach*, he posited that shareholders were best served when all stakeholders were well served. Freeman defined a stakeholder as "any group or individual who can be or is affected by the achievement of a firm's objectives." He disdained Milton Friedman's idea of shareholder supremacy, preferring instead to view shareholders as one among others in a constellation of interdependent stakeholders.

A distinguishing core value of FoEs is service to all stakeholders without favoring one over another. This is an irreplaceable factor in these companies' ability to outperform most if not all their direct competitors. We found this all the more remarkable after learning that companies listed in Jim Collins' management best seller *Good to Great* dramatically trailed FoEs in returns to shareholders over the past 10–20 years (details in Chapter 6, "Investors: Reaping What FoEs Sow").

Collins claimed in that book there are no specific "right" core values for becoming an enduring great company. That may have once been true, but no longer is. Collins writes, "A company need not have passion for its customers (Sony didn't), or respect for the individual (Disney didn't), or quality (Walmart didn't) or social responsibility (Ford didn't) in order to become enduring and great."[23]

In our view, the "shareholder versus stakeholder" debate presents a false dichotomy. Judging by the superior financial performance achieved by the exemplary companies cited in this book, we believe that the best way to create value for shareholders in the long run is by consciously creating value for all stakeholders. Take Costco, for example. Costco pays its employees very well compared to its retail industry peers, with generous benefits to boot. It pays much more than its direct competitors do, but it also *generates significantly more sales and profit per employee*. It achieves this seeming act of alchemy by being far more efficient and having very low employee turnover. Costco's better paid and happier employees are highly motivated and productive. Moreover, with deeper company loyalty than is common in retail, these more highly motivated employees are sure to be a constant source of new ideas for further improving productivity.

Like other FoEs, Costco has designed a business model that enables it to pay its employees well, make good money for investors, have highly satisfied customers and suppliers, and generally be welcomed with open arms into every community it wants to enter.

Still, Wall Street has many analysts who think that Costco is guilty of robbing investors to line the pockets of undeserving, pampered employees. It's difficult for analysts bent on looking at companies through a traditional lens of numbers to comprehend the value-producing potential of the stakeholder relationship management business model. Here is Bill Dreher of Deutsche Bank Securities: "From the perspective of investors, Costco's benefits are overly generous. Public companies need to care for shareholders first. Costco runs its business like it is a private company."[24]

Dreher appears to us to be misguided. Public companies that are managed as though they were enlightened private companies often turn out to be great investments. Listen to former CEO Jim Sinegal elaborating on why Costco is "overly generous" to employees:

> "Paying your employees well is not only the right thing to do but it makes for good business. In the final analysis, you get what you pay for."[25]

He goes on to state that paying rock-bottom wages is "wrong. It doesn't pay the right dividends. It doesn't keep employees happy. It keeps them looking for other jobs. Plus, managers spend all their time hiring replacements rather than running your business. We would rather have our employees running our business. When employees are happy, they are your very best ambassadors.... If we take care of the business and keep our eye on the goal line, the stock price will take care of itself."[26] And indeed it has; Costco has been a stellar performer in the stock market.

The problem is that many financial analysts are uncomfortable with anything other than conventional business models. They rely on extensive data on "norms" against which to judge companies. When a company spends more than the norm in one category—as Costco does in the wages category—analysts often overlook offsetting gains. Costco's higher wages—in conjunction with a culture of respect and empowerment—buy it lower recruiting and training costs and better relationships with customers that lead to higher sales per customer and deep customer loyalty.

One of the biggest "secrets" of FoEs' successes is how they become preferred companies to do business with in every stakeholder group. For example, manufacturers of high-quality products such as Titleist and Cuisinart initially shunned warehouse-style retail stores because of their "bare-bones" image. Today, such companies eagerly sell their products at Costco, which attracts a high proportion of affluent shoppers. The best employees woo FoEs. For example, UPS has a multiyear waiting list of highly qualified drivers. Patagonia receives about 10,000 resumes annually to fill a hundred new openings. Most FoEs do little costly advertising. Customers come into a company's space without being called by pitches, Madison Avenue style. Sometimes FoEs' primary problem is not getting customers, but keeping up with customer demand. Communities often are anxious to attract FoEs to locate in them. The family-owned grocer chain Wegmans receives hundreds of letters monthly from customers pleading with it to open a store in their community.

Apparent recent interest in an SRM business model by industry titans General Electric and Walmart probably makes it safe to say, "The tide is turning." The rising assertiveness of members in every stakeholder group toward companies they invest in, buy from, work for, and permit to operate through public license is causing companies to lean toward the SRM business model. We see this not as a management fad destined to pass quickly, but an enduring trend helped along by a moral revolution in the executive suites of America, a demographics-driven value shift in the population at large, and keener understanding among business leaders that this is ultimately a matter of enlightened self-interest.

What's the bottom line here? Placing shareholders far above all other stakeholders may be the worst long-term position a company can put them in. The record of the exemplary firms in this book indicates that shareholders can gain more when their interests are aligned with the interests of all other stakeholder groups. We say this without regard for day-traders and other high-churn speculators. They only *take* transient value; they do not invest in creating long-term value. Indeed, short-term investing is a contradiction in terms; all true investing is for the long term. In the SRM economic ecosystem, only stakeholders that create long-term value make long-term sense.

Emotionally Intelligent Management in FoEs

Ever since Howard Gardner published his landmark book *Frames of Mind: The Theory of Multiple Intelligences* in 1983, there has been intense interest in understanding the specific types of intelligence that lead to greater or less success in various endeavors. In 1990, Peter Salovey and John Mayer published an article titled "Emotional Intelligence," which dealt with "one's ability to be aware of one's own feelings, be aware of others' feelings, to differentiate among them, and to use the information to guide one's thinking and behavior."[27] This academic work was later popularized and brought into the cultural mainstream by Daniel Goleman, a former reporter for *The New York Times*. His 1995 book *Emotional Intelligence: Why It Can Matter More Than IQ* was a worldwide bestseller, and was followed by *Working with Emotional Intelligence* in 1998.[28]

Goleman defines emotional intelligence (EI) as "the capacity for recognizing our own feelings and those of others, for motivating ourselves, for managing emotions well in ourselves and in our relationships." It includes the components of self-awareness, self-regulation (self-mastery or self-management of emotion), social awareness (empathy), and social skills (relationship management).[29] Goleman believes that self-awareness is the most fundamental aspect of emotional intelligence, but has generally been ignored in business settings.[30] He and many academic researchers have shown that there is a strong link between the ability of individuals to manage their own emotions and their ability to positively impact the emotions of others.

Emotional intelligence is vitally important for long-term success in management as well as in business and life generally. It is no coincidence that all the firms of endearment described in this book can also be described as companies with a high degree of EI, not just in their senior management team, but woven throughout the fabric of the organization, and reflected in the dealings of employees with each other, with customers, with business partners, and with society at large.

Researchers have shown that EI leads indirectly to competitive advantage because it is a prerequisite for the kind of leadership necessary to effect positive and sustainable strategic change.[31] EI is increasingly viewed as a characteristic, not just of individuals, but of work groups as well as of organizations. Under this "systems" view, individuals contribute energy that adds to organizational EI. However, organizational EI is also "a dynamic output of the function and structure and energy of the organizational system itself." In turn, organizations with high EI exert a strong influence on individuals within those organizations to exhibit similar traits.[32]

The importance of EI in the workplace can be appreciated by seeing the consequences of its absence: low morale, a climate of fear or apathy, intense conflict, and high levels of stress, which clearly impact business effectiveness. Such environments inevitably foster costly defections and even lawsuits by employees who feel "bullied, intimidated, and exploited."[33]

Most companies strive to create work environments that are strictly rational, with no place for emotional concerns. However, it is impossible to remove emotion from the workplace, just as it is impossible to remove emotions from any sphere of human activity.[34] In the twenty-first century, we can no longer view business organizations as merely "rational machines." Rather, they must be viewed as "dynamic and increasingly unpredictable organisms." This perspective requires that managers shed their traditional hierarchical command-and-control mindset and embrace flat, flexible structures that depend on "interactive, interdependent, and creative processes."[35]

In their 2002 book *Primal Leadership: Realizing the Power of Emotional Intelligence*, Goleman and his co-authors describe a study of 3,871 executives and their direct reports. This study showed that leadership style matters in emotional as well as pragmatic bottom-line terms. "The tone of the workplace, the emotional tone drives bottom-line results, that is, how much people give, how much people want to give, how much people care...those things show up on the balance sheets. And the rule of thumb that our research points to is that the leader's style determines about 70 percent of the emotional climate, which in turn drives around 20 percent—and sometimes 30 percent—of business performance."[36] Given this, the results of a study reported in Harvard Business Review in 2005 are particularly worrisome. Based on 100,000 measurements of EQ, the researchers found that "EQ scores rise as executives climb the ladder, peaking at the manager level, falling off thereafter, and bottoming out, alarmingly, at the CEO level."[37]

Finding the Will to Change

The remaking of capitalism into an instrument of broader purpose appears unstoppable. Companies that fail to recognize this court disaster. Stakeholders are increasingly demanding more socially aware management from companies. Customers will vote for this by closing their wallets to companies that don't comply. The best employees will hire on elsewhere. Suppliers will favor companies that treat them with respect. Communities will make it tougher for companies that place shareholders high above all. And financial markets will restrict the flow of capital and raise its cost.

Most companies today still operate by rules of the past because they are hapless captives of outmoded mental frames. Cognitive scientist George Lakoff observes that our behavior is framed by "mental structures that shape the way we see the world."[38] Mental frames impart stability to our lives by serving as benchmarks for making sense of the world. But mental frames also predispose us to reflexively accept as fact something that agrees with what we believe, and mindlessly deny as error anything that is inconsistent with what we believe. This "confirmation bias" can also be expressed in the following brief statement:

Belief follows need.

How often have you presented a spouse, a friend, a colleague, or other person with an objectively verifiable fact that they dismiss out of hand? For the most part, people and companies believe what they feel a need to believe.

We *need* to preserve our mental frames or worldviews because we need to maintain mental equilibrium. Thus, we select and organize incoming information to preserve the integrity of those worldviews. This is why protection of our belief system often overrides a pragmatic need to change what we believe. George Lakoff explains:

> Neuroscience tells us that that each of the concepts we have—the long-term concepts that structure how we think—is instantiated in the synapses of the brain. Concepts are not things that can be changed just by someone telling us a fact. We may be presented with facts, but for us to make sense of them, they have to fit what is already in the synapses of the

brain. Otherwise, facts go in and then they go right back out. They are not heard, or they are not accepted as facts, or they mystify us: Why would anyone have said that? Then we label the fact as irrational, crazy, or stupid."[39]

Einstein famously said, "A problem cannot be solved by the same consciousness in which it arose."[40] The consciousness that has ruled business enterprise over the past two centuries is rooted in classical notions that reason is superior to emotions in the affairs of people (intimate affairs excluded). This has rendered stakeholders (including shareholders) as largely bloodless, statistical entities.

FoEs offer evidence that this has been a mistake. Right brain emotionality deserves no less than equal attention with left brain rationality in business analysis, planning, and operations. Recent research resoundingly confirms the primacy of the emotional over the purely rational. In an overwhelming majority of cases, top performers are not those executives with the highest level of intellectual intelligence but those with the highest level of *emotional intelligence.* In his book *Working with Emotional Intelligence,* Daniel Goleman provides data from studies of more than 500 organizations showing that self-confidence, self-awareness, self-control, commitment, and integrity are factors that lead to more successful employees as well as more successful companies.[41]

The affectionate regard that FoEs have for their stakeholders has value that cannot be accounted for by classical economic and management theory. Neither body of thought has any way of reckoning the value of mutual affection between a company and its stakeholders. Calculating its influence on financial return is beyond their reach. But if the economic value of something as intangible as a brand can be assessed in absolute dollar terms, why not also the amount of heart a company invests in its stakeholders? This means giving caring a prominent place in economic and management theory.

Classical capitalism is heartless by design. The same holds true for traditional management theory. This heartlessness is ancestrally rooted in René Descartes' scientific method, formulated some 400 years ago. The Cartesian approach to scientific inquiry discounted the value of emotion in truth-seeking. Emotion was considered the antithesis of reason. Philosophers laid the foundations of economics and capitalism with this in mind. In *The Wealth of Nations*, Adam Smith famously talked about market outcomes being shaped by an *invisible hand* moved by the *reasoned* decisions of people acting in their own interests. The invisible hand was emotionless. But Adam Smith also wrote movingly and insightfully about the human need to care in his earlier book *The Theory of Moral Sentiments*. That need and the drive to pursue one's self-interest are the two fundamental human drives. For most of us, the need to care often overrides the pursuit of self-interest when one is forced to make such a choice (as any parent would recognize). A great tragedy of the last two centuries was that we built the intellectual foundations of capitalism on only one of those two pillars, setting in motion the inevitable backlash of exploited workers rising up to demand better treatment and Karl Marx channeling that angst into creating an even more deeply flawed approach to how human activity should be organized.

Some may wince when hearing talk about promoting affectionate relationships between a company and its stakeholders. However, anyone wanting hard proof that "going soft" in business has a big payoff will find it in contemporary neuroscience.[42] Loyalty of any sort turns out to be more a function of *how one feels* than *what one thinks*. This is supported by a study in which brain scans traced people's mental responses to brands. Researchers found that brands engaged the emotional right side of the brain more than other proper nouns generally do.[43] Coupling that finding with neurologist Antonio Damasio's discovery[44] that emotion—not reason—is how we determine the relevance of anything to us provides substantial support for the central premise of this book:

Endearing behavior by a company toward its stakeholders is one of the most decisive competitive differences ever wielded in capitalistic enterprise.

Assuming sound management is in place, we argue that Company A will outperform Company B in the long term if its stakeholders regard it with greater affection than do the stakeholders of Company B. Company A's margins are likely to be greater than Company B's. Consumers will pay more for Company A's products because they love the company and its products. The outdoor apparel and equipment maker Patagonia discovered this. A much-loved company,

Patagonia's customers pay an average premium of 20 percent or more over competitors' prices. This helps to produce a gross profit margin of close to 50 percent.[45]

Emotions are not some vaporous essence in our consciousness. They are concrete physiological states. Emotions are the touchstone of relevance arising from changes in body states. Changes in adrenalin flow, heartbeat, blood pressure, galvanic skin response, breathing, salivation, and other body states generate emotions. The greater the importance of a matter, the stronger the emotional response. Without emotional responses to connect us viscerally as well as cognitively to something, we can have no sense of affinity to it. We are incapable of affection toward that something.

A brand or company that fails to arouse a customer's emotions in positive ways will not engender true loyalty in that customer. But the same holds true for employees. Their bonds with a company are less based on left-brain quantitative issues of salaries and benefits than many managers believe. They are based more on the right brain qualitative issues of recognition and appreciation. Yes, a high salary and generous stock options may keep an employee on the payroll (as long as the stock price holds up), but absent recognition and appreciation that person will not be bonded with the company. Being unbonded, the employee will not give the company her best efforts. She will not be engaged, inspired, cooperative, creative, happy, or fulfilled. She will care little about the wellbeing of customers and speak ill of the company to anyone who will listen.

The subject of customer, employee, and shareholder loyalty began to command higher attention following the publication of Frederick Reichheld's book *The Loyalty Effect: The Hidden Force Behind Growth, Profits and Lasting Values* in 1996.[46] But even Reichheld did not discuss the role of emotion in fostering stakeholder loyalty. Emotion has been the elephant in the living room waiting to be acknowledged by business academicians, corporate executives, economists, and Wall Street. Daniel Goleman has made great strides in pointing this elephant out to the business community.

Reflecting back on Einstein's dictum about solving a problem created by an old consciousness, the new consciousness that will lift a company successfully into the loftier realms of New Capitalism recognizes that all reality is personal and infused with affect. Objectivity has proven to be an overreaching affectation of science. Subjectivity rules in the Age of Transcendence in terms of garnering stakeholder loyalty and affection. We need to find the right blend between the two.

Endnotes

1. Claudia H. Deutsch, "New Surveys Show That Big Business Has a P.R. Problem," *The New York Times*, December 9, 2005.

2. Jeffrey M. Jones, "Americans Most Confident in Military, Least in Congress," GALLUP News Service, 2011. http://www.gallup.com/poll/148163/Americans-Confident-Military-Least-Congress.aspx.

3. Regina Corso, "Big Companies, PACs, Banks, Financial Institutions and Lobbyists Seen by Strong Majorities as Having Too Much Power and Influence on DC," The Harris Poll #65, Harris Interactive, 2011. http://www.harrisinteractive.com/NewsRoom/HarrisPolls/tabid/447/ctl/ReadCustom%20Default/mid/1508/ArticleId/790/Default.aspx.

4. GfK Custom Research North America, "State of Distrust—New Survey Indicates Corporate Trust Waning Among Influential Americans," GfK 2011 Corporate Trust Survey, 2011.

5. The Futures Company, Tom Morley, email to author, "State of the Consumer," 2011 U.S. Yankelovich Monitor, 2011.

6. Craig Wood, "2004 Yankelovich State of Consumer Trust: Rebuilding the Bonds of Trust," Yankelovich, Inc., 2004.

7. When discussions were underway for rebuilding the House of Commons, which had been severely damaged by the German blitzkrieg, Winston Churchill nixed proposals to rebuild those hallowed premises on a grand scale. He argued that the House of Commons should be rebuilt on an intimate scale to facilitate democratic processes of face-to-face debate. The great man observed, "Man shapes his buildings and thereafter they shape him."

8. See Walter Isaacson's masterful book *Jobs* for a description and examples of this at Apple Inc.

9. John L. Perry, "What Matters Most," http://www.newsmax.com/archives/articles/2003/6/18/155248.shtml, Jun. 18, 2003.

10. Rick Warren, *The Purpose Driven Life: What on Earth Am I Here For?* Zondervan Publishing, 2002.

11. Mihaly Csikszentmihalyi, *Good Business: Leadership, Flow and the Making of Meaning,* Penguin Group, 2004; William Greider, *The Soul of Capitalism: Opening Paths to a Moral Economy,* Simon & Schuster, 2004; Richard Barrett, *Liberating the Corporate Soul: Building a Visionary Organization,* Butterworth-Heinemann, 1998; and Marc Benioff and Karen Southwick, *Compassionate Capitalism: How Corporations Can Make Doing Good an Integral Part of Doing Well,* Career Press, 2004.

12. Erich Fromm, *To Have or To Be?* Bantam Books, 1981.

13. The Bruntland Commission, made up of representative from 22 countries and named after its Norwegian chairman, Gro Harland Bruntland, popularized the term *sustainability* and provided this definition in its final report, *Our Common Future,* to the UN General Assembly in 1987.

14. Contrary to common belief, Maslow did not coin the term *self-actualization* or originate the theory of self-actualization. He adopted the term and concept of self-actualization after meeting neurologist Kurt Goldstein, who introduced the term and concept in his famous book *The Organism* (1934). Goldstein's study of brain-damaged soldiers from World War I formed the foundation of his ideas about self-actualization. He noted that many of the soldiers (who were mostly in their late teens and early 20s) had developed worldviews that Goldstein and others typically associated with much older people—people in their 60s and beyond. To Goldstein, brain trauma had accelerated the actualization of their developmental potential.

15. Abraham H. Maslow, *Toward a Psychology of Being,* Van Nostrand Reinhold, 1968. p. 26. Explanations in italics added by authors.

16. http://www.ga-institute.com/nc/issue-master-system/news-details/article/number-of-companies-in-sp-500R-and-fortune-500-R-reporting-on-sustainability-more-than-doubles-1.html.

17. Milton Friedman, "The Social Responsibility of Business is to Increase it Profits," *New York Times Magazine,* September 13, 1970.

18. Guerrera, Francesco, "Welch rues short-term profit 'obsession,'" *Financial Times,* March 12, 2009.

19. Joel Bakan, *The Corporation, the Pathological Pursuit of Profit and Power,* Free Press, New York, 2004, pg. 31.

20. See John Mackey and Raj Sisodia, *Conscious Capitalism: Liberating the Heroic Spirit of Business,* Harvard Business Review Publishing, 2013.

21. Daniel Pink, "Will Search for Meaning Be Big Business?" Oct. 17, 2005, http://finance.yahoo.com/columnist/article/trenddesk/1228.

22. Marc Gunther, "Money and Morals at GE," *Fortune,* November 1, 2004.

23. Jim Collins, *Good to Great,* HarperCollins, New York, 2001, pg. 195.

24. Ann Zimmerman, "Costco's Dilemma: Be Kind to Its Workers, or Wall Street?" *The Wall Street Journal,* March 26, 2004.

25. Stanley Holmes and Wendy Zellner, "The Costco Way," *Business Week,* April 12, 2004, pp. 76–77.

26. Michelle Conlin, "At Costco, Good Jobs and Good Wages," *Business Week Online,* May 31, 2004.

27. Peter Salovey and John D. Mayer (1990), "Emotional Intelligence," *Imagination, Cognition and Personality,* Volume 9, Issue 3, pp. 185–211; Daniel J. Svyantek and M. Afzalur Rahim (2002), "Links Between Emotional Intelligence and Behavior in Organizations: Findings From Empirical Studies," *International Journal of Organizational Analysis,* Volume 10, Issue 4, pp. 299–301.

28. Howard Gardner (1983), *Frames of Mind: The Theory of Multiple Intelligences,* Basic Books; Daniel Goleman (1995), *Emotional Intelligence: Why It Can Matter More Than IQ,* Bantam; Daniel Goleman (1998), *Working with Emotional Intelligence,* Bantam.

29. Cliona Diggins (2004), "Emotional Intelligence: The Key to Effective Performance," *Human Resource Management International Digest,* Volume 12, Issue 1, pp. 33.

30. Stephen Bernhut (2002), "Primal Leadership, with Daniel Goleman," *Ivey Business Journal,* May/June, Volume 66, Issue 5, pp. 14–15.

31. Ranjit Voola, Jamie Carlson, and Andrew West (2004), "Emotional Intelligence and Competitive Advantage: Examining the Relationship from a Resource-Based View," *Strategic Change,* Mar/Apr, Volume 13, Issue 2, pp. 83–93.

32. Susan P. Gantt and Yvonne M. Agazarian (2004), "Systems-Centered Emotional Intelligence: Beyond Individual Systems to Organizational Systems," *Organizational Analysis*, Volume 12, Issue 2, pp. 147–169.

33. Mike Bagshaw (2000), "Emotional Intelligence—Training People to be Affective so They Can be Effective," *Industrial and Commercial Training*, Volume 32, Issue 2, pg. 61.

34. L. Melita Prati, Ceasar Douglas, Gerald R. Ferris, Anthony P. Ammeter, and M. Ronald Buckley (2003), "Emotional Intelligence, Leadership Effectiveness, and Team Outcomes," *International Journal of Organizational Analysis*, Volume 11, Issue 1, pp. 21–40.

35. Prati et al, *op. cit.*

36. Stephen Bernhut (2002), "Primal Leadership, with Daniel Goleman," *Ivey Business Journal*, May/June, Volume 66, Issue 5, pp. 14–15.

37. http://hbr.org/2005/12/heartless-bosses/ar/1.

38. Ibid, pg. 59.

39. Ibid, pg. 59.

40. This is an oft-used idea attributed to Einstein with some variation in the words. However, we could not determine the exact quote, much less where it first appeared. But that hardly matters; it is a salient and useful piece of wisdom.

41. Daniel Goleman, *Working with Emotional Intelligence*, Bantam Books, 1998.

42. *Serving the Ageless Market* (McGraw-Hill, 1990) by this book's co-author David Wolfe was the first business book to link neuroscience to marketing. Since its publication 16 years ago, brain science has become a major player in marketing thought. The marriage of brain science and marketing is often referred to as *neuromarketing*. Quite possibly, every global consumer brand has by now begun looking at customers through the lens of brain science. The area that has commanded the most attention is emotions.

43. Possidonia F. D. Gontijo, Janice Rayman, Shi Zhang, and Eran Zaidel, *Brain and Language*, Vol. 82, Issue 3, Sep. 2002, pp. 327–343.

44. The line between reason and emotion has been dissolving in cognitive science, the science of intelligence that examines mental capabilities such as the ability to reason, plan, solve problems, think abstractly, comprehend ideas and language, and learn. The inability of people who have no emotional capacities in the cortical regions of their brain has highly flawed reasoning processes. Reason allows us to convert sensual readings and the emotions they arouse into abstract concepts that can then be mentally manipulated via the process we call thinking. However, there are strong indications that the results of this manipulation must be "juried" by the emotions and will only be assimilated into a person's worldview and belief systems if the results "feel" right as determined by emotions.

45. Forest Reinhardt, Ramon Casadesus-Masanell, and Debbie Freier, *Patagonia*, Harvard Business School Case 703035.

46. Frederick F. Reichheld, *The Loyalty Effect: The Hidden Force Behind Growth, Profits, and Lasting Value*, Harvard Business School Press, 1996.

3

Dealing with Disorder

Tom Stoppard's *Arcadia* character Valentine first uttered, "The future is disorder," before an audience in London's National Theater in April 1993. Twenty years later, that future has clearly arrived in the world of business. Virtually every major industry is beset with dramatic changes and fresh challenges, driven by multiple technological revolutions that have followed rapidly upon one another, widespread globalization, quantum shifts in customer preferences, and rapidly evolving value systems.

The Western mind is accustomed to meeting disorder with force. Step on it. Hammer it down. Rein it in. Order *will* be restored at all costs. Ahem, sir, how do you box the wind?

For more than two centuries, business has operated under the influence of Newtonian science, which evolved in response to the restless desire of humans to understand the forces of nature well enough to harness if not conquer and control them. Business management came to view markets in much the same way. But the traditional ethos of conquest and control is losing sway. Procter & Gamble chairman/CEO A.G. Lafley acknowledged this when he said, "We need to reinvent the way we market to consumers. We need a new model. It does not exist. *No one else has one yet.*"[1] (Italics added.)

That new marketing model may not be as remote as Lafley thinks. FoEs profiled in this book have solidly performing marketing models. For the most part these models depend little on traditional marketing. FoEs Starbucks and Google, for example, became enormously valuable global brands with virtually no advertising. At New Balance, the percentage of sales consumed by marketing is far less than at the other big sneaker companies. FoE Boston-based Jordan's Furniture, which grosses about five times more per square foot of sales space than the national average, spends less than a third as much on marketing as the average furniture retailer does.

Everywhere, companies face the challenge of operating in a world in which they no longer have the control over markets that they once had. The Internet and other advanced information technologies give the masses enormous power to resist companies' attempts to take control of their minds and wallets. This has changed the rules of marketing and management, and given life to new forms of organizational architecture.

FoEs reflect in varying ways the fluid architecture of natural ecosystems. They reject the hierarchical control-minded templates inspired by Newtonian science that have long been central to organizational theory. FoEs transcend that tradition by tapping natural laws governing *complex adaptive system*—networks of entities that continuously form and reform in response to evolving needs and environmental changes.

"Complex adaptive system" is a term biologists use to describe self-organizing systems. Ant colonies are self-organizing systems. So are ecosystems. And so is the Internet; no one runs it, but it magically works. And now, a growing number of companies are embracing the idea of self-organization. This doesn't mean they lack executive direction and leadership. But leadership at the top is more catalytic and inspirational than directive. The leadership that makes things work is down in the lower echelons where the rubber meets the road, and it is often not from a single person but from the group. The GE jet engine factory in Durham, North Carolina is such a place. It has no factory leader. Rank and file workers manage everything from process-improvement and work schedules to overtime budgets.[2] Happily for us frequent fliers, defects have been less than traditional in this leaderless factory. Managers who have never held an engine-making tool in their hands no longer shape happenings on the factory floor.

Kevin Kelly, founding executive editor of *Wired*, anticipated self-organizing systems replacing rigid corporate hierarchies in his colorfully written book *Out of Control: The New Biology of Machines, Social Systems and the Economic World*. He says it will happen because information technology is remolding human culture into networked systems.[3] To be "out of control," in Kelly's context, is to be *free of control*. It is to be emancipated from organizational constraints that keep you from being all you can be. You are free to transcend the wretched dailyness of life that stunts your inner self.

Like skilled helmsmen in strong winds, consciously or unconsciously, FoE leaders align their organizations to tap the energy of human transcendence. They reject the "command-and-control" business models of tradition. They don't retreat to an executive restroom when nature calls and hobnob with their peers in executive cafeterias. The C-suite (if one exists) is open to all, from mailroom clerks up. Employees at all levels have broad authority to spend company money to send customers away happy. Southwest Airline flight attendants have been known to give an aggrieved passenger a free ticket. An L.L. Bean employee may give a new mackinaw to a customer who returned one she mistakenly thinks was originally bought there. FoE leadership knows that extraordinary confidence in employees causes them to perform extraordinarily—to transcend, or "to rise above, surpass, excel, exceed," per the *Oxford English Dictionary*. Employees so regarded usually rise to levels of performance well above those of their peers in competing companies where employees still sweat under the heels of command-and-control suits.

In natural ecology systems, the end game is balanced relationships between system participants. Without balance, an ecosystem loses its capability to support its stakeholders. Under these conditions the system will eventually *dis*-integrate.

Rather than holding out one stakeholder group or another as *the* most important stakeholder group, FoE companies attend to the well-being of the total economic ecosystem in which they operate. Without a healthy economic ecosystem, the interests of all stakeholders are at risk. In the organizational equivalent of self-actualization, FoEs are not centered on the interests of the corporate self or of any single stakeholder group. Rather, they take into account the interests of all: They are ecosystem-centric. Whole Foods Market reflects this perspective in its holistic vision of stakeholders, described in its "Declaration of Interdependence."

Paul Hawken, cofounder of the gardening supply outfit Smith & Hawken, co-authored *Natural Capitalism* (Little, Brown & Company, 1999) after writing *The Ecology of Commerce* a few years earlier. It is a manifesto for epochal change in how companies operate. It calls for companies to take bigger roles in making the world a better place.

Natural capitalism is a framework "for harnessing the talent of business to solve the world's deepest environmental and social problems."[4] This is not Milton Friedman's brand of capitalism, for sure.

Peter Senge, author of *The Fifth Discipline*, said "If Adam Smith's *The Wealth of Nations* was the bible for the first industrial revolution, then *Natural Capitalism* may well prove to be it for the next."[5] Whether or not Senge's words prove prophetic, *Natural Capitalism* is but one of many signs of the growing role of business in solving problems that have traditionally been mainly the concern of government.

Hawken and his co-authors wrote the following: "We believe that the world stands on the threshold of basic changes in the conditions of business. Companies that ignore the message of natural capitalism do so at their peril." FoEs such as BMW, Patagonia, and Starbucks are showing the way. BMW is a world leader in corporate sustainability and goes beyond the boundaries of its own *direct* interests in addressing social issues (for example, its program against juvenile violence). Patagonia levies a self-imposed "earth tax," consisting of one percent of sales or ten percent of profits, whichever is greater. Starbuck's coffee bean buying is structured to help preserve small family farms.

The Communications Challenge

Johannes Gutenberg's invention of a movable type press around 1450 began the democratization of information flow. Still, in the ensuing five and a half centuries, information flow to the public remained mostly under the control of its originators. Governments have often been as restrictive in what the masses were permitted to read as the Church once was. Similarly, business enterprise has fostered a policy of tightly controlled communications. Legal counsel has played a large role in this by promoting the wisdom expressed by Euripides almost 2,500 years ago in his play *Orestes*: "Least said, soonest mended." But the Internet has dissolved business's information hegemony. The balance of information power is now in the hands of the masses. This has changed the rules of communication between companies and their stakeholders, especially customers.

Instead of business-controlled monologues, the marketplace is now dominated by conversations. People talk to each other as never before about companies they work for, buy from, and invest in. This is forcing companies to operate with greater transparency. But that's not a problem for thoughtful companies committed to treating all their stakeholders well, as FoEs have discovered. Transparency helps customers, employees, and other stakeholders develop trust in a company. It has proven to be effective as a motivating force among employees.

Though privately held, sneaker maker New Balance shares production and financial data with employees to give them a clear picture of their output and the competitive challenges they and the company face. Seeing measured outcomes fixes performance benchmarks in workers' minds. Under inspiring leadership, it spurs them on to reach higher levels of output. New Balance Chairman Jim Davis is convinced that openness with information is a big reason why his U.S. factories are ten times more productive than the overseas factories it contracts with to make sneakers, as we will detail in Chapter 4, "Employees: From Resource to Source."

The Container Store, privately held until October 31, 2013, shared detailed financial information with employees. This gives employees a stronger feeling of connection with management and management's objectives. It also is a sign that management trusts employees with information that in most private companies is top secret.

Transparency can also reduce vulnerability to outside threat. Johnson & Johnson recognized this in dealing with the crisis that arose when someone slipped cyanide into Tylenol containers on Chicago area store shelves in 1982. It began with the mysterious death of 12-year-old Mary Kellerman of Elk Grove Village, Illinois. Over the next two days, six more people, including three from one family, were felled by mysterious deaths. Tylenol was soon found to be the common denominator. A firestorm of media coverage turned a ghastly local event into a nationally experienced horror. Tylenol faced ignominious dispatch into the dustbins of brand history. Advertising maven Jerry Della Femina proclaimed, "There may be an advertising person who thinks he can solve this and if they find him, I want to hire him, because then I want him to turn our water cooler into a wine cooler."[6]

J&J CEO James Burke apparently agreed with Della Femina. The problem was just too big for an advertising solution. So Burke chose the route of transparency. Nothing would be hidden from media. In fact, the media—including Mike Wallace with his *60 Minutes* camera crew—were invited to sit in on unstaged meetings dealing with the crisis. Meetings and press conferences were timed for pickup by primetime news. Walter Cronkite's evening news was a key target, since polls had tagged Cronkite the most trusted person in America. Burke figured that Cronkite's audience would trust stories gleaned from J&J's open meetings and press conferences. The rest of the story is history. The brand was saved. After its restoration to store shelves in tamperproof containers, it garnered an even larger market share.

It might seem that Burke's approach would have increased J&J's vulnerability. And perhaps it did. But it also lowered J&J's risks. Risk does not necessarily increase in proportion to increases in vulnerability. In fact, increased vulnerability can lower risk, as it did in the Tylenol case.

The cheeky *Cluetrain Manifesto* talked about the marketplace as an arena for conversations.[7] Most people think of this as stemming from the mainstreaming of the Internet. However, James Burke solved the Tylenol problem through conversations with the media and the marketplace well before the Internet became a mainstream artifact. What the Internet has done is to make conversations (a.k.a. dialogues) less optional. But not all companies have yet mastered the crucial principles of effective dialogue, which we summarize in four principles.

Principle #1: Establish a positive relationship (or reinforce an existing one) before getting down to business.

By J&J inviting the media into its inner sanctum, a relationship that could otherwise have taken an adversarial turn developed positively. This predisposed positive outcomes in the news, and ultimately in the marketplace.

FoEs gain extraordinary loyalty by endearing themselves to stakeholders. This predisposes positive outcomes all around. Customers spend more, employees work more productively and creatively, suppliers are more responsive, communities are more welcoming, and shareholders are better satisfied with their investments.

Principle #2: Show willingness to be vulnerable.

This is the transparency principle. Undoubtedly, many corporate legal departments don't like this principle. However, it's essential to getting the best outcomes from conversations with stakeholders. When one party to a dialogue holds back, the other party is inclined to do likewise. Strategic vulnerability helps to build and maintain trust. Vision and mission statements often speak to the objective of building trust, but how many indicate a company's willingness to be vulnerable?

FoE leaders practice this principle with fervor. Honda ritualizes managerial vulnerability through the practice of *waigaya*, a protocol by which rank is put aside to facilitate problem solving. *Waigaya* permits employees to challenge any policy, procedure, or decision made by higher-ups. Whole Foods Market, L.L. Bean, Harley-Davidson, and most other FoEs have their own versions of *waigaya*.

Principle #3: Foster reciprocal empathy, whereby stakeholders reciprocate the company's empathy.

In *A Whole New Mind*, Daniel Pink cites empathy as one of six key cultural dimensions in what he calls the "Conceptual Age," which parallels the Age of Transcendence. Every customer wants to be understood. The same goes for every employee, supplier, and business partner. This yearning arises from expectations that people have of their relationships. Companies that don't understand their stakeholders' expectations from an empathetic perspective will inevitably have low stakeholder loyalty scores.

Some corporate "left brained" number crunchers may roll their eyes when hearing the word *empathy* invoked in a business context. However, even they appreciate the economic value of loyalty, which is just another term for affection. Empathy generates affection. Projecting empathy to customers, employees, and other stakeholders is like fertilizing a tomato plant. The relationship between stakeholders and company will grow, blossom, and bear fruit.

Discussion of the value of empathetically connecting with customers is commonplace, especially in sales training. However, little time is spent discussing the value of encouraging customers to empathetically connect with a company. The insurance giant USAA, which serves military personnel and their families, has a story to tell that testifies to the value of customers empathetically connecting with a company. With an empathetic understanding of the difficulties that going to war poses for military families, USAA decided to do something about it after the first Gulf War. It sent refunds to policyholders who had gone to the Gulf, covering the period they weren't driving back home. Some 2,500 policyholders mailed the refunds back to USAA. They included notes of appreciation in which they said "thanks" but were returning the refunds to help keep USAA financially sound.

Thirty-three years ago, when he was starting fresh in the natural food business, Whole Foods Market co-founder John Mackey saw his dream turned into a nightmare by floodwaters from heavy rains inundating his first store in Austin, Texas. As he reflected on how the cruel finger of fate had devastated his business, customers began flowing in from everywhere to help him rebuild his store. Mackey's empathetic regard for his customers was reciprocated by their empathetic response to his situation.

We are awash in a sea of complexity and disorder—not just in business, but in daily life. Companies can help customers and employees find simplicity and order. Connecting empathetically with people helps make this happen. FoE Trader Joe's understands this. Stores are small (10,000 square feet) and carry only about 2,000 items (the average supermarket carries 30,000 items). But regular shoppers of Trader Joe's miss neither the size nor the overabundance of choices found in supermarkets. In fact, one might call Trader Joe's environment a breath of fresh (tropical?) air. With its old-hat Don Ho–type humor, Trader Joe's offers customers respite from complexity and disorder.

Principle #4: Conduct conversations with genuine reciprocity.

Conversational reciprocity makes for good and lasting friendships. One friend speaks, the other acknowledges what has been said. Each intermittently signals to the other person that he or she is not only being heard, but is having an influence. Customers and employees may get some satisfaction from sounding off, but they get even greater satisfaction if they know that someone has not only heard them, but has also been influenced by them.

The Body Shop began life without relying on traditional types of market research. But Anita Roddick kept her ear to the customer rail via suggestion boxes at each outlet. The ideas were gathered and carefully catalogued while staff members wrote a personal reply to the author of every message. In this way, Roddick and her staff were fulfilling the fourth principle of business dialogues.

✿ ✿ ✿

So, yes, we are experiencing upheavals in the world of business on an unprecedented scale, sowing seeds of disorder all about us. However, the forecast for the future is bright for companies whose leaders are blessed with high levels of managerial competence and who inspire employees, customers, suppliers, shareholders, and the communities in which their companies operate with the transcendent vision we've seen uniformly throughout the FoE universe.

Endnotes

1. Jack Neff, "P&G chief: We Need New Model—Now," *Advertising Age*, Nov. 15, 2004.

2. Charles Fishman, "How Teamwork Took Flight," *Fast Company*, Oct. 1999, pg. 188.

3. Kevin Kelly, *Out of Control: The New Biology of Machines, Social Systems, and the Economic World,* Addison-Wesley Publishing, 1994, pg. 28.

4. Paul Hawken, Amory Lovins, and L. Hunter Lovins, *Natural Capitalism*, Back Bay Books division of Little, Brown and Company, Boston, 1999, Preface, pg. ix.

5. Back cover remarks for *Natural Capitalism.*

6. Jerry Knight, "Tylenol's Maker Shows How to Respond to Crisis," *The Washington Post,* October 11, 1982.

7. Rick Levine, Christopher Locke, Doc Searls, and Dave Weinberger, *The Cluetrain Manifesto: The End of Business As Usual*, Perseus Books, 2000.

4

Employees: From Resource to Source

Wegmans Food Markets, Inc., has been has been named to *Fortune's* "100 Best Places to Work" 16 years in a row, including finishing in the top ten for 11 consecutive years and being #1 in 2004. That is an astonishing accolade for a company in an industry notorious for razor-thin margins, low pay, and high employee turnover. The company fosters extraordinary customer loyalty. A writer on CBS Money Watch asks, "Could this be the best company in the world? I don't know how a company could be better.... Customers are fiercely loyal and will tell you they feel like Wegmans is 'their' store. Actor Alec Baldwin told David Letterman about his mother's refusal to leave upstate New York because there are no Wegmans stores in Los Angeles."[1]

Wegmans' philosophy is that "good people, working toward a common goal, can accomplish anything they set out to do." In the highly competitive supermarket industry, Wegmans differentiates itself through the customer experience. It sells 60,000 different products, 20,000 more than the average supermarket. Many of its stores have play areas that allow parents to shop without their children. Market cafés, seating between 100 and 200, serve a wide array of dishes to customers.[2]

Most retailers deliberately hire low-skilled employees who can be easily replaced, keeping wages low while accepting—even welcoming—high turnover rates. FoEs provide solid evidence to the contrary. They know that higher wages and benefits can actually *lower* employee-related costs. This paradoxical outcome is made possible by lower employee recruiting and training costs and higher productivity.

Wegmans is not unique in believing that if it takes care of its employees, its employees will better serve customers. What is unique (except among other FoEs) is the extent to which Wegmans delivers on that belief. The family-owned company pays well above average wages in its industry. It offers affordable health insurance to employees, along with a 401(k) plan under which the company matches employee contributions at 50 cents to the dollar up to allowable tax limits.

Even part-time workers fare unusually well at Wegmans. High school cashiers and baggers can earn a scholarship bonus of up to $6,000 over four years.[3] Over the past 27 years, Wegmans has paid out $81 million in college scholarships for more than 25,000 full- and part-time employees.

This nearly $6 billion company provides extensive training to all employees. CEO Danny Wegman says knowledgeable employees are "something our competitors don't have and our customers couldn't get anywhere else."[4] They gain this knowledge not only by reading or by attending local classes, but "many department heads travel overseas to work in French patisseries or to tour the countryside to learn about cheese."[5]

Karen Shadders, vice president of people at Wegmans, says, "If we take care of our employees, they will take care of our customers. If employees can't take care of their families, they cannot do their jobs. The focus is on freeing up people so that they can be more productive.... Our pay and benefits are at or above our competitions. It helps us attract a higher caliber of employee." Good employees ensure higher productivity, she says, and that translates into better bottom-line results.[6]

Wegmans puts great faith in its employees. Every employee has wide latitude to do whatever is necessary to ensure that a customer leaves the store fully satisfied—without needing to consult a manager. One employee cooked a customer's Thanksgiving turkey in the store after the customer found the bird was too big for her oven. On another occasion, a Wegmans chef went to a customer's home to help finish cooking a meal for guests that she had messed up.[7]

Wegmans' experience shows the direct connection between trust placed in employees and employee loyalty. Its annual voluntary turnover rate for full-time employees is just six percent in an industry in which the average annual turnover rate exceeds 100 percent for part-timers and 20 percent for full-timers.

The company promotes almost exclusively from within. More than half of its store managers started with Wegmans in their teen years. The company primarily uses exceptional employees from existing stores to staff new ones, and trains all employees extensively before opening a new store. The company spent $5 million on training employees for just one new store in Dulles, Virginia. One of the store managers for its new location opening in Burlington, Massachusetts in 2014 said that he had participated in 87 different training courses in 27 years with the company.[8]

Wegmans' direct labor costs are approximately 15 to 17 percent of sales. That's significantly higher than the 12 percent for a typical supermarket. Certainly, were Wegmans a publicly traded company, it would be soundly criticized by some analysts for paying wages at rates that are 25 percent or more than most of its competitors' pay. However, research has shown that the supermarket industry's annual turnover costs exceed its annual profits by approximately 40 percent.[9] No wonder that former Chairman Robert Wegman, son of cofounder Walter Wegman, said, "I have never given away more than I got back."

So, what does Wegmans get back from paying higher wages than most of its competitors? Doubtless, quite different from what most grocery industry analysts might expect. Wegmans' operating margins are *double* those of other big grocers. Its sales per square foot are 50 percent higher than the norm.

In describing the importance of his staff, Robert Wegman said, "When I visit our stores, customers stop me and say, 'Mr. Wegman, you have a great store, but, wow, your people are wonderful.'"[10] Consider how much money that saves in advertising and other marketing costs. That consideration indicates why employee compensation should not be evaluated in a vacuum. Employee compensation is not an independent variable. Employees either benefit or burden every dimension of a company's existence. The extent to which they deliver one or the other is primarily a function of company culture and leadership's view of employees' value to the company.

FoEs Put Meaning into the Work Experience

There was a time when work was simply a means of collecting a paycheck for most people. Work was generally drudgery, and conditions often inhumane. Over time, working conditions have improved dramatically, but the work itself remains boring, repetitive, and one-dimensional for far too many people.

Gallup has earned a well-deserved reputation for its work in tracking employee engagement. The company's findings paint a rather dismal picture of the typical workplace: Over a 13-year period between 2000 and 2012, average employee engagement in the United States ranged between 26 and 30 percent. The proportion of employees described as "actively disengaged" (in other words, deeply unhappy and even hostile) has ranged from 16 to 20 percent. This is a shocking state of affairs and points to a colossal and tragic waste of human potential. The blame for this must be laid at the feet of business leaders; most have simply failed to create the conditions in which people can give of their gifts and truly thrive.

In the Age of Transcendence, people look for more than a paycheck from their work; they crave "psychic income" as well as monetary income. Education levels have risen, and global awareness of life options and possibilities has exploded because of the Internet. More and more, people want work that engages them wholly, that fulfills their emotional and social needs, that is meaningful—in short, work that is psychologically rewarding. Emblematic of the scope of the cultural shifts taking place in the early years of the Age of Transcendence, people want to view their work as a calling, something they were born to do, that answers to a higher need. This goes far to give FoEs the inspirational character of their business models. Their employees feel a calling to help customers have a better life and to do what they can to improve society and the planet we live on.

FoE leaders facilitate, encourage, reward, recognize, and celebrate their employees for being of service to their communities and the world at large, simply because that it is the right thing to do. The best form of corporate social responsibility is not making monetary donations to charities, but the dedicated involvement of everyone in a company in meaningful pursuits beyond the bottom line. In FoEs, it is common to see executives, managers, and frontline workers working shoulder to shoulder, forging unshakeable bonds through shared service to others in all stakeholder groups. This fosters a sense of cooperation and support within the company. It gets employees to help each other succeed rather than viewing each other as rivals for advancement.

Outdoor wear and equipment company Patagonia has an environmental internship program that gives employees up to two months a year, with full pay and benefits, to volunteer with an environmental organization of their choice. The Harley-Davidson Foundation draws on some 50 employees to help review grants and guide company giving. Outfitter REI supports community organizations ($4 million in grants in 2012), but only issues grants to organizations nominated by employees. The sum total of all of these activities by Patagonia, REI, Harley-Davidson, and the like is not just another exercise in CSR. The other components of the FoE and SRM models that surround these clearly socially responsible human resource activities constitute a strategic system that reduces costs, improves productivity, and engenders superior customer and employee loyalty, enabling these companies to outperform their competitors on a consistent basis and deliver exceptional returns to shareholders.

FoEs can afford to be highly selective in employee recruitment because they are attractive places to work and rank well above average in their categories for wages and benefits. Yet, an interesting question to consider is whether this high degree of selectivity in employee recruitment is a *cause* or *effect* of these companies' success. If keen selectivity in recruiting is a driver of FoE success, then firms working with lower caliber employees would be unlikely to duplicate FoE success. It would also suggest that the number of FoEs will ultimately be limited by the number of high caliber employees that are available in the workforce. On the other hand, if it is an *effect* of the FoE way of being, then other firms might indeed be able to emulate FoE success. Nissan offers us a lesson on this point that demonstrates how ordinary, inexperienced workers can become extraordinary, highly skilled contributors (see the sidebar, "Mississippi Miracle").

Mississippi Miracle

Nissan CEO Carlos Ghosn has executed a remarkable turnaround at the company, taking it from steep losses and massive debt in the late 1990s, to the highest profit margins of any major carmaker in the world. Consider what Nissan has been able to do with its factory in Canton, Mississippi, which opened in May 2003. One of the poorest and least industrialized states in the U.S., Mississippi is an unlikely place to put a state-of-the-art $2 billion factory. The plant had to rely on an untested, largely inexperienced workforce, the product of the state's dismal educational system. Nissan offered pay that was nearly double the prevailing industrial wage in the state. The company held job fairs in all 82 of the state's counties, and some lines of job seekers were more than half a mile long. The governor of the state asked Ghosn to promise that half the workers at the new plant would be African-American; the company exceeded that threshold by 2005. The Canton plant has achieved some of the highest quality ratings in the world. Its success has far exceeded expectations, and the pride and joy of the workers is palpable. Employee meetings have taken on the air of religious revivals. At a graduation ceremony for new supervisors, one said, "Coming to Nissan was one of the best decisions I ever made." Another said, "If you don't know how to build relations with people, Nissan will show you." A woman got up to speak, her voice shaky and eyes filled with tears, and said, "I can't even talk because I'm so full of joy."

Many skeptics thought that locating a highly sophisticated auto factory in one of the most educationally and economically backward slices of land in the U.S. was the height of poor judgment. But those skeptics have changed their tune. By 2013, the plant's workforce had grown to 5,200, and it now produces 450,000 cars a year. One prominent former critic says that what Nissan achieved in Mississippi is "a miracle."[11]

Based on his research, Prof. Charles O'Reilly of Stanford has concluded that "ordinary people" can help to build great companies and achieve extraordinary results. In his book *Hidden Value: How Great Companies Achieve Extraordinary Results with Ordinary People*, he shows that if companies create a culture in which employees take psychological ownership, even average employees can perform at high levels. Employees need to feel that they are listened to and appreciated, and that they can make a difference. If that happens, they certainly do make a difference.

Most FoEs, especially those catering to particular customer lifestyles, try to hire employees with a passion for the purpose of the business. For example, Patagonia, L.L. Bean, and REI try to hire only outdoors enthusiasts. This tightens bonds between employees and customers. Trader Joe's, Wegmans, and Whole Foods recruit foodies. Design firm IDEO's employees come from an amazing array of systems-thinking backgrounds, from physicians to architects.

Executive leadership in FoEs typically comes up through the ranks. This is a big motivator for new employees, giving them hopeful and bright dreams about their future with the company. CarMax and Trader Joe's both have clearly laid-out career ladders. At CarMax, new employees choose one of four career tracks: Sales, Purchasing, Operations, or Business Office. The employee can be promoted through several levels within each track. At Trader Joe's, new hires generally start as "Novitiates," and then progress through Specialist, Merchant, First or Second Mate, and then Captain or Commander.

The Partnership Advantage in Management-Union Relationships

Prof. Jeffrey Pfeffer of Stanford University argues that if management and unions can maintain a cordial relationship, unionized companies tend to perform better than non-unionized ones. Of course, if the relationship turns adversarial, the opposite is the case. Unionization's most direct benefit is higher wages, which attracts better employees and reduces turnover. The net profit impact tends to be zero (and can even be positive) because turnover is expensive and experienced workers are more productive. When Kaiser Permanente finally launched a partnership with its unions, results improved dramatically. Employee satisfaction soared, customer satisfaction rose, and the partnership led to cost savings of $100 million.[12]

FoEs fall into one of two labor relations profiles: strong management partnerships with a union (such as Southwest and Harley-Davidson have) or management partnerships directly with employees in companies with excellent working conditions and strong compensation and benefit packages such that little is left for a union to bargain over (as with Whole Foods Market).

Most of Harley-Davidson's employees are union members. When the company's future was seriously in question in the early 1980s, the union stuck with it to help get through the rough period. Ever since, management has maintained an uncommonly open relationship with the union. Both company and employees benefit, as do shareholders.

At Harley-Davidson, management and union have the same objective: working together for the benefit of both company and employees with balanced service to the needs and objectives of each. Harley tries whenever possible to use "in-sourcing" to bring work back home to avoid layoffs. The union has been known to reprimand its own members for unsatisfactory work. Management and the union have worked closely together to improve the safety environment of the company.[13]

At Southwest, the company's relationship with the pilots' union is one with very little finger pointing. Both sides share opinions openly, and there is respect for everyone involved.[14] This respectful relationship between management and the unions was put to a real test after the terrorist attacks of 9/11. CEO Herb Kelleher responded to the aftermath of that tragic day by refusing to make any layoffs. He said, "We could have furloughed at various times and been more profitable, but I always thought that was shortsighted. You want to show your people that you value them and you're not going to hurt them just to get a little more money in the short term."[15]

Leaders in non-unionized FoEs tend to view the first signs of interest in unionization as a warning signal that they are letting their employees down. That is certainly how Whole Foods Market's founder and CEO John Mackey sees it. When employees at the Madison, Wisconsin store voted (65 to 54) to unionize because of rising healthcare costs and concerns about the dress code, Mackey reacted quickly. He publicly acknowledged, "There's room for improvement.

As Whole Foods has grown to a $3.2 billion company, the balance between the company's attention to its employees and to the company's other stakeholders may have gotten a little out of whack."[16]

Mackey went back to the company motto—"Whole Foods, Whole People, Whole Planet"—to recharge himself. He decided to visit all 145 stores to reconnect and hold meetings with team members. After these meetings, Mackey decided to hold a company-wide vote on how employee benefits should be restructured. Because of the Madison "wake-up call," the company decided to pay 100 percent of health insurance premiums. But it went further: It issued "personal wellness cards" to all full-time employees in the form of debit cards with $1,700 to spend on medical and dental expenses. The union at the Madison store refused to allow its members at that store to receive these benefits, since it had not negotiated them. Employees at the store responded by voting to decertify the union in November 2003.

Building Trust

A distinguishing mark of FoEs is the high degree of trust that exists within them. Building trust is a slow process, and sustaining it always a challenge. Consider how The Container Store builds and sustains trust among its employees. The company is clearly highly successful in doing this because it is regarded as one of the best companies to work for in the U.S. *Fortune* twice rated it #1 (in 2000 and 2001), #2 in 2002 and 2003, and #3 in 2004, and the company has made this coveted list 14 years in a row. New employees go through a weeklong orientation, known as Foundation Week, during which they learn the inner-workings and philosophy of the company. This is step 1 in building a relationship of mutual trust. Barbara Anderson, former manager of employee relations, said the following:

> "Many of our new employees have worked for other firms that have let them down. When they first hear about our culture, they want to believe it, but they have learned to be cautious. Our Foundation Week doesn't completely resolve this problem; trust takes time. But it does speed things up. The store manager spending the entire day with new hires makes a huge statement."[17]

FoEs draw on four key elements to build trust with employees: respect for individuals, transparency, team building, and empowerment.

Respect for Individuals

FoEs view each individual employee as a "whole person" rather than an impersonal "factor of production." Respect for individuals is demonstrated by management's encouragement of employees to participate in company decision making, regardless of an employee's rank. For example, recall our earlier discussion about FoEs consulting employees about worthy causes for corporate philanthropy (REI and Harley-Davidson), about empowering employees to make decisions on their own to send customers away fully satisfied (Wegmans), and about supporting employees' contribution of time and expertise to worthy causes (Patagonia and L.L. Bean).

Transparency

FoEs do not share the paranoia many companies have about sharing information with all employees as well as with other stakeholders. The FoE way is the sunshine way, even in privately owned companies such as New Balance and The Container Store (which recently went public). Both companies open up their books to employees. New Balance shares information on manufacturing processes, production numbers, and costs of production. This builds trust but also helps its U.S.-based manufacturing employees to understand what it costs the company to produce shoes in the U.S. versus in offshore locations. Management considers this an important factor in improving efficiency and remaining competitive, which protects domestic jobs.

Team Building

FoEs cultivate an uncommonly strong sense of team participation, a major factor in their low job turnover rates. At San Francisco–based industrial design firm IDEO, teams are encouraged to take an afternoon off now and then and see a movie or a ballgame together. Employees develop a distinct sense of identity. Google employees are called Googlers—a breed apart. Trader Joe's has created a distinct identity for its employees, who wear Hawaiian shirts at work and are known as Captain, First Mate, and so on. The Jordan's Furniture management team created the concept of the "J-team," to institutionalize the fact that all employees must work together to delight customers and deliver memorable customer experiences. The idea of equality between customer and employee, and even between management and part-time hire, is central to the J-team credo.

Empowerment

FoE employees generally have the authority (and the obligation) to spend the resources necessary to make a customer happy or fix a production problem. This, of course, builds employee trust in the company because the company trusts them. IDEO asks new employees to manage a project as soon as they are hired. Southwest, in its early years, was forced to sell one of its four planes. Rather than operate a reduced schedule (which would require fewer people), employees came up with a plan to maintain the existing four-plane schedule with only three planes. To accomplish this, they reduced turnaround time at the gate to ten minutes by having everyone pitch in: pilots and management helped with baggage handling, flight attendants streamlined the cabin clean up, and ground crews revamped the beverage restocking process. At Jordan's, through the concept of the J-team, all employees are empowered to do what it takes to serve customers. Viewed by management as ambassadors to the customer, employees feel a sense of purpose in their daily actions. Knowing that their performance directly affects the customer experience promotes autonomy and provides satisfaction for a job well done.

The Joy of Work

FoEs foster a fun, collegial, productive, and purposeful work environment. This is a key factor in attracting, motivating, and retaining employees. These companies create an atmosphere that enables people to give their best without feeling pressured. Employees are productive without being stressed out. They are serious about their work but do it with a sense of humor. They experience a form of "relaxed concentration" that maximizes the potential of each employee.

Until the late 1970s, Toyota did not treat its assembly line workers well. Accounts tell of hours spent in front of conveyor belts that never stopped. "Free time" during working hours was often taken away to increase production without increasing the number of workers. The workers were bound to the conveyors until they stopped, which didn't happen until the day's production goal was reached. According to Satoshi Kamata, a former assembly line worker, the company did not tolerate absence from work, suicides were rather frequent, and many employees developed shoulder, arm, and neck problems due to long hours spent in unnatural body positions and movements.[18]

Fortunately, Toyota saw the light and started to recognize that the health and safety of all its employees is a matter of paramount importance. It focused heavily on eliminating accidents and occupational diseases through education and awareness. The company conducts annual employee health checks and launched a lifestyle improvement campaign to promote better health among employees. Concern for mental health inspired Toyota to implement active listening courses for supervisors as a means of prevention and early detection of mental problems among employees.

FoE work environments are fun, flexible, and balanced (between work and personal life) and offer employees creative quality-of-life benefits.

Fun

At Southwest, Herb Kelleher performed numerous stunts to create a fun atmosphere and promote the airline, such as arm-wrestling another company's chief executive for the rights to an advertising slogan (an event that drew huge media publicity and featured 1,800 Southwest employees dressed as cheerleaders), and dressing up in drag or like Elvis Presley.[19] Kelleher's fun-loving personality permeates the culture of Southwest Airlines and its wisecracking employees. The culture is now deeply engrained. To ensure that it continues, the company has created a "Culture Committee" consisting of nearly a hundred employees nominated by their peers from all levels and locations. This group has responsibility for "doing whatever it takes to create, enhance, and enrich the special Southwest spirit and culture that has made it such a wonderful company/family." It organizes special events throughout the Southwest system, such as employee appreciation parties, station parties for meeting goals, and an annual awards banquet that honors employees for their length of service.

Google's logo (the company creates hundreds of variations on it, to suit every occasion and context) connotes fun and playfulness. The Container Store's tongue-in-cheek positioning tagline for customers is "Contain Yourself," while it encourages employees to "Think Outside the Box." The company has a "Fun Committee" that sponsors activities and events that connect employees to one another. It was created to combat the depersonalization and employee anonymity that typically set in as a company grows. As Len Berry wrote in his book *Discovering the Soul of Service*, "Families invest time and money in having fun together and so do high-trust organizations. Fun is a great trust builder because it conveys caring."[20]

A few years ago, Jordan's Furniture surprised all its employees by closing down its stores and chartering four jumbo jets to fly the entire J-team—then 1,200 employees—to Bermuda for a day, treating them to a "90-degree day of beach, BBQ, live music, water games, and dancing."[21] This reward reinforced the philosophy of the J-team. The company wanted to thank its employees for their hard work and loyalty. Rather than giving a trip to each employee separately, the entire company traveled together, tightening the sense of teamwork. They all enjoyed the trip together because they had all worked together to earn it.

At IDEO, founder David Kelly believes that "play ignites the innovative spirit."[22] Unplanned breaks are the norm, and diversions and silly little pranks on other employees are valued. Employees take many field trips together and are encouraged to play at work. Many play miniature golf inside and throw Nerf balls in the hallways.

Balance and Flexibility

"Balance" in a person's life is a delicate state of equilibrium that can be disturbed by any number of events. If a company allows employees flexibility in how, when, and where they do their work, employees can continue to meet their personal needs and obligations while also delivering on their professional commitments.

FoEs are disposed toward accommodating their employees' unique scheduling needs. Patagonia and New Balance offer flexible work schedules, allowing mothers, for example, to be home with their children after school. Former Timberland CEO Jeffrey Swartz believes, "Executives fool themselves if they fail to acknowledge that the people they manage have important needs outside of work." He used to check Timberland's security logs periodically to see if any employees were coming to the office consistently on weekends. When he spotted a trend, he figured there must be a problem—lack of sufficient equipment or understaffing. "Nothing is more wasteful than to burn up people," says Swartz.[23]

Pernille Spiers-Lopez, President of IKEA North America, tries to keep regular hours and not take work home, avoids business travel on weekends, and expects her employees to do the same. IKEA demonstrates a commitment to its employees and nurtures them through slumps. The company expects all supervisors and managers to serve as mentors, and to match their stores' needs with those of employees. To accomplish this, it offers flexible work schedules, job sharing, and compressed workweeks. IKEA conducts regular employee surveys to gauge morale and identify issues that it needs to address.

A unique aspect of Google's business model and culture is "20 percent time." Google grants employees the right to spend 20 percent of their time at work on independent projects of their own choosing. Several of these have developed into important new offerings for the company, including Ad Sense for Content, Google News, and Orkut (social networking).[24] There's little corporate hierarchy, and everyone wears several hats. For example, the international webmaster who creates Google's holiday logos spent a week translating the site into Korean. Southwest also has a culture of job boundary flexibility, which ultimately helps the airline operate more efficiently than its competitors do. Managers and supervisors work side by side with frontline employees.[25]

An amazing story of balance, flexibility, and employee empowerment comes from a company in Brazil.

In the mid-1980s, Semco was a struggling ship-parts company based in São Paulo, Brazil. The company manufactured pumps and propellers for merchant ships. Like the Brazilian economy, it was slowly sinking. Ricardo Semler took over the business from his father, and launched an ambitious plan to diversify the business. He took control of every aspect of the business, delegating very little and alienating many experienced employees. He set such a hectic pace for himself that he finally collapsed while touring a factory in upstate New York, and had to check himself into the Lahey Clinic near Boston. Doctors there told him to slow down or he would soon have a heart attack.[26]

Ricardo took the warning to heart. He set about changing his company as well as himself. He decided to create balance between his work and his personal life, and do the same for his employees.

To his surprise, he found this new, more temperate pace improved not only his performance and that of his employees, but the performance of Semco as well. Employees became more productive, loyal, and versatile as he gave them more freedom to chart their own course. He did away with receptionists, organizational charts, and even the central office. Semler asked employees to suggest their own pay levels, assess the performance of their bosses, and learn how to do each other's jobs. He opened the books to all employees, and set up a transparent profit-sharing plan.

Semler didn't stop there. In an almost weird reversal of tradition, he made all meetings voluntary and vacation time compulsory. The company tells employees that they can and should leave any meeting if they are no longer interested. This way, the only people remaining are those who are truly interested and have a real stake in an issue.

How did Semco do financially through all this? Sales increased from $35 million to $212 million in six years. The number of employees grew from several hundred to 3,000—with an unheard-of job turnover rate of just one percent.

Semler has written two books about his experience.[27] Here he is in his own words regarding employees setting their own hours:

> We always assume that we're dealing with responsible adults,
> which we are. And when you start treating employees like
> adolescents by saying you can't come late, you can't use this

bathroom—that's when you start to bring out the adolescent in people.... Our people balance their lives much better, and there's an unusually high number of people who take their kids to school, etc. But a recent statistic showed that 27 percent of our people are online on Sunday at 8 p.m. So they probably do work hard.

And here are his words regarding a stakeholder perspective:

I think what we've done is being emulated because of the amount of dissatisfaction that is rampant among workers, but also among stakeholders.... Consider the airline industry. I think that is the only industry so far that has managed to make all of the stakeholders lose. The shareholders don't make any money. The executives don't last. The planes don't get better. The air-traffic controllers have the worst job in the world. The crew is never happy. The pilots are on strike. The food is just awful. There's not a good thing you can say about the business of flying. So...the traditional model isn't working. And there's incentive to start looking for something else.[28]

Creative Quality-of-Life Benefits

Small things make a big difference when it comes to employee quality of life. IDEO encourages employees to design their own work-spaces in ways that express and encourage creativity. It once agreed to spend $4,000 on an old aircraft wing that an employee wanted as part of his office decor. More conventionally, Timberland offers lactation rooms and on-site childcare. Google provides employees with on-site physicians, free massages, a game room, showers, subsidized childcare, a free gourmet lunch five days a week, dry cleaning, counseling on tax matters, personal and family services, and business legal services. Toyota offers 24-hour childcare at its manufacturing facility in Georgetown, Kentucky. The 19,000-square-foot facility has 115 staff members, including 90 teachers, and holds classrooms, homework rooms, activity spaces, beds, and a wellness center. Patagonia offers employees "green" benefits, in keeping with its culture. It regularly offers "brain food" classes covering topics such as surfing, yoga, time management, introduction to French culture, business communication, and nonviolent civil disobedience. Employees who purchase hybrid vehicles are reimbursed $2,000.

The impact of such benefits can be huge. Patagonia's subsidized on-site childcare "allows the company to integrate the parent's workplace into children's everyday environment, minimizes friction and anxiety for both parent and child, and increases workplace satisfaction and employee productivity."[29] It is a common sight to see parents eating lunch with their children in the subsidized company cafeteria, which offers only healthy, local, and organic food made fresh daily. Is it any surprise that Patagonia receives 10,000 applications for about 100 open positions each year? For the lucky few who are hired, the company offers an ideal way to integrate their home life, their professional life, and their recreational life.

When it comes to providing employees with the "right" benefits, it is clear that doing everything is not an option. However, there is plenty of research-based evidence to guide enlightened CEOs on how they should design benefit packages for optimal impact.[30]

Training and Development Are Priorities in FoEs

People should develop and grow throughout their lifespans, and employees are no exception. Even the most experienced and highly qualified employees need and benefit from continuous education. FoEs are exemplary in their focus on helping employees maximize their potential through training, development, and mentoring. They constantly celebrate their employees' achievements and successes, large and small.

The Container Store has a long-standing reputation as one of the best employers in the country. In addition to repeatedly being cited at or near the top of *Fortune's* annual list of best places to work, The Container Store has also won *Workforce* magazine's award for general excellence in people management strategies. A major reason for its success is its commitment to training. The average company in the retailing sector provides seven hours of training. New employees at

The Container Store receive 263 hours of training during the first year alone, and at least 160 hours a year after that.

Most FoEs have their own "Universities" to train employees. Southwest has its University for People, where new employees receive months of training. Toyota employees receive extensive technical training through experienced peer-to-peer *kaizen* (continuous improvement) and technology transfer instructors. Ongoing training at UPS includes programs that provide 1.3 million hours of training per year to more than 74,000 drivers. The company provides 3.8 million hours of safety training annually to employees, spending approximately $120 million a year. Overall, UPS spends $300 million a year on training.

In 1999, UPS rolled out its "Earn and Learn" program. Within two years, it had helped more than 20,000 part-time employees attend college. Within the first year alone, UPS spent more than $9 million in tuition, fees, and books for part-time employees. UPS management believes that this helps develop future full-time employees and provide the skills necessary for part-timers to be promoted to full-time supervisory positions. UPS designed the program to work with 242 colleges to allow deferred billing to students, making the opportunity that much more affordable and encouraging involvement.[31] Today, all employees are eligible for up to $20,000 in assistance to attend college over their tenure with the company.

At IDEO, project mentors play the role of the HR department; they help new employees enroll in required training classes and adapt them to their first project and the office environment.

Recall our earlier discussion about the importance of emotional intelligence (EI) in organizations. Nowhere is this more important than in the process of selecting and training employees. Employees that do possess high EI are very careful to select companies to work for that mirror their own values and are able to resonate with them emotionally. To such candidates, it is important that their jobs are meaningful extensions of themselves, and not just a way to make a living.[32] Employees and work teams that have a high level of EI enjoy many benefits, such as lower stress levels, higher job satisfaction, higher organizational commitment, increased creativity, lower turnover, and higher productivity.[33]

Recognition and Celebration Have High Priority in FoEs

Most FoEs have celebration-intensive cultures. Says former Southwest COO and President Colleen Barrett (who started as Herb Kelleher's legal secretary, and as company president was responsible for helping to maintain the company's culture), "We aren't uptight. We celebrate everything. It's like a fraternity, a sorority, a reunion. We're having a *party!*"[34]

Google excels at empowering its employees and recognizing them for their important role in helping the company achieve its objectives. It gives an award worth millions of dollars to employees who work on outstanding projects. The first two Founders' Awards consisted of restricted stock worth $12 million, awarded to two teams of a dozen or so employees each. Says co-founder Sergey Brin, "We have people who just do phenomenal things here. I wanted a mechanism to reward that."[35]

Bob Chapman has crafted an extraordinary business success story. He runs a $1.5-billion industrial conglomerate called Barry-Wehmiller, with dozens of stand-alone manufacturing businesses. Chapman has implemented a philosophy that he calls "Truly Human Leadership," which has created an extraordinary shared culture filled with caring and celebration. The company uses phrases such as "Building great people is our business" and "We measure success by the way we touch the lives of people." As Bob puts it, "We believe that business enterprise has the opportunity to become the most powerful positive influence on our society by providing a cultural environment in which people can realize their gifts, apply and develop their talents, and feel a genuine sense of fulfillment for their contributions in pursuit of a common inspirational vision." A big part of the company's culture is celebration based on peer recognition. Employees are frequently nominated by their peers for awards, and a committee of their fellow workers reviews each nomination and interviews the nominee. The recognitions don't cost a lot of money; a typical reward is the use of a special company vehicle for a week. These cars have become well known in the small communities in which the company operates, and generate a lot of attention and pride. Recognition ceremonies include the awardee's extended family. Barry-Wehmiller's emphasis on creating such cultures has been a major part of the company's success in rescuing and growing its many acquired businesses.[36]

How FoEs View Part-Time Employees

In recent years, the proportion of people working part time has risen. Those working fewer than 35 hours a week account for nearly 20 percent of the workforce in 2013, up from 18 percent in 1996, according to the U.S. Bureau of Labor Statistics. The trend will likely continue as baby boomers shift in growing numbers to work part time in their retirement years.

Relatively few companies offer benefits to part-time workers. In 2000, only 13 percent of part-time workers in large and mid-sized firms received healthcare benefits, and only 12 percent received any contributions toward their retirement. However, FoEs are generally exceptions to this norm. Most offer generous benefits to part-time employees, in some cases to those working as few as 15 hours a week. Wegmans' employees become eligible for free health coverage and profit sharing retirement plan contributions if they work 17.5 hours a week. The company specifically tries to hire single moms as part-time workers, viewing that as a win-win: the company gets staffing during difficult hours, and single moms get what they most need—health coverage. Unionized part-time employees at UPS get free health insurance as well as college tuition assistance. This has beneficially transformed the lives of countless employees and their families. Part-time worker Christine Virelli started with UPS as a package sorter after her husband was injured and could no longer work. She was a ninth grade dropout who had been out of the workforce for 16 years. UPS paid for her to get her graduate equivalency diploma and then for her to attend college. "I can't leave UPS. They've done so much for me that I can't imagine not working for them," said Virelli. "Someday I want to work in the HR department here at UPS. UPS helped me turn my life around, and I'm still growing. My main goal is that I want to grow in the company."[37]

Connecting Top to Bottom

Unlike at traditional companies, frontline workers at FoE companies often have the opportunity to interact directly with senior leaders. In fact, it is rare to find employees who have been with these companies for any time who have not had personal contact with the leader of the company—in the case of the smaller firms, quite regularly.

FoEs try to enhance such connections for two reasons. First, they are highly energizing for the CEO and motivating to employees. Second, their leaders know that they are not the source of all strategic wisdom in the company; if asked, employees at any level can offer brilliant ideas that could greatly benefit the company.

REI's senior management team visits each store several times a year to hand out awards and get suggestions, and shares all significant decisions with lower echelon employees. The company gives more than $4 million in grants to nonprofit organizations annually, based on nominations by employees. L.L. Bean has an employee "Speak-Up" program that encourages employee feedback and incorporates it into its quality improvement programs. Costco regularly organizes employee appreciation days where the management waits on the regular employees. Harley-Davidson has developed a practice called "Freedom with Fences," in which employees are encouraged to take risks by challenging the ideas and concepts developed in the organization. The company follows an "open door" policy that gives each employee access to all levels of the organization, including the CEO.

BMW encourages its employees to question the necessity of the job they are doing. In the company's culture of trust, employees can do so without any fear of losing their jobs. Instead of laying them off, BMW trains them to fill another role in the company. Honda has instituted a practice called *waigaya*, which roughly translates as "noisy-loud." It refers to an informal session in which participants put aside rank in order to address the problem at hand. Any employee can invoke a *waigaya*, and executives must participate if called on. It was through a *waigaya* that Honda chose its original advertising campaign for its motorcycles: "You Meet the Nicest People on a Honda." Senior managers had favored a more conservative approach, but a low-ranking employee was able to convince them otherwise in a *waigaya* session.[38]

The HR Department of the Future

The human resources (HR) function is vital to the very existence of FoEs. Above all else, these companies are exemplary recruiters, managers, developers, and motivators of human talent. They know how to build empathetic bridges to people's minds.

The innovative and humanistic practices that FoEs follow in dealing with employees reflect a deep understanding of what people are looking for in their work lives today. For a long time, relatively few companies saw a connection between employees' personal needs and their performance at work. Employees were generally seen as resources, akin to capital, technology, and war materials. That is why the traditional personnel department became "human resources" in the last half of the twentieth century. But now, the term "human resources" is increasingly coming under fire. Just as customers have been objectified as consumers, employees have long been objectified as resources or assets to be exploited in service of company objectives. That is all now changing, and FoEs are leading the way.

Here is a better way to think about people: a human being is not a resource but a *source*.[39] A resource is like a lump of coal; once you use it, it's gone, depleted and worn out. A source is like the sun—virtually inexhaustible and continually generating energy, light, and warmth. There is no more powerful source of creative energy in the world than a turned-on, empowered human being. FoEs consciously create conditions that energize and empower people and engage their best contribution in service of their personal passions and the firm's noble higher purposes.

Reflecting the new mindset, many companies have started referring to HR as the "People" department. Here is how the People Department at Southwest puts it: "Recognizing that our people are the competitive advantage, we deliver the resources and services to prepare our people to be winners, to support the growth and profitability of the company, while preserving the values and special culture of Southwest Airlines."[40]

In the past, the HR function was something of a corporate backwater, a primarily administrative function dealing with payroll and staffing. This is fast changing, as companies have outsourced the basic

functions of administering benefits plans and payrolls. This frees HR
to focus on more strategic issues, such as employee engagement, performance, and retention, which can directly affect the bottom line.
Companies are beginning to see that hiring, developing, and retaining
the right employees can be a great source of competitive advantage.
HR professionals have a key role to play in sustaining the corporate
culture and instilling ethical values in employees. CEOs now look for
HR leaders who can be trusted advisers to them. More CEOs are now
coming from the HR function.[41]

Pernille Spiers-Lopez, President of IKEA North America, is one
such leader. She spent four years as manager of human resources
before being named President. She created a culture at IKEA that
balances work and family, with the family taking precedence. In 2003,
Working Mother magazine awarded Spiers-Lopez its Family Champion Award. IKEA provides full benefits and flexible schedules for
employees working more than 20 hours a week. According to Spiers-
Lopez, leadership is "about what I stand for and my values." Managers must strive to be authentic and open, and try to engender two-way
trust with employees. People who are trusted deliver way beyond
their own expectations.[42]

Essentially, it comes down to treating employees the way customers should be treated: with respect and a deep understanding of their
needs. The ultimate goal of the Jordan's Furniture management team
is to create "raving fans"[43] out of its employees by providing internal growth opportunities, offering extensive benefits, and considering
them as another form of Jordan's customers. Costco, SAS Institute,
and Toyota monitor employee satisfaction through surveys. UPS
conducts a survey that assesses employees' opinions on employee
recruitment, retention, and motivation to measure what is called the
"Employer of Choice Index."

Benefits That Flow to Shareholders from Doing It Right

The bottom-line message of this chapter is quite simple: Good
people management is great business. Even as more and more activities become automated, the importance of human capital in the

performance of an organization continues to grow. Just as companies now track brand equity and customer equity, they should also track their employee equity.

The two main indicators of strong employee equity are low turnover and high productivity. Without exception, every FoE has an employee turnover rate that is far lower than its industry's norm. FoEs employees are also highly productive. They exceed their non-FoE competitors by large margins in revenue per employee. Jordan's generates $950 per square foot of sales, compared to $150 for the average furniture store, and turns over its inventory 13 times a year, compared to 1–2 times for the average furniture store. Toyota leads automakers globally in sales per employee. Honda ranks second worldwide in assembly productivity and first in engine productivity.

New Balance has continued to manufacture shoes in the U.S. and the UK long after its competitors sent all manufacturing to low-wage nations. The company does this with pride but not out of any sense of charity. In a 2002 interview with *Industry Week*, New Balance CEO Jim Davis had the following comment:

> The philosophy here is we wouldn't be doing as well as we are if all the people who work here weren't so committed. It's because of them we're able to do so well, it's because of them we're able to give back.... It's providing the right machinery, developing new [manufacturing] techniques and empowering the associates so they continuously improve the process.[44]

Low turnover and high productivity are related to one another because low turnover creates more experienced employees over time, which translates to higher productivity. As a result, companies can have relatively low overall costs and be highly competitive while paying good wages and providing generous benefits to employees. Companies owe it to their shareholders to elevate the working conditions of the men and women on their payrolls, materially, emotionally, and experientially. FoEs show us that the mother lode of wealth runs not through the executive corridors but through the vocational landscape of frontline employees.

Endnotes

1. http://www.cbsnews.com/8301-505143_162-45340815/could-this-be-the-best-company-in-the-world/.

2. Overview from www.wegmans.com and http://www.wegmans.com/about/pressRoom/overview_printable.asp.

3. Matthew Swibel, "Largest Private Companies—Nobody's Meal," *Forbes*, November 24, 2003.

4. Michael A. Prospero, "Moving the Cheese: Wegmans Relies on Smart, Deeply Trained Employees to Create a 'Theater of Food,'" *Fast Company*, Issue 87 (October 2004), pg. 88.

5. Prospero, *op. cit.*

6. Swibel, *op. cit.*

7. Matthew Boyle & Ellen Florian Kratz, "The Wegmans Way," *Fortune*, January 24, 2005, pg. 62.

8. http://homenewshere.com/daily_times_chronicle/news/burlington/article_0fcaf680-de78-11e2-b275-0019bb2963f4.html

9. Study by Coca Cola Retailing Research Council, cited in Boyle & Kratz, *op. cit.*

10. Overview from www.wegmans.com and http://www.wegmans.com/about/pressRoom/pressReleases/FortuneTop100.asp?sd=home&dt=top100.

11. G. Paschal Zachary, "Dream Factory," *Business 2.0*, June 2005, pp. 97–102.

12. Jeffery Pfeffer, "In Praise of Organized Labor," *Business 2.0*, June 2005, pg. 80.

13. Lois Caliri, "Harley-Davidson: Win-Win for Workers," *Central Penn Business Journal*, April 18, 1997.

14. Jody Hoffer Gittell, *The Southwest Airlines Way: Using the Power of Relationships to Achieve High Performance*, McGraw-Hill, 2002, pg. 169.

15. Gittell, *op. cit.*, pg. 243.

16. Michelle Breyer, "Whole Foods Market Woos its Staff," *Knight Ridder Tribune Business News*, June 6, 2003.

17. Leonard L. Berry, *Discovering the Soul of Service*, New York: The Free Press, 1999.

18. S. Kamata, *Employee Welfare Takes a Back Seat at Toyota*, Pantheon Books, 1982.

19. David Field, "Southwest Succession," *Airline Business*, April 2002, Vol. 18 Issue 4, pg. 34.

20. Leonard L. Berry, *Discovering the Soul of Service*, New York: The Free Press, 1999.

21. Arthur Lubow, "Wowing Warren," *Inc. Magazine*, March 2000.

22. "Seriously Silly" (interview with David M. Kelley, CEO and founder of IDEO) *Business Week*, Sept. 13, 1999. pg. 14; Tom Kelley and Jonathan Littman, *The Art of Innovation* (New York: Double Day 2001), pg. 95.

23. Pam Mendels, "When Work Hits Home: Few CEOs Seem to Realize That It Pays to Offer a Balance," *Chief Executive*, March 2005, Vol. 206.

24. SEC 8/13/04, File 333-114984, Accession Number 1193125-4-139655, pg. 28. http://www.secinfo.com/d14D5a.148c8.htm (April 11, 2005).

25. Gittell, *op. cit.*, pg. 157.

26. Brad Weiners, "Ricardo Semler: Set Them Free," *CIO Magazine*, April 1, 2004.

27. *Maverick: The Success Story Behind the World's Most Unusual Workplace* (1993) and *The Seven-Day Weekend: Changing the Way Work Works* (Portfolio, 2004).

28. Weiners, *op. cit.*

29. Leslie Goff, "What it's Like to Work at Patagonia," *Computerworld*, November 2, 1999.

30. See, for example, Thomas Davenport, *Thinking for a Living: How to Get Better Performances and Results from Knowledge Workers*, Harvard Business School Press, 1995; also, consulting firms such as Watson Wyatt Worldwide have developed considerable expertise on the "right" employee benefits for a given context.

31. Greg Gunsauley, "UPS Delivers Tuition Aid to Recruit Army of Part-Timers," *Employee Benefit News*, June 1, 2001.

32. Cliona Diggins (2004), "Emotional Intelligence: The Key to Effective Performance," *Human Resource Management International Digest*, Volume 12, Issue 1, pp. 33.

33. Cited in L. Melita Prati, Ceasar Douglas, Gerald R. Ferris, Anthony P. Ammeter, and M. Ronald Buckley (2003), "Emotional Intelligence, Leadership Effectiveness, and Team Outcomes," *International Journal of Organizational Analysis*, Volume 11, Issue 1, pp. 21–40; "lower stress levels": K. S. Rook (1987), "Social Support Versus Companionship: Effects on Life Stress, Loneliness, and Evaluations by Others," *Journal of Personality and Social Psychology*, Volume 52, Issue 6, pp. 1132–1147; "higher job satisfaction": N. Eisenberg R.A. Fabes (1992), "Emotion, Regulation, and the Development Of Social Competence," in M. Clark (Ed.), *Review of Personality and Social Psychology: Emotion and Social Behavior* (Volume 14, pp. 119–150), Newbury Park, CA: Sage Publications; "higher organizational commitment": S.G. Scott and R.A. Bruce (1994). "Determinants of Innovative Behavior: A Path Model of Individual Innovation in the Workplace," *Academy of Management Journal*, Volume 37, Issue 3, pp. 580–607; "increased creativity": T.P. Moses and A.J. Stahelski (1999), "A Productivity Evaluation of Teamwork at an Aluminum Manufacturing Plant," *Group and Organization Management*, Volume 24, Issue 3, pp. 391–412; "lower turnover and higher productivity": P.E., Tesluk, R.J. Vance, and J.E. Mathieu (1999), "Examining Employee Involvement in the Context of Participative Work Environments," *Group and Organization Management*, Volume 24, Issue 3, pp. 271–299.

34. Andy Serwer, "Southwest Airlines: The Hottest Thing in the Sky," *Fortune*, March 8, 2004, pg. 101.

35. Katie Hafner, "New Incentive for Google Employees: Awards Worth Millions," *The New York Times*, February 1, 2005, Section C, pg. 10.

36. www.trulyhumanleadership.com.

37. Elayne Robertson Demby, "Nothing Partial about These Benefits," *HR Magazine*, August 2003.

38. Henry Mintzberg, Richard T. Pascale, Michael Gould, and Richard P. Rumelt, "The Honda Effect Revisited," *California Management Review*, Volume 38, No. 4, Summer 1996, pg. 88.

39. This metaphor was suggested by Debashis Chatterjee, director of the Indian Institute of Management, Kozhikode.

40. Charles O' Reilly and Jeffrey Pfeffer, "Southwest Airlines (A): Using Human Resources as a Competitive Advantage," *Harvard Business School Case HR-1A*, pg. 7.

41. Kris Maher, "Human-Resources Directors Are Assuming Strategic Roles," *The Wall Street Journal*, June 7, 2003, pg. B8.

42. *Knowledge@Wharton*, "IKEA: Furnishing Good Employee Benefits Along with Dining Room Sets," April 6, 2004.

43. http://www.jordans.com/careers/reviewed on November 15, 2003.

44. Patricia Panchak, "Manufacturing in the U.S. Pays Off," *Industry Week*, December 2002, pg. 18–19.

5

Customers: Healing vs. Hucksterism

We do not lack for ideas on how to keep customers coming back: Delight your customers. Exceed their expectations. Listen to what they say. Give them what they want. In the end, keeping customers coming back again and again boils down to the "wow" index of their experiences. How they *feel* usually has more binding power than how they *think*. Customer loyalty is like love: It grows not from reason but from the heart.

Heart is not a word that is often heard in business schools. But heart—a symbol of empathy, love, nurturing, caring, giving—has recently made a quantum leap and landed smack dab in the middle of mainstream business consciousness. It's okay now to talk about love in the office—in a Platonic sense, of course. It's okay now to promote love between supervisors and line staff (same ground rules). It's okay now to think of customer/company relationships in terms of love.

The New Marketing Paradigm

We have left the twentieth century, but you wouldn't know it by looking at much of the marketing still being done 14 years into the twenty-first century. Marketing remains heavily committed to a twentieth century paradigm based on the seduction, conquest, and manipulation of customers. Reflect a moment on the title of an end-of-century marketing book on sales: *Triggers: 30 Sales Tools You Can Use to Control the Mind of Your Prospect to Motivate, Influence and Persuade* (1999). *Triggers* continues to sell well 15 years after its initial publication. This and many other similar books suggest that legions of marketers and salespeople are still obsessed with figuring out how to control consumers' minds. The idea of collaborating with customers to better meet their needs is largely foreign to them. Most sales training is still about seizing control of consumers' minds. Ever hear the term *market capture rate*? That's straight out of the twentieth-century marketing paradigm, which FoEs in this book rejected even before the twenty-first century ended.

The main trait of the twentieth-century marketing paradigm was of hucksterism—aggressive promotion and selling that put sellers' objectives ahead of the *real* needs of consumers. The elements of snake oil salesmanship in this paradigm were never completely masked by Madison Avenue glamour, glimmer, and glitz. Sales quotas were used everywhere to keep pressure on managers, sales agents, and others to sell, sell, sell. Little thought was given to the fact that when job security is tied to quotas, ethics and moral principles are at great risk. Customers become prey. Marketers and salespeople become predators. We believe that this model of marketing and sales is headed for the ashbins of business history.

Yes, there will always be individuals and companies that are bent on exploiting customers, but we are talking about the dominant moral character of marketing in the future. Melinda Davis, CEO and lead seer of The Next Group, a futurist think tank in New York, offers a refreshingly new view of the marketing profession:

> "The possibility for real differentiation comes not in the product itself but in how you collaborate with the consumer's need to heal.... This is the new imperative: The marketer must now be a healer."[1]

Welcome to marketing in the Age of Transcendence. Like a velvety fog rolling in over the cold earth of a dying winter to signal the emerging warmth of a new spring, a culture of love and healing is spreading throughout the business landscape. It permeates workplaces everywhere, from executive suites to mailrooms. It laces the brain cells with a seductive disposition to reverse the tides of customer exploitation that reached peak heights in the last quarter of the twentieth century. That is when companies gained unprecedented information advantage over customers. Companies used information technology to disembody us all as dehumanized data sets. We were variously labeled by such sterile terms as *seats, eyeballs, lives,* and faceless *end users*. We were reduced to stimulus-response mechanisms virtually devoid of volition by predictive modeling programs that supposedly knew us better than we knew ourselves. This mindset was pithily captured in the title of a 1990 PBS documentary on direct marketing with the ominous title, "We Know Where You Live."

Love is the antidote for this dehumanization. Sounds too New Agey, maybe? Pause for a moment and consider: the former head of Meredith Publishing Magazine Group, the Chief Solutions Officer of Yahoo!, the CEO of Whole Foods Market, and the CEO of one of the world's largest advertising agencies talk about love in the marketplace without being concerned about raising eyebrows. Perhaps love has indeed established a secure beachhead in mainstream business thought. In any event, it's not possible to fully understand how FoEs outperform their closest competitors without understanding the role of love in their success. FoE executives lead with strong spines and dedicated resolve, but they retain their capacity to love and inspire love—in the workplace, in the marketplace, and across the full spectrum of their stakeholder groups.

Interestingly, participants in our seminars and workshops usually get the love idea quicker than they get the healer idea. "Marketers as healers? You've got to be kidding." But we're not kidding. Love and healing are inseparable, like gems and their facets.

New Balance is a loving FoE with a healing-based market strategy. This comes through strongly in its marketing communications. Given its history, it's not surprising that New Balance was an early practitioner of the ennobling idea that marketing should be about healing. The following is from New Balance's website:

> The story of New Balance begins at the dawn of the 20th century (1906) in Boston, Massachusetts when William J. Riley, a 33-year-old English immigrant, committed himself to helping people with problem feet by making arch supports and prescription footwear to improve shoe fit.

> When Jim Davis bought the company... on the day of the Boston Marathon in 1972, he committed himself to uphold the company's founding values of fit, performance, and

manufacturing. When Anne Davis (Jim's wife) began her journey with New Balance in 1978, her focus became building a superior culture for NB associates and those who do business with the company around the globe.

Now you know why New Balance offers more shoe widths than other major sneaker companies.[2] Podiatric comfort and healing depend on the right fit. New Balance was founded on principles of healing that Jim and his wife and business partner Anne Davis continue to uphold a century after the company's founding. Healing is in New Balance's DNA. As society ages and podiatric problems become more commonplace, New Balance seems even more dedicated to the healing model of marketing. The company has made major efforts aimed at raising awareness of its commitment to proper shape and fit among podiatrists and other professionals who minister to unhappy feet. But it's not just through the functional attributes of its shoes that New Balance reveals it culture of healing. This is especially evident in its sensitivity to boomers in their midlife years.

Midlife is a time ripe for crisis, or at least new, unfamiliar challenges. Perennial midlife urgings to shift psychic energy away from *social actualization* toward *self-actualization* disturb the personal status quo. Social actualization is a developmental process concerned with gaining social acceptance that facilitates vocational and material success. This requires us to subordinate part of our inner self to the demands and expectations of others in the outer world. However, this changes as we approach midlife. We begin to experience a need acknowledged by New Balance's slogan, "Connect With Yourself. Achieve New Balance." The gravitas of the process of shifting psychic energies more toward the inner self is reflected in words set down in *The Seasons of a Man's Life* by Daniel Levinson et al., whose research was the primary source of insights on midlife that Gail Sheehy wrote about in her famous bestseller *Passages*. Levinson wrote:

> In the Mid-life Transition, as a man reviews his life and considers how to give it greater meaning, he must come to terms in a new way with destruction and creation as fundamental aspects of his life. His growing recognition of his own

mortality makes him more aware of destruction as a universal process. Knowing his own death is not far off, he is eager to affirm life for himself and for generations to come. He wants to be more creative. The creative impulse is not merely to "make" something. It is to bring something into being, to give birth, to generate life.... Thus, both sides of the Destruction/Creation polarity are intensified in mid-life.[3]

A commonly expressed midlife theme is "It's now my turn," or "my time," as Abigail Trafford says in her book *My Time: Making the Most of the Rest of Your Life,* about how to "connect with yourself."[4] However, this is not "my time" in the sense of greater self-absorption, but rather in the sense that Levinson talks about when he describes the core developmental tasks of midlife and regards them as based on creativity as opposed to consumption.

In midlife, ancient catalysts of personality development in our genes nudge us toward ever higher levels of psychological maturation, provided we are beyond struggling to meet our basic survival, security, and social belonging needs. As Maslow suggested, this is when self-actualization, a developmental process that decreases the influence of the outside world on our worldviews and behavior, begins to emerge. We begin turning more attention toward the inner self. In Jungian terms, we begin dissolving the self-conscious and socially pretentious *persona*[5] that we needed during adolescence and the early adult years.

From FoE New Balance's headquarters in Boston, not far from Abraham Maslow's Brandeis campus, Chairman Jim Davis has shown a remarkable intuitive understanding of self-actualization needs and the influence they have on people's behavior in the second half of life. His insights show up clearly in a comparison of values promoted by New Balance and Nike, respectively, in their marketing (see Figure 5.1). Note that the values promoted by Nike are perfectly legitimate and likely to be highly successful in a youth-dominated culture with a strong bias toward masculine values. The values promoted by New Balance, on the other hand, are increasingly well suited to a culture that is becoming dominated by the values of middle age and the rise of feminine values.

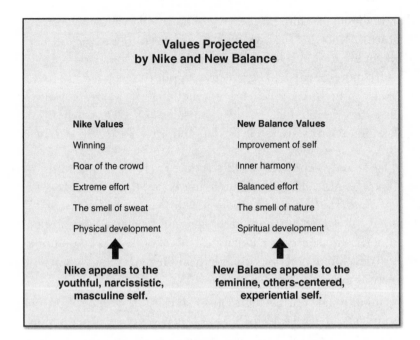

Figure 5.1 Comparison of values projected by Nike and New Balance

In one New Balance ad, a man is running along a road carved into the side of a mountain overlooking a shimmering sea. The ad headline reads, "The shortest distance between two points is not the point." Nike might have run a visually similar ad but stressed superior performance and winning. With New Balance, it's a person against him- or herself, or Man *with* Nature—never *mano a mano,* as often seen or implied in Nike ads.

When we're scrappy youngsters or freshly minted adults hell-bent for big-time success, we spend much of our energy trying to get ahead of our competitors in love, work, and play. But as midlife comes upon us, our very humanness inclines us to shift our energies into other pursuits. New Balance's marketing reflects this. Its ads have none of the machismo that generally underlies sneaker marketing. New Balance ads posit that one's worth is not measured by superiority over others, but by the measure of one's fidelity to one's *real self.*

Thus, when people begin wakening to the fact that they can't run and play as hard as they once did, when they start wondering why "things" no longer satisfy the soul as they once did, when they begin to ask perennial midlife questions such as "Is this all there is?" and "What is the meaning of life... of *my life*?" New Balance is there with its comforting messages about self-discovery and new vistas.

A New Consciousness

It takes a different mindset than the one that produced the twentieth-century marketing paradigm of huckstering to get in sync with the new twenty-first century marketing paradigm. Recall the evergreen wisdom of Einstein about the importance of changing consciousness when old ways no longer work: A problem cannot be solved by the same consciousness in which it arose.

By nearly all accounts, marketing is sodden with problems. Abandoning old ways of thinking, whose rules you know, for new ways of thinking, whose rules you don't know, is challenging. It is challenging intellectually, and also emotionally. Grief over the passing of "the good ol' days" and the stress of feeling lost in new mental territory unsettles the spirit. As a result, most people continue flailing away at a problem in the same consciousness in which it arose, doing the same thing over and over, expecting different results each time. Haven't we all heard by now that doing the same thing over and over, expecting different results, is a definition of insanity?

The enviable success of FoEs flows from inspired leadership working from a different consciousness than used by their non-FoE competitors. Nike founder Phil Knight is an inspiring leader in his own right, but he operates from a very different consciousness than New Balance's Jim Davis does. Nike views the sneaker market through the lens of competitiveness. Seeing the market through that view, it makes sense to spend tens of millions of marketing dollars for iconic athletes to endorse products and tens of millions more publicizing those endorsements. Consider that Adidas signed up soccer star David Beckham for an estimated $160 million, the largest endorsement contract in history. Nike signed up basketball neophyte LeBron James for an estimated $90 million agreement in the biggest sneaker endorsement deal in history—after signing Tiger Woods on for $100 million—the biggest golf endorsement deal in history.

New Balance views sneaker markets through the lens of a different consciousness. First, it sees itself as a sneaker-*making* company. Thirty percent of its inventory is manufactured at its own factories in the U.S. Jim Davis views his closest competitors, including Nike, as sneaker-*marketing* companies. They don't make sneakers. They outsource all sneaker manufacturing.

The foundation of New Balance's marketing is fit and performance. But some people also buy New Balance sneakers because they want to acknowledge New Balance's resistance (to the extent it feasibly can) to outsourcing. We make no moral judgment on outsourcing, but bring attention to an increasing *meta* need of consumers to patronize companies and brands that share their values.

Styling, which is primary among New Balance's biggest competitors, is secondary at New Balance. Nike and others view customers primarily in terms of the social self (fitting in, impressing others, and competitiveness). New Balance views customers in terms of the inner self (life with balance and meaning). This view of customers doesn't depend on expensive endorsements and extensive advertising for expression.[6] It leaves a lot of money for research as well as the care and feeding of retail partners (at which New Balance excels). Also, it helps in covering the higher salary costs of manufacturing operations in the U.S., although the superior productivity of New Balance's American employees goes far in accomplishing that.

"But how successful has New Balance been with its unconventional view of sneaker markets?" you might ask. Enormously successful. It rose from 12th place in the sneaker category in 1990 to second place in 2004, prior to the Adidas-Reebok merger. It made these gains during a time when sneaker markets were becoming smaller as a result of shrinking youth and young adult populations. During the 1990s, the 18-to-34-year-old population shrank by nearly 9 million potential sneaker wearers. In U.S. markets, Nike, Reebok, and Adidas experienced decline in both sneaker sales and market share. During the same period New Balance's sneaker sales and market share grew dramatically. Its annual sales growth averaged around 25 percent between 1990 and 2003. By 2013, its revenues were close to $2 billion, and its global market share was 6%, trailing only Nike, Adidas, and Puma and tied with Reebok. Being an FoE has indeed paid off handsomely for New Balance.

The marketers of Unilever's Dove brand of skincare products have also entered a new consciousness. They have done so in a radical departure from traditional marketing in the personal care products category: Dove has embraced the idea of the marketer as healer. It has shifted from a consciousness that perceives beauty in idealized terms to a consciousness that sees beauty in real-life terms. This shift in consciousness was motivated by a survey that revealed that only two percent of women considered themselves beautiful. A meager 13 percent were "very satisfied" with their body weight and only 13 percent were "very satisfied" with their beauty. Dove's marketers saw this as signs of a previously unrecognized opportunity.

They began thinking about the beginning of women's attitudes of physical inadequacy in adolescence. Low self-esteem and hang-ups that emerge from these attitudes sentence countless girls to a life that fails to measure up to their potential. So Unilever established the Dove Self-Esteem Fund, which serves as an agent of change in young girls' attitudes about themselves. It inspires them with a wider definition of beauty than traditional marketing of personal products encompasses.

The vast majority of females—young, middle aged, and old—do not identify with sensual depictions of youthful beauty in advertising. Dove marketers saw in this an opportunity. It launched its much-lauded global campaign to redefine beauty. A website devoted to "Real Beauty" was set up, offering "Inspiration from and for Real Women," and promising "to help real women reveal their own real beauty with articles meant to inform, inspire and instill confidence in you." One Dove ad featured three older women with a crucial question adjacent to each picture:

- Gray or Gorgeous?
- Wrinkled or Wonderful?
- Flawed or Flawless?

The power of Dove's healing message draws from its empathetic connection with customers. "But does it sell soap?" one might ask. Yes. Resoundingly, yes. In Europe, where the campaign first broke, results surpassed all expectations. Dove Firming Lotion sales, for example, exceeded forecasts by 110 percent in Western Europe in 2004. In the UK, Dove Firming Lotion sales rose from 280,000 bottles in 2003 to 2.3 million bottles in the first six months of 2004. In 2013, Dove launched another innovative campaign to get women to recognize and acknowledge their own beauty. Called "Dove's Real Beauty Sketches," the campaign featured an artist sketching women's faces based on their self-descriptions as well as based on descriptions provided by others. The ones based on self-descriptions were invariably less attractive and less reflective of reality. The publicity attracted by the campaign generated 4.3 billion impressions in less than a month.

Make no mistake about it: healing, a distinguishing trait in FoE corporate culture, is replacing hucksterism as the soul of marketing.

It's Not News: Committed Employees Yield Committed Customers

Just about everyone in business seems to recognize the truth embodied in the title to this section. But how many companies fully put that truth to work? FoE companies do. They know that great customer care begins with hiring people who have a high capacity for caring about their work and the customers they serve. They know that the work of immensely satisfied employees yields immensely satisfied customers. They take the long view that paying their employees higher wages and benefits than their competitors can often reduce employee-associated costs and improve the customer experience. They also know that this long view leads to decreased marketing costs and higher sales per customer. All this may seem counterintuitive, but in case after case, FoEs with higher labor costs actually have lower labor costs per dollar of income as well as lower marketing costs. Seen through the lens of the proverbial bean counter's consciousness, it's not easy to see how higher wages and benefits can lead to such felicitous results.

The line-by-line way of looking at costs, treating each line item as an independent variable, inescapably obscures crucial connections between compensation and productivity, income and profits.

Everything in business is part of a piece. Companies are participants in economic ecosystems in which all participants are interrelated and interdependent. Actions in one group of participants can influence the well-being and behavior of participants in other groups. Given this, wages and benefits need to be viewed in the context of the whole picture. Look at the issue this way: Low wages and meager benefits inevitably lead to low employee engagement and high turnover. This puts a damper on productivity as well as increases recruitment and training costs. Last but not least, it lowers revenue per customer and promotes higher customer turnover.[7]

To us, it is self-evident that greater employee engagement leads to superior performance. Corporations are a form of embodied human energy. That energy increasingly seeks to express itself toward nobler ends. If a leader can help create the conditions for that to happen, financial performance inevitably follows.

In 2008, the Kenexa Research Institute found that the top quartile of firms on engagement have net incomes that are double those of the bottom quartile. Shareholder returns were seven times greater over five years.[8] A Towers Perrin study in 2011 found that companies with high engagement had six percent higher net profit margins.

Kevin Kruse calls the process whereby this happens the "engagement-profit chain," similar to the classic service-profit chain described by Jim Heskett and Earl Sasser:

"Engaged employees lead to...

higher service, quality, and productivity, which leads to...

higher customer satisfaction, which leads to...

increased sales (from more repeat business and referrals), which leads to...

higher levels of profit, which leads to...

higher shareholder returns (stock price)."[9]

Doug Conant became CEO of Campbell's Soup in 2000, and found a company with dismal levels of employee engagement. He made it a top priority to improve that, and succeeded dramatically. By 2009, Campbell's had 23 engaged employees for every disengaged one, and its stock was dramatically outperforming the market.

FoEs pointedly look for hires who have a genuine interest—who are even a bit fanatical about the purpose of the FoE's existence. For example, FoE Patagonia's market focal point is climbing enthusiasts. It wants employees who are passionate about "the dirt bag culture" of climbing. L.L. Bean's market focus is also the great outdoors, so it looks for employees who are zealous about nature. In the same industry, REI cares deeply about reconnecting people with nature, and its employees are inevitably hiking and camping enthusiasts.

As we mentioned earlier, Whole Foods Market's business philosophy is summed up by its motto, "Whole Food, Whole People, Whole Planet." It doesn't want just warm bodies, but enthusiastic "foodies" who take life in with gusto in the spirit of the motto. They know that this enthusiasm will not only give customers an enjoyable shopping experience, but that it will lead to more income per dollar of employee cost.

Employee enthusiasm is a big reason why Whole Foods Market and other FoEs outperform their competition. People patronize FoEs in part because of the fun they experience. One of us is a foodie who divides his shopping time between FoE Trader Joe's for basics and fun, FoE Whole Foods Market for health and fun, and FoE Wegmans Food Market for fun and... well, fun. Wegmans is a foodie's paradise!

Earlier in the book, we discussed the importance of emotional intelligence (EI) in employees and senior management. In addition to its benefits within the organization, EI is also critical in dealings with customers. For example, consider the often-conflicting and ambiguous demands placed on professional salespeople. They are called on to simultaneously generate immediate profits through sales, build customer satisfaction, promote lifetime customer loyalty, and contribute to the long-term economic viability of the company. Research has shown that a salesperson's ability to perform well in juggling and delivering on all of these priorities is strongly related to his or her level of EI.[10] FoEs are characterized by high levels of EI among all employees, and especially among employees who deal with customers on a regular basis.

How Not to Build Trust

Countless vision and mission statements cite building trust with customers as a primary objective. That puts a nonproductive spin on why a company is in business. Trust should not be a primary business objective. It is more properly regarded as an outcome from consistently meeting or exceeding customers' expectations. In other words, trust is a measure of how well a company serves its customers, and in a broader sense, how well it serves all stakeholders.

Lee Surace, L.L. Bean's former CFO, was not your garden variety chief bean counter. He felt a deeply engrained sense of mission in his work, unrelated to dollars. He didn't think about strategies for building trust. He thought about strategies for helping all L.L. Bean stakeholders. He approached his work with almost priestly humility and reverence:

> "For me, this business is not all about money. You have a sense that you are really improving people's life…. When you become aware of the social responsibility that you have not only with your workers, but also with all your suppliers, vendors, customers, and your community, you realize that this business is not about how much money you are going to make as a company."[11]

The culture defined nearly a century ago by passionate outdoorsman L.L. Bean, who was named by *The Wall Street Journal* as one of the Top Ten Entrepreneurs of the twentieth century, remains intact today. Unlimited guarantees are part of that culture. As one story has it, several years ago a customer returned a threadbare coat bought in the 1950s and received a new coat in exchange in fulfillment of L.L. Bean's guarantees without time limits. The $1.5 billion outdoor equipment and apparel company knows that its unlimited guarantees say to customers, "We trust you." Customers' respond, "We trust you, too," by giving the company their undivided loyalty.

Costco is another FoE that scores high in customers' trust. However, founder and former CEO Jim Sinegal didn't spend much time thinking about building trust with customers. He was more devoted to maintaining consistency in expressing Costco's core values on a daily basis (the core values are listed in Chapter 8, "Society: The Ultimate Stakeholder").

Sinegal's passion for taking care of customers began by limiting the markup of any branded product to 14 percent and to 15 percent on its Kirkland private label products. Some years ago Costco's Kirkland brand 35mm film started flying off the shelves. The supplier kept lowering the wholesale price to Costco as sales continued rising. This increased margins on the film above Costco's 15 percent margin limit. Concern arose in management that lowering the price to stay within the 15 percent margin limit could erode brand equity. The solution Costco adopted was lowering the price per roll, but adding more rolls to the pack to keep the package price about the same.

Much like L.L. Bean and some other FoEs, Costco customers have blanket permission for returns: no receipts; no questions; no time limits, except for computers, which have a six-month grace period. Costco trusts customers, and customers trust Costco. Trust is always strongest in relationships where it runs in both directions. Countless companies want customers to trust them, but they do not reciprocate that trust. But FoEs understand the payoff in nurturing and trusting customers. Yes, occasionally a customer will abuse the system, but FoEs won't compromise the benefits that flow to the many because of the transgressions of a few.

Costco's disposition to trust its stakeholders begins in its dealings with employees. Sinegal set an example that made it clear to employees that Costco executives aren't in the game to take advantage of employees, customers, suppliers, or anyone else they can for personal gain. He demonstrated this by taking compensation that is pocket change in comparison with what most other chief executives of large corporations take. The average total compensation (including stock options) for CEOs in the top 350 companies in revenue in 2010 was approximately $12 million. Though Costco racked up an impressive (and profitable) $71 billion in revenues in 2010, Sinegal's total income that year was $540,000 ($350,000 in salary with a $190,000 bonus).

Sinegal was deeply committed to the idea that it makes more business sense to make a nice profit, but not a killing, and to invest more in Costco's now 175,000 workers. "I don't see what's wrong with an employee earning enough to be able to buy a house or having a health plan for the family," he says.[12]

FoEs Are Soulful

Harvey Hartman is into soul. Not soul music or soul food, but the soul of companies and their cultures. Most people believe the human soul is what most distinguishes us from other animals. Hartman believes the corporate soul is what most distinguishes companies from each other. Hartman is the founder and CEO of the Hartman Group, a soulful market research firm in Bellevue, Washington. He sees the issue of company soul as increasingly important to business survival and growth. "It's the result of our shifting from the industrial era Age of Reason to the postmodern Age of Soul," he says.

Asked what he means when referring to a company as "soulful," Hartman replied, "I mean a company that has an authentic product-origin narrative that champions nonmaterialistic attributes and moral values." That's another example of the Age of Transcendence *zeitgeist* that is driving the social transformation of capitalism.

People don't go to Walmart for soulful experiences. But they do go to Whole Foods Market with that in mind. They also go in battalion-sized mobs to the service-rich, family-owned Wegmans Food Markets for soulful experiences. They shop at Jordan's Furniture (now owned by Warren Buffet's Berkshire-Hathaway, Inc.) with its shoppertainment bonanza for a fun-filled soulful experience. People go out of their way to catch a flight on Southwest, the jester FoE airline with a perpetual smile on its face that takes some of the pain out of flying—a distinctly soulful experience.

Soulfulness is a hallmark of FoE companies. It is a distinctive component of culture in the Age of Transcendence that is reflected by an upsurge of interest in spirituality—in turn, a reflection of the aging of society. Aspirations for more soulful experiences in daily life are reducing the materialistic flavor of society. Consumers are looking more and more beyond the raw functional character of products and services for experiences that enhance life satisfaction. Joe Pine and Jim Gilmore richly document this in their business best seller, *The Experience Economy*.

Sure, "value" retailers such as Walmart will continue drawing in people for whom price is the primary criteria in choosing where to shop. But in the Age of Transcendence—similar to Hartman's Age of Soul, and Dan Pink's Conceptual Age—price is not the primary criteria in shopping decisions for a growing proportion of customers. By now, most people who know about Whole Foods Market have probably heard the tongue-in-cheek faux plaint that Whole Foods is "Whole Check." But millions of people shop there anyway. They accept the reality that it costs more to produce foods organically and more to produce meats and dairy products from free-range animals. So, Whole Foods Market shoppers gladly pay $3.49 a dozen for large grade-A eggs laid by free-range chickens even though they can get "normal" eggs at Safeway for less.

So "high price, high soul" is indeed a feasible business strategy. But is "low price, high soul" as feasible? Look no further than Costco, Trader Joe's, Southwest Airlines, Jordan's Furniture, Toyota, IKEA—all companies that offer great value and low prices.

Costco and other FoEs survive and prosper using a business model that inspires feelings of love among their customers as well as among employees and other stakeholders—love, the ineffable feeling of affection that bonds us to another being, and in the marketplace, to brands, companies, and employees of the companies we love. We readily talk about the value of a company's intellectual property; why not take its emotional property into account when assessing its investment value?

Endnotes

1. Bill Breen, "Desire: Connecting with What Consumers Want," *Fast Company*, Feb. 2003, pg. 86.

2. In a recent Chicago marathon, runners used 140 variations of size and width of the Model 991 running shoe.

3. Daniel J. Levinson, et al., *The Seasons of a Man's Life*, Ballantine Books, 1978, p. 223.

4. Abigail Trafford, *My Time: Making the Most of the Rest of Your Life*, Basic Books, 2003.

5. *Persona*, Latin for "mask."

6. In recent years, New Balance has started signing baseball players to endorsement deals—the influence in part of a new marketing head who came from Nike. The company is doing this to attract younger customers. We believe this is a misguided approach, as they are very strongly positioned for an aging market. But conventional wisdom has a way of asserting itself in the most forward-thinking of companies.

7. Frederick F. Reichheld, *The Loyalty Effect: The Hidden Force Behind Growth, Profits and Lasting Value,* Harvard Business School Press, 1996. This seminal book examines customer, employee, and shareholder loyalty and quantitatively shows the linkage between all three and makes the case that companies with low customer, employee, and shareholder turnover have the highest returns for shareholders.

8. http://www.kenexa.com/getattachment/8c36e336-3935-4406-8b7b-777f1afaa57d/The-Impact-of-Employee-Engagement.aspx.

9. http://www.openforum.com/articles/how-employee-engagement-leads-to-higher-stock-prices.

10. Elizabeth J. Rozell, Charles E. Pettijohn and R. Stephen Parker (2004), "Customer-Oriented Selling: Exploring the Roles of Emotional Intelligence and Organizational Commitment," *Psychology & Marketing,* June, Volume 21, Issue 6, pg. 405.

11. Eduardo Araiza and Pablo Cardona, "L.L. Bean Latin America," *International Graduate School of Management,* Case #ISE088.

12. Jim Hightower, "A Corporation That Breaks the Greed Mold," *Working for Change,* http://www.workingforchange.com/article.cfm?itemid=16603, July 17, 2005.

6

Investors: Reaping What FoEs Sow

Chris is an accomplished investment manager for one of the largest financial institutions in the U.S. For reasons that will be obvious, we can identify neither him nor the institution with further specificity. At a meeting convened in the fall of 2005 to discuss the establishment of an FoE investment fund, Chris said he had been following FoE Whole Foods Market for some time. "When each quarter's reports come in I say to myself, 'The PE [stock price to earnings per share] ratio can't go any higher.' But it always does." At the time of the investment fund meeting, Whole Foods' stock had gained 70 percent for the year. Who would have believed that a grocery company in perhaps the narrowest margin business of all could turn in such a performance? Chris confessed to being bewildered by this phenomenon. But when he was introduced to the FoE business model, the picture of Whole Foods Market's remarkable financial performance became clearer.

Recall from an earlier discussion that the firms of endearment we've cited collectively performed exceptionally well for investors over multiple time horizons. And remember, we selected FoEs for inclusion in this book based on their dedication to the interests of all stakeholders, which we believe bodes well for their future success. Only then did we analyze them in detail for their past financial performance. As we said earlier, we intuitively expected good performance, but nothing close to what we discovered to be the case.

We provided a brief summary of the impressive financial results generated by these companies in Chapter 1, "Building Business on Love and Care." We contrasted them with the overall stock market, represented by the S&P 500. We also compared FoE performance with that of companies identified by Jim Collins as having made the transition from "Good to Great."

In this chapter, we present further details on the financial performance of FoEs. Before getting into the numbers, however, we would like to discuss several issues related to investors as stakeholders.

The Whole Foods Way to Shareholder Wealth

FoE Whole Foods stands as a vivid exemplar for the stakeholder relationship management (SRM) business model, generating cumulative returns to investors of 2270% for the 20 years ending September 30, 2013. The company's business philosophy is embodied in its "Declaration of Interdependence," which is posted in every store and reflects the interconnectedness of its stakeholders. In part, it states the following (the entirety can be read at www.wholefoods.com/company/declaration/html):

"Whole Foods Market is a dynamic leader in the quality food business. We are a mission-driven company that aims to set the standards of excellence for food retailers. We are building a business in which high standards permeate all aspects of our company. Quality is a state of mind at Whole Foods Market.

"Our motto—Whole Foods, Whole People, Whole Planet— emphasizes that our vision reaches far beyond just being a food retailer. Our success in fulfilling our vision is measured by customer satisfaction, Team Member excellence and happiness, return on capital investment, improvement in the state of the environment, and local and larger community support.

"Our ability to instill a clear sense of interdependence among our various stakeholders (the people who are interested and benefit from the success of our company) is contingent upon our efforts to communicate more often, more openly, and more compassionately. Better communication equals better understanding and more trust."

Later on in the *Declaration of Interdependence*:

"Satisfying all of our stakeholders and achieving our standards is our goal. One of the most important responsibilities of Whole Foods Market's leadership is to make sure the interests, desires and needs of our various stakeholders are kept in balance. We recognize that this is a dynamic process. It requires participation and communication by all of our stakeholders. It requires listening compassionately, thinking carefully and acting with integrity. Any conflicts must be mediated and win-win solutions found. Creating and nurturing this community of stakeholders is critical to the long-term success of our company."

Whole Foods Market provides an interesting illustration of how the stock market can overreact to external events. After bidding up the stock to unreasonable heights and unsustainable price-earnings ratios, the market swung to the other extreme when the great recession of 2008 hit. From a high of around $70, the stock was beat down all the way to $7. The company's same-store sales growth had slowed and even showed a small negative trend. But as CEO John Mackey put it, it was still the same company that had been deemed to be worth ten times as much some time earlier. Refusing to let the Wall Street tail wag the business dog, the company stayed true to its purpose and its management philosophy. The stock soon went on a historic run, reaching approximately $112 (split-adjusted) at this writing.

Who Are Today's Investors?

Owning stocks and bonds used to be the preserve of the wealthy and the privileged. This is no longer the case. The Federal Reserve's Survey of Consumer Finances found that the percentage of American households owning stocks rose from 19 percent in 1983 to 32 percent in 1989, 41 percent in 1995, and 51.9 percent in 2001.[1] (The percentage actually declined to 46.9 percent in 2010.) Even more significantly, investors have become a major political force. In the 2004 election, exit surveys found that 70 percent of voters owned stock.[2]

The mainstreaming of stock ownership has helped drive the move toward greater corporate transparency. But it's having another effect, too. Many individual investors are bringing their personally held moral values into their investment decisions. They subscribe to the idea of sustainable and responsible investing that has a positive impact on the world. Steven J. Schueth, President of First Affirmative Financial Network, LLC, wrote the following on his company's website:

> "The motivations of investors who are attracted to socially responsible investing tend to fall into two, often complementary, categories. Some wish to put their money to work in a manner that is more closely aligned with and reflective of their personal values and social priorities. Others are interested in putting investment capital to work in ways that support and encourage improvements in quality of life in society at large. This group is more focused on what their money can do to catalyze movement toward a more economically just and environmentally sustainable world that works for all inhabitants. They tend to be more interested in the social change strategies that are an integral part of socially responsible investing in the U.S."[3]

Twenty years ago, America's premier management guru, the late Peter Drucker, wrote, "The rise of pension funds as dominant owners and lenders represents one of the most startling shifts in economic history."[4] Continuing, he said:

> "All told, institutional investors, including pension funds, controlled close to 40 percent of the common stock of the country's large (and many midsize) businesses. The largest and fastest-growing funds, those of public employees, are no longer content to be passive investors."[5]

When reflecting on Drucker's insights and the fact that over half of U.S. households own stock, Frederick Reichheld's revealing insights about how investors both add to and subtract from stock value come to mind. He faulted day traders and other short-term speculators for being destroyers of value by exerting pressure on executives to take shortsighted decisions at long-term cost. Reichheld advises companies to develop strategies that court the interests of such long-term investors as pension funds and mainstream American households. He shows with compelling metrics how long-term investors add value to a company. This is a key feature of *all* stakeholders in the FoE business model. From customers to communities, FoE management sees value creation as Reichheld does. All major stakeholders add value and benefit from gains in value. By involving all stakeholders, companies can tap into a broader and deeper set of resources to create far greater value.

FoEs are Warren Buffet's kind of investment. When asked how long he prefers to retain an investment, he often says, "Forever."[6] Commenting on his view of churn in Berkshire Hathaway's 1992 annual report, Buffett stated the following:

> "...we believe that our shares turn over far less actively than do the shares of any other widely held company.... The frictional costs of trading—which act as a major "tax" on the owners of many companies—are virtually nonexistent at Berkshire Hathaway."[7]

We put a lot of stock in Reichheld's and Buffet's views. The first has diligently studied the relationship between stock churn and erosion of shareholder value; the second became the world's second-richest man in part by understanding that relationship as well as the drivers of long-term value creation and investing accordingly. So why is it that more companies do not have similar views? Could it be that boards of directors incite top executives to make short-term, value-destroying decisions by rewarding them only for short-term gains?

The Zen Way of Viewing the Pursuit of Profit

The view we've promoted throughout this book—one that growing numbers are buying into in this new era—is that achieving business success is less a matter of obsessing over the financials than about focusing on how a business can create value for all of its stakeholders. FoEs do so by contributing to solving stakeholders' problems and enabling them to better achieve their potential and otherwise improve their quality of life. In support of this indirect approach to pursuing profits, noted British economist John Kay reminds us that most objectives are best pursued indirectly or tangentially.[8] For example, if you try to learn how to juggle, you will be told, "Focus on the throw, don't worry about the catch."[9] The trick is that if you get the throw right, the catching takes care of itself, and in fact becomes quite trivial. What this means for business is that they should heed a very spiritual principle: They should focus on consistently taking the right actions, and not be driven by a predetermined goal, or as the Buddha put it, a "cherished outcome." A business that is obsessively focused on that desired outcome is quite likely to undertake "wrong" actions, ones that eventually and inevitably lead to negative consequences all around.

The principle of indirectly pursuing an objective is reflected in the following Zen-like paradox: Trying harder to make money often leads to making less money. To put it another way, the most profit-driven companies are usually not the most profitable, whereas most companies that are highly profitable are not principally focused on profit making. As Peter Drucker explained, "Profit is not the explanation, cause or rationale of business behavior and business decisions, but rather the test of their validity."[10] Recall from the last chapter former L.L. Bean CFO Lee Surace saying, "For me, this business is not all about money. You have a sense that you are really improving people's life...." Those are words you never expect from a CFO—except from the CFO at a firm of endearment.

Research by McKinsey, the world's leading consulting firm, clearly demonstrates the efficacy of taking a long view and letting profits take care of themselves, so to speak, like a juggled ball finding its way almost mysteriously into the juggler's hands. In a 2005 edition of *The McKinsey Quarterly*, Richard Dobbs examined the relationship between a company's short-term performance and its long-term health. Healthy companies sustain superior performance over time. They are characterized by "a robust strategy; well-maintained assets; innovative products and services; a good reputation with customers, regulators, governments, and other stakeholders; and the ability to attract, retain, and develop high-performing employees."[11]

Unfortunately, especially for investors, too many companies fail to realize that seeking to achieve exceptional short-term results can be damaging to their long-term health. This is analogous to elite athletes who take steroids and other performance-enhancing drugs in order to win a contest, but suffer devastating long-term consequences. Companies can certainly boost short-term performance by reducing staff, cutting back on service levels, eliminating employee benefits, and other such actions. However, such actions significantly increase the odds for poor performance in the future. It is certainly common to see a company's stock rise when large-scale layoffs are announced. That may heat up trading and produce gains for day traders, but long-term investors should read it as a warning about the future health of the company.

Here is McKinsey's take on the pursuit of profits:

> "Paradoxically, the language of shareholder value... hinder(s) companies from maximizing their shareholder value. Practiced as an unthinking mantra, 'the business of business is business' can lead managers to focus excessively on improving the short-term performance of their businesses, thus neglecting important longer-term opportunities and issues, including societal pressures, the trust of customers, and investments in innovation and other growth prospects."[12]

Too many managers remain highly susceptible to short-term pressures. A study by the National Bureau of Economic Research found that most managers would *not* make an investment that offered an attractive return if it meant that they would miss their quarterly earnings target. Shockingly, over 80 percent of executives would cut R&D expenditures for the same reason, even if they truly believed that doing so would hurt the company in the long run.[13] And many boards award them cash bonuses and stock options for thinking this way.

The quarter-to-quarter pressures put on companies by influential stock analysts is a well-known phenomenon. The good news is that though many analysts do indeed exert pressure on management to deliver short-term results, the stock market as a whole rewards actions that produce long-term value.

Companies must decouple managerial compensation from short-term results and link it more closely with multidimensional indicators of long-term corporate health.[14]

Bonding Investors, Employees, and Customers

The investors, employees, and customers of a company can be bound together in a way that results in greater stability for the company and the harmonization of interests across those stakeholder groups (see Figure 6.1). For instance, at most well-run companies, and certainly at FoEs, employees are encouraged to become customers of the company, enjoying sizable discounts on the company's products and services. In many cases (especially with lifestyle products), companies find that their best hires come from within the ranks of their most loyal and demanding customers. Most such companies also have generous ESOPs (employee stock ownership programs). Rather than simply awarding stock options (which can be short-term in nature) to employees, FoEs encourage employees to purchase and hold the company's stock for the long run.

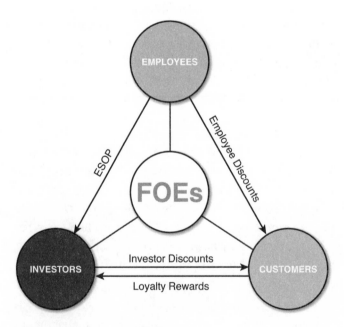

Figure 6.1 Hybrid relationships

The possible linkages between customers and investors are more unusual and in some ways more interesting. Companies should encourage hybrid relationships by getting their investors to become customers. In fact, they should consider offering long-term investors discounts similar to those employees get. On the flip side, some companies have started experimenting with new types of loyalty programs for their best customers by rewarding them with stock. For example, Jameson Inns rewards customers who stay three or more nights a year in its hotels with company shares worth 10 percent of their nightly room rate.[15] When Boston Beer Company went public in 1995, CEO Jim Koch wanted to move the company's customers to the front of the line, rather than favoring professional investors. Customers were able to buy shares at $15, versus $20 for those who bought at the public offering.

The advantages of bonding stakeholders together in this manner are obvious. Stakeholders with multiple relationships with the company are more likely to be valuable to the company, and they are also more likely to stay with the company when it goes through turbulent times. Stakeholders should be bonded not just with each other, but also directly with the company. Companies should not hesitate to bring representatives of all stakeholders (not just the three mentioned here) directly into their long-term strategic planning process.

Shareholder Returns

What makes FoE firms different in the eyes of investors? What makes their stock prices outperform the *Good to Great* companies over the long run?[16] We've found out that FoE firms generally earn higher shareholder returns, typically have premium price-to-earning (P/E) ratios, but incur no more risk than the overall stock market.

To compare shareholder returns, we researched the historical price activity for the 28 public U.S. FoE firms, the 11 *Good to Great* (G2G) firms, and the S&P 500 over the three-, five-, ten-, and 15-year time periods ending September 30, 2013. These time frames span a range of market conditions, including the dawning of the Internet boom, the bursting of the tech bubble, a slow recovery, and the Global Financial Crisis of 2008–2009.

Here is how we calculated returns:

- Quarterly holding period returns calculated using closing prices and dividends pulled from Bloomberg terminals from 10/01/1998 to 09/30/2013.

- Total return calculated by accumulating holding period returns (HPRs) to account for reinvested dividends.

- Beta calculated by a linear stock price regression from 10/01/1998 to 09/30/2013 as per Bloomberg.

- Companies that became public during this period were added in once stock price data was available; that is, not having a stock price did not result in a 0% return for the company, as it would drag down returns for the group.

Table 6.1 and Table 6.2 show that the stock price performance of FoE firms has dwarfed that of the S&P 500 for all included time horizons. FoE firms also outperform G2G firms over the longer time periods.

Table 6.1 Cumulative Returns

Cumulative Performance	15 Years	10 Years	5 Years	3 Years
U.S. FoEs	1681.11%	409.66%	151.34%	83.37%
International FoEs	1180.17%	512.04%	153.83%	47.00%
Good to Great Companies	262.91%	175.80%	158.45%	221.81%
S&P 500	117.64%	107.03%	60.87%	57.00%

Table 6.2 Annualized Returns

Annualized Performance	15 Years	10 Years	5 Years	3 Years
U.S. FoEs	21.17%	17.69%	20.24%	22.40%
International FoEs	18.53%	19.86%	20.48%	13.70%
Good to Great Companies	8.97%	10.68%	20.91%	47.64%
S&P 500	5.32%	7.55%	9.98%	16.22%

P/E Ratios and Beta

P/E ratios can be used to gauge whether stocks are overvalued, undervalued, or fairly valued. Traditionally, stocks that have a P/E below their historical or industry mean can be considered undervalued. In this study, however, we were trying to prove a different theory, which is that FoE firms outgrow and outdistance themselves from traditional P/E valuations, and earn premium P/E ratios. A premium P/E ratio is an indicator that a firm has balanced its major stakeholders effectively and is positioned for sustained growth in the future (partially at the expense of its more traditional profit-driven competitors). We expect firms of endearment to continue to carry higher P/E ratios relative to their industries and the general market (S&P 500) as long as they continue to operate in this manner.

Beta is a measure of the risk or volatility of a stock. We found that the beta for the Combined FoEs is currently at 1.02, a slightly higher risk relative to the S&P 500 (see Table 6.3). But a lower beta isn't always better. The idea is to reward investors with above-market returns without incurring much additional risk. This is exactly what FoE firms typically do, delivering much higher risk-adjusted returns than the market as a whole (see Table 6.4).

Table 6.3 Key Ratios*

Ratios	P/E	Beta
U.S. FoEs	26.15	1.02
Good to Great Companies	17.20	0.91
International FoEs	23.57	0.81

* As of 10/4/13

Table 6.4 U.S. FoE Returns

Company	15 Years	10 Years	5 Years	3 Years
3M	222%	72%	74%	37%
Adobe Systems	1096%	164%	32%	99%
Amazon.com	1580%	546%	330%	99%
Autodesk	526%	383%	23%	29%

Company	15 Years	10 Years	5 Years	3 Years
Boston Beer Company	3268%	1434%	414%	265%
CarMax	629%	284%	172%	43%
Chipotle	-	674%	673%	149%
Chubb	182%	174%	62%	56%
Cognizant	16239%	801%	260%	27%
Colgate Palmolive	244%	111%	57%	53%
Costco	388%	271%	77%	78%
FedEx	411%	77%	45%	34%
Google	-	576%	119%	67%
Harley-Davidson	333%	33%	71%	125%
IBM	188%	109%	58%	37%
JM Smucker	359%	148%	88%	72%
Marriott International	277%	109%	72%	24%
MasterCard Worldwide	1302%	1302%	279%	200%
Nordstrom	353%	351%	94%	50%
Panera	5103%	287%	211%	79%
Qualcomm	2147%	223%	56%	49%
Schlumberger	287%	264%	13%	43%
Southwest Airlines	62%	-18%	0%	11%
Starbucks	1602%	435%	418%	200%
T Rowe Price	388%	247%	33%	43%
UPS	55%	43%	44%	36%
Walt Disney	157%	224%	110%	95%
Whole Foods Market	1011%	324%	484%	215%

Conclusion

We harbor no fantasy that the traditional narrow view of business's sole purpose as profit maximization will become obsolete anytime soon. But we are confident that the number of companies following that philosophic direction will be fewer in number and increasingly put at a disadvantage by companies with a more connected view of their place in the lives and communities of all their stakeholders. This is the business philosophy preferred by growing numbers of customers, employees, suppliers, and other stakeholders. FoEs demonstrate that shareholders stand to have higher long-term gains by investing in companies with humanistic cultures. Of course, sound management and adequate capitalization remain critical. However, given the presence of those conditions, investors stand to reap significant gains with less risk when investing in companies that are firms of endearment.

Endnotes

1. http://www.federalreserve.gov/pubs/oss/oss2/scfindex.html.

2. Matthew Continetti, "I, Eliot," *The Weekly Standard,* March 7, 2005, Vol. 10, Issue 23, pp. 24–30.

3. http://www.firstaffirmative.com/news/sriArticle.html, as of Nov. 11, 2005.

4. Peter F. Drucker, *Managing the Future: The 1990s and Beyond,* Truman Talley Books, 1992, pg. 237.

5. Ibid, pg. 235.

6. Frederick Reichheld, *The Loyalty Effect: The Hidden Force Behind Growth, Profits, and Lasting Value,* Harvard Business School Press, 1996.

7. 1992 *Annual Report,* Berkshire-Hathaway, Inc., pg. 20.

8. John Kay, "The Role of Business in Society," February 3, 1998 (www.johnkay.com).

9. Michael J. Gelb, *Lessons From the Art of Juggling: How to Achieve Your Full Potential in Business, Learning, and Life,* Harmony, 1994.

10. Peter F. Drucker, *Management: Tasks, Responsibilities, Practices,* Harper & Row, 1974.

11. Dobbs, *op. cit.*

12. Richard Dobbs, Keith Leslie, and Lenny T. Mendonca, "Building the Healthy Corporation," *The McKinsey Quarterly*, 2005 Special Edition: Value and Performance.

13. John R. Graham, Campbell R. Harvey, and Shivaram Rajgopal, "The Economic Implications of Corporate Financial Reporting," *NBER Working Paper* Number 10550, January 11, 2005.

14. Dobbs, Leslie, and Mendonca, *op. cit.*

15. *Business Week,* Upfront, August 8, 2005, pg. 12 (also see www.jamesoninns.com).

16. Jim Collins, *Good to Great*. New York: HarperCollins, 2001.

7

Partners: Elegant Harmonies

Coffee farmers in Chiapas, Mexico darkly joke that that theirs is the business of the future—because it will always be better *next* year. Erwin Pohlenz toiled, worried, and sweated for years before *that* next year came. In 1998, his 1,250-acre coffee plantation Santa Teresa lost an entire mountainside of plants in torrential rains. The same year, bandits broke into his home and tried to extort $100,000. Pohlenz found himself in the role of a modern day Job. Scorching heat in successive years wreaked havoc on his plantings. A borer worm infestation swept over the plantation. Santa Teresa's production plummeted. Then, prices plunged worldwide. What else could go wrong? That was the question Pohlenz awoke to every day. One thing that could go wrong would be a change in people's coffee tastes. And just that happened. Demand shifted toward higher quality specialty grades than Santa Teresa was producing. Failure of the plantation started by Pohlenz's German immigrant father Ernesto over a half a century ago seemed imminent.

Then the relentless tide of misfortune began to turn. Commodities trader Agroindustrias Unidas de México S.A. (AMSA) came to the rescue of the Pohlenz family farm. AMSA is the Mexican unit of one of the world's largest commodities trading groups. Eduardo "Teddy" Esteve, AMSA's coffee chief, knew Santa Teresa was blessed with high altitude and the desirable *mundo novo* variety of arabica coffee—key ingredients in growing the specialty grades buyers were beginning to demand. But when Esteve sent technicians to investigate, they found Santa Teresa's operations suffered numerous quality problems: Green cherries were not pre-separated from mature fruit, and inferior "floaters" were not sifted out in the milling. Santa Teresa also fermented the beans longer than necessary, risking dehydration and the loss of flavorful oils. Pohlenz diligently pondered AMSA's advice. He tackled the processing glitches and successfully negotiated a contract with AMSA for the following year's crop.

Over the next four years, AMSA managers coached the Santa Teresa operation in making quality upgrades and targeted its sales to the coffee market's leading specialty client, Starbucks. In the 2001–2002 season, Starbucks bought a sample lot. A year later it contracted for Santa Teresa's entire first-grade harvest at 30 percent above local market prices. In 2003, Pohlenz signed a three-year contract for as much as 76 percent above the then-going Chiapas rate. "We were in crisis," Pohlenz says, "and Starbucks saved us from dying."

The transformation of Santa Teresa was only beginning. In 2003, conservationists from Rainforest Alliance and Conservation International visited Santa Teresa. What they saw inspired them to recommend Santa Teresa as a pilot farm for Starbucks' then-new incentive purchasing program, C.A.F.E. (Coffee and Farmer Equity) Practices.

Starbucks established C.A.F.E. Practices to evaluate, recognize, and reward producers of high-quality sustainably grown coffee. The program was developed in collaboration with Scientific Certification Systems (SCS), a third-party evaluation and certification firm. It promotes activities that yield social and environmental benefits. Growers that make progress by following the C.A.F.E. Practices Guidelines are awarded points toward preferred supplier status or preserving that designation once they've earned it. During a 2003 meeting with suppliers, AMSA's Esteve laid out the financial and social benefits such a program could bring. "At that point," Pohlenz says, "our vision took shape for a farm where nature, the producer, and workers together would all be better off."

Pohlenz began giving the comfort and well-being of his workers more attention. He built a concrete barrier to prevent rains with a smelly muck from washing downhill through worker housing. He installed biodegradable latrines. He built two open-air kitchens with wood-burning grills to replace campfires workers had been using in preparing meals.

Pohlenz realized that more was needed. The agenda of needed improvements was partly driven by a new management vision, partly by a contractual obligation to Starbucks to set aside 10 cents per pound of sales for social or environmental upgrades. But the preferred supplier credit that Santa Teresa received under the C.A.F.E. incentive system was also a driver. Each improvement earned points toward a preferred supplier status. Pohlenz knew he couldn't afford to rest on past achievements. "I don't think Starbucks has total confidence yet that Santa Teresa will be a long-term supplier," he said. "But it's not up to them to come save us—we have to do it for ourselves. If we produce a quality product under best practices, then Starbucks will pay us a fair price that will enable us to continue over a long time."

Keeping in mind Starbucks' C.A.F.E. Practices sustainability standards, AMSA plies its producers with services of the kinds that proved valuable in turning Santa Teresa from near disaster into a model operation. Such assistance runs contrary to the traditional image of middlemen like AMSA preying on farmers and taking a slice of profits for minimal value. But as Santa Teresa's success with Starbucks has demonstrated, "it really pays off in the long run to do the right thing," says Eric Ponçon, AMSA's commercial director. "And that means extending the vision for our own business to take on environmental and social responsibilities of the farm." Indeed, as buyers such as Starbucks demand increasing volumes of quality coffee over the coming years, the future of AMSA and other traders depends on finding and nurturing more producers who can deliver the goods with an animated social and environmental conscience. "The story of Santa Teresa," Ponçon promises, "is not an isolated case."

Of all the stories we heard in our research, none make the point about companies being participants in economic ecosystems with greater poignancy than the story of the Pohlenz family coffee farm in Chiapas, Mexico. Because Starbucks is a people-driven rather than a numbers-driven vessel of commerce, it has a nurturing influence on the lives and organizations within its economic ecosystem. Starbucks inspires bureaucrats, commodity traders, farm operators, field hands, and others in coffee-growing countries to reach beyond immediate, self-serving objectives to contribute to making life better for all that fall within Starbucks' sphere of influence.

Starbucks' leadership in spearheading solutions to social and environmental issues within its economic ecosystem exemplifies a remarkable development in private enterprise: the expanding role of business in areas of public welfare traditionally dominated by government. And who would have the temerity to charge Starbucks founder and CEO Howard Schultz with squandering shareholder wealth? Starbucks' stock appreciated six fold over the past decade, and tenfold between 2009 and 2013. It's worth pointing out here that Starbucks did not become a global brand by following the traditional Madison Avenue route of heavy advertising and promotion. It did so by diligently devoting attention to the needs of every stakeholder group, starting with its suppliers. Call it a social conscience at work if you wish, but we simply think that under Howard Schultz's inspired and inspiring leadership, Starbucks is just a very well-managed company that has achieved the concinnity that distinguishes companies operating under the nontraditional FoE business model.

Measures That Matter

Concinnity is an ancient English noun, little used today. Perhaps it's a sign of our times. Chronic impatience for getting to the "bottom line" or to "the point" dulls sensitivity to what concinnity stands for. Refined attention necessary to appreciate concinnity is scarce in a society that parses reality in sound bites and crudely renders it in "reality" shows on TV that are not reality at all.

Concinnity means "a skillful blending of the parts achieving an elegant harmony." It is found in poetic descriptions of finely crafted artifacts. It's also used to describe elegantly constructed thoughts. But organizations can achieve a state of concinnity, too.

Companies that operate beyond the moral boundaries of Milton Friedman's self-focused model of corporate purpose have a higher likelihood of achieving concinnity. They are like a person who has achieved a state of self-actualization: Everything has come together in elegant harmony. Abraham Maslow would probably view FoEs as companies that project self-actualization behavior. Self-actualization, he said, was about "being all you can be." (He said that many years before it became a slogan in the U.S. Army's marketing.) Reaching the vaulted state of "being all you can be" involves letting go of the ego. This mellowing act changes a person's worldview from self-centeredness to others-centeredness. But this doesn't mean sacrificing one's self-interest. Self-interest can be well served at the highest levels of maturity when the ego's desire to control all within its compass is diluted by a broader perspective on life. This holds true for companies as well as for human beings. We believe strongly that in the Age of Transcendence, winning companies will be those that strive to create value for all stakeholders, not just shareholders, and in doing so operate in a state of concinnity in which stakeholders in every category sustain the sublime experience of interacting with each other in elegant harmony.

Inevitably, the question arises, "How can a company be less self-focused, yet more successful?" Traditionalists believe that broadening a company's concern to encompass all stakeholders can only be done at a cost to shareholders. They claim this dilutes corporate focus on profit making to the point that profits fail to reach optimum levels. The error in their argument draws from *either/or* and *if/then* modes of thinking, which narrow options to as few as two. FoEs are run by CEOs who are able to chart their companies' directions in the more inclusive terms of *both/and* thinking. Options drawn from such thinking are literally limitless.

Concinnity Between Competitors

On November 9, 2005, after years of anticipation, IKEA opened its first Massachusetts store in the South Shore town of Stoughton. In preparation for the opening, IKEA had plastered its yellow-and-blue logo over subways and distributed more than a million catalogs to area households. It had also towed a bedroom set in a glass display case around the city. The president of IKEA North America, Pernille Spiers-Lopez, was on hand for the traditional Swedish good luck tradition of sawing a log in front of the store before it opened. The 350,000-square-foot store (six and a half times the size of a football field) drew approximately 25,000 customers, some from as far away as Atlanta. Many customers had camped out for more than a week to be among the first shoppers (the first 100 received free Poang chairs, a $99 value), and thousands took a day off from work to make it to the Wednesday opening. IKEA employees greeted the shoppers with whoops and cheers, banging blue and yellow thunder sticks. Shoppers headed for the 99-cent breakfast and later for the $3.99 Swedish meatball lunch, while their kids played in the supervised ball room.

Why all this excitement over the opening of a furniture store? It is because IKEA enjoys a cult-like following among customers (as do many FoEs), and its Boston-area fans had been waiting for this day for years. What was perhaps most interesting about this opening was the reaction of IKEA's next-door neighbors in Stoughton: fellow FoEs Jordan's Furniture and Costco. Both companies offered to let IKEA use their adjacent parking lots for the grand opening, and Jordan's lined the street with signs saying "Jordan's Welcomes IKEA."[1] This from a direct competitor in the furniture business!

In the dog-eat-dog, "Darwinian" image of competitors in the traditional capitalistic mindsets, one never helps a competitor. But FoEs extend their caring to everybody, even their competitors. Remember Yahoo!'s Tim Sanders' words in Chapter 1, "Building Business on Love and Care":

> "I don't think there is anything higher than Love.... Love is so expansive. I had such a difficult time coming up with a definition for Love in my book, but the way I define Love is the selfless promotion of the growth of the other."[2]

And remember Saatchi & Saatchi CEO Kevin Robert's follow on statement:

> "At Saatchi & Saatchi our pursuit of Love and what it could mean for business has been focused and intense. Human beings need Love. Without it they die. Love is about responding, about delicate, intuitive sensing. Love is always two-way. When it is not, it cannot live up to the name Love. Love cannot be commanded or demanded. It can only be given.[3]

Customers, employees, suppliers, community members, and others beholding the welcome mat put out by Jordan's and Costco can hardly do other than to admire the congeniality of two settled competitors as a third competitor enters their midst. It's a true example of concinnity.

Some may find it strange to hear of companies being talked about as self-actualizing entities. However, it's not in the least strange. After all, companies are extensions of people. Especially, they are extensions or analogs of the personalities that run them. So, it makes sense to describe a company's behavior in the same terms we use to describe people's behavior.

For example, some companies are wantonly aggressive, just as some people are. These companies pursue their self-interests to the point of ruthlessly overriding the interests of others. Some companies can be accurately described by the clinical term *borderline personality disorder*. BPD is characterized by long-lasting rigid patterns of thought and behavior including extreme "black and white" thinking, mood swings, and excessively emotionally grounded reasoning. BPD sufferers continuously experience disrupted relationships and difficulty in functioning in a way society accepts as normal. Most of us could quickly come up with a half a dozen companies that have the symptoms of a borderline personality. We describe such companies as *developmentally retarded* because they operate at the lower levels of "human beingness."

Then there are companies that seem to have everything together. Included in this felicitous group are firms of endearment. They operate with a human heart and follow a moral course with uncompromising intention. But let there be no mistake: FoEs are well managed. Their leaders know that intentions to do good can only be fulfilled when their companies do well. But they also know that by tending to the interests of every stakeholder group on whom their success depends, they are more likely to do better in meeting financial objectives. We describe such companies as *developmentally mature*.

The famous Milton Friedman view of corporate purpose fails to see connections between organizational concinnity and a company's evolution into an *enduring* great company. Organizational greatness is more qualitative than quantitative. Notwithstanding the exhaustive metrics used in selecting exemplar companies in Jim Collins' *Good to Great*, what it takes to be an enduring great company cannot be as precisely measured as financial activities and results can. The stuff of corporate greatness can only be approximated. It is more a product of the unseen than of the seen. It cannot be fathomed through accounting paradigms. Traditional Wall Street–styled analyses of companies overly depend on "hard" data to the exclusion of rigorously examining "soft" data. In the end, corporate greatness draws from how well organizational parts mesh together and how those parts give life to the whole. How that is done is largely told by "soft" data. What investors need is a "concinnity index" that tells them how well a company has integrated its parts.

Stakeholder Concinnity vs. Exploitation

FoE leaders view stakeholders as partners, not as objects of exploitation or means to their financial ends. They don't *objectify* stakeholders. Instead, they encourage stakeholders to collaborate with them in moving their companies forward. Every five years Whole Foods brings together representatives of its primary stakeholder groups to collaborate in designing the next five-year strategic vision. It's a process called *Future Search*. Customers and vendors participate alongside several other company stakeholder groups to shape plans for Whole Foods' future.

Several decades ago, feminist Gloria Steinem famously charged that men demean women by *objectifying* them. Many companies do the same with stakeholders. The main difference is that companies objectify stakeholders in pursuit of money, not sex. Steinem also said society pays a great price for tolerating the objectification of women: It is cruel, inhumane, and keeps many women from achieving their potential. Similarly, stakeholders—especially investors—pay a stiff price when companies objectify them. Doing so keeps them and the company from realizing their fullest potential.

The era of stakeholder exploitation is waning. Companies can no longer take advantage of their stakeholders with impunity. This is not pontification. It's marketplace reality in the dawning light of a new era in business. Freed from the distorting effects of excessively materialistic appetites, today's older, more experienced, and wiser population is quicker to recognize and react to signs of exploitation. Additionally, the Internet has vastly increased the power of consumers, employees, and other stakeholders to share and distribute information. When the emperor has no clothes, the Internet will reveal it. Comedian George Allen famously observed, "The most important thing in life is sincerity—if you can fake that, you've got it made." What it takes to be an FoE cannot be faked; it must be real.

Making Stakeholders Partners Increases Success Potential

In the wake of 9/11, one of the most calamitous days in U.S. history, an unprecedented wave of bankruptcies swept the airline industry. As the airlines pursued layoffs and big pay takebacks to regain viability, management's relationships with employees and their unions plummeted to new lows. Southwest Airlines was a notable exception. Alone among the major airlines, Southwest chose to ride out the storm without making any layoffs. And it never asked for any pay givebacks.

Kim Cameron, a University of Michigan business school professor, studied corporate resilience in the wake of 9/11. He found that "Airline companies that avoided layoffs and invested in preserving relationships... showed more resiliency than those that violated contractual commitments, instituted layoffs, and cancelled severance benefits. By foregoing downsizing, these companies created coping resources that enabled their employees to respond cohesively to the crisis in innovative ways and allowed organizational performance to return more quickly to pre-crisis levels."[4]

But there is more to Southwest's post-9/11 resilience than rejection of layoffs and pay cuts. Southwest experiences the same economic challenges as American, United, Delta, and other large airlines. However, for more than four decades, Southwest has come through every economic downturn without once having had a money-losing year. This in an industry that has lost more money than it has made.[5] Remember (from Chapter 4, "Employees: From Resource to Source") how Southwest faced selling one of its four planes in its early days? Frontline employees solved the loss-of-revenue threat by designing a way to have three planes do the work of four. When times are tough, Southwest employees rise to the occasion. So do the unions representing them.

Not long ago, a top airline analyst tried to explain to a gathering of MIT students how in an industry frequently beset by unprofitable years, Southwest never has a money-losing year. "Southwest is not shackled by traditional unions," he told the students.[6] But he was wrong. Southwest is one of the most highly unionized airlines in the U.S. What Southwest has going for it that none of its major competitors has is a strong partnership relationship with every stakeholder group. This includes its employees' unions. Unions are stakeholders, too. Treating them as partners can be as profitable as doing so with customers and suppliers.

Most companies with unionized workforces view unions as hindrances. Southwest sees them as partners. This outside-the-box company, with the personality of a jester and spirit of love for all stakeholders (its stock symbol is LUV), has become the nation's largest carrier of domestic traffic not in spite of unions, but in part because of them.

Southwest's corporate culture is based on five basic principles laid down years ago by its longtime CEO Herb Kelleher:

- Focus on the situation, issue, or behavior—not the person.
- Maintain the self-confidence and self-esteem of others.
- Maintain constructive relationships with your employees, peers, and managers.
- Take initiative to make things better.
- Lead by example.

Note the "others-oriented" bent of those principles. Each principle conforms to Maslow's description of self-actualizing personalities. In no principle is there a hint of the more prevalent command-and-control-guided business model. Self-actualizing people do not seek to control others. Instead, they gain greater effectiveness by leading through examples and mentoring rather than through commands and demands. Self-actualized companies do the same.

When asked about his leadership philosophy, Herb Kelleher answered, "A company is much stronger if it is bound by love rather than by fear." There's that word *love* again! Relationships form the backbone of the Southwest business model—correction: *loving* relationships form the backbone. Yes, we know that the word love has almost never been used in a book on economics, but how can one argue against its economic value after examining the incredible story of an airline whose stock symbol is LUV and whose cofounder unabashedly touts the practice of love as the foundation of the airline's success?

The Southwest business model is distinguished from the business models of its major competitors in two crucial ways. First, it rests on a foundation defined by principles of human behavior. Second, its operations are driven by a flexible organizational structure that changes to suit circumstances. The business models of the other major airlines rest on a foundation of numbers. The operations of the traditional airlines are driven by inflexible hierarchical structures in which employees are organized by specialty functions. Who has ever seen pilots at other airlines help flight attendants and ground crews ready a plane for its next leg? This happens routinely at Southwest. The turnaround time saved translates into millions of dollars in additional revenue annually—without a dollar's worth of added cost involved. This could only happen in a company without a hierarchical structure where love between frontline employees, their unions, and management prevails.

Harley-Davidson also views unions as partners. Retired Harley CEO Richard Teerlink deserves much of the credit for the harmonious relationship that exists between management and employees and their unions: "It was up to us managers to be drivers of change. For the business to work, everything must work well and function together, everyone must be excited about going to work in the morning."[7] Harley's union partners have been key in making that philosophy work.

The unions stuck with Harley-Davidson during rough times in the early 1980s, when 13 executives bought the nearly bankrupt company from AMF. Harley's management has never forgotten the unions' help in its struggles for survival after AMF management brought it to the brink of extinction. Despite many ups and downs in the economy, Harley didn't lay off workers for economic reasons for 25 years. At times, rather than lay off workers, the company brings outsourced tasks back in house. In recent years, the company has had to make some reductions in its workforce, but has been able to do so in a humane manner, working closely with its unions to determine the best way to do so.

Reflecting its close ties with management, Harley's unions have been known to reprimand workers for unsatisfactory performance. Its unions and Harley have long worked in a dedicated partnership to improve occupational safety. This has fostered open communications that enable employees at all levels to talk about any problem. Again, every stakeholder group, not the least of which are shareholders, benefits from this.

Under AMF, Harley's relationship with dealers hit rock bottom. Dealers were simply marketing targets for motorcycle sales. But from the first days of its emancipation from AMF, Harley has viewed dealers as business partners. Early in its reincarnation, Harley kicked off a program to help dealers hone their business and marketing skills. Today, that program continues under the auspices of the Harley-Davidson University.

Harley management came up with an idea in 1983 for turning Harley bikers into missionaries for the brand. It organized the HOGs—the Harley Owners Group. The HOGs played a major role in buying time with both bikers and dealers while the company dove into a crash program to restore levels of quality that had prevailed before Harley merged with AMF in 1969.

Harley's life under AMF management had turned into a disaster. Its market share in the U.S. plummeted from 77 percent in 1973 to 23 percent in the early 1980s. Harley-Davidson's revival was not the result of commands and control from a hierarchical organization. What brought Harley-Davidson back from the dead and restored its iconic luster was attentive nurturing of relationships that were skillfully knit together by 13 executives who still believed in one of the greatest vehicle brands of all time.

New Balance co-owner and Chairman Jim Davis drew on the principles of SRM to move from the #12 position among sneaker makers in 1990 to the #2 position before the Adidas-Reebok merger took place in 2005. As we wrote in Chapter 4, New Balance's partnership mindset with employees has been a huge factor in elevating productivity to levels that are ten times greater than has been achieved by factories abroad. That same spirit of partnership prevails in New Balance's relationships with dealers.

Jim Davis told us in an interview that retail dealers are New Balance's best friends—and vice versa. He said he spends most of his time on the road to visit retailers, working with them to improve sales and share trend data. An important competitive difference New Balance has over its top competitors is that it is able to restock retailers more quickly because its U.S. factories can deliver product faster than overseas factories whose products may take months to reach retailers' shelves. The ability of New Balance's domestic factories to restock shelves in weeks rather than months lowers retailers' inventory costs and enables them to more quickly respond to sudden changes in consumer preferences.

Suppliers also benefit from New Balance's SRM philosophy. In 1994, New Balance teamed up with leather supplier Prime Tanning Co. to create better waterproof leather for New Balance's then-new casual shoe line, American Classics. Kenneth Purdy, Prime's CEO, described the relationship as follows: "It's like a marriage.... It's like having a baby."[8] By forming close relationships with suppliers, New Balance has decreased the cycle time for shoes. The Prime Tanning and New Balance relationship led to a 50-percent reduction in the time required to take a new shoe style from concept to retailers' shelves.

If New Balance were publicly traded, stock analysts would undoubtedly criticize it for paying its American workers $15 per hour in wages and benefits while factories in China can turn out the same shoes for 30 cents an hour. But it's exactly that kind of linear thinking that sends many companies down pathways to calamity and investors into disappointing stocks. Everything is of a piece. You can't look at $15-per-hour employees as a problem that can be cured by 30-cents-per-hour employees. Those $15-per-hour employees are crucial to New Balance's strategy for securing a preferred position with retailers. They enable New Balance to outdo even the mighty Nike in responsiveness to retailers' needs. New Balance could never have made it into the big time as quickly as it did without the enthusiastic support of retailers. Cultivating retailers, as no other sneaker maker does, has turned out to be an enviably productive strategy.

If companies such as Whole Foods Market, Starbucks, Google, Panera, New Balance, and other FoEs have rewarded their owners as handsomely as they have, why don't more companies find out what has made these companies truly great companies and follow suit?

Accounting paradigms are linear. Their purpose is to yield pictures of certainties. However, the certainties they reveal are of the past, relied on by analysts and others in tribute to the Shakespearian bon mot, "What's past is prologue." But were that true in business, bankruptcy would be a rare occurrence. While poring over financial data is important in evaluating a company's prospects, a full picture cannot be obtained without also considering such contextual influences as relationships with stakeholders, corporate culture, and organizational architecture. In fact, such qualitative attributes have greater influence on future performance than quantitative attributes of the past. For instance, loyalty—a qualitative dimension of stakeholder relations—can be a stronger predictor of future performance than any balance sheet data. Reichheld makes a good case for this in *The Loyalty Effect*.

Collaboration Is More Profitable Than Exploitation

FoEs are intent on helping stakeholders gain from their relationships with the company. This includes helping suppliers become financially more successful.

For years, many large retailers have annually mandated suppliers to reduce their prices. Any adverse impact on a supplier's profitability and prospects for surviving is the supplier's problem. However, as FoEs know, this unsympathetic approach to cost control is myopic and detrimental to the integrity of the supply chain. Worse, by pitting suppliers against procurers in a price tug-of-war, the benefits of a partnership approach become unobtainable.

There is a growing realization that imposing annual pro forma mandates on suppliers to lower prices is not a sustainable strategy. IBM began recognizing this when its dependence on outsourcing increased dramatically in the 1990s. Bill Schaefer, vice president, procurement services for IBM in Raleigh, North Carolina, said the following:

"I've been in purchasing for a long time, and the traditional caricature of old-school procurement is that the supplier is treated as someone who's not to be trusted and who's totally dispensable. However, our view is that's not a desirable or sustainable model for procurement. We believe that there has to be close teamwork, a trust and a sharing that has to occur between IBM and our suppliers in order to be successful."[9]

Honda Motor Co. is widely regarded as a worldwide leader in supply chain management. It has gained this reputation because of successful outcomes from its focus on building and maintaining long-term, value-driven supplier relationships.

Honda is more an assembler than a manufacturer; it does not make most of what a new car owner drives away with from a dealer. In the United States, Honda buys approximately 80 percent of what makes up every car from external suppliers.[10] This is why it makes eminent sense to treat suppliers as partners rather than as expendable resources. Heavily stressed suppliers and high turnover in supplier ranks can deeply impair quality and significantly raise manufacturing costs.

Collaboration is key. Nothing is dictated; everything is negotiated. By definition, collaboration is bidirectional. Honda not only helps suppliers reach higher levels of productivity, quality, and profitability, it also encourages suppliers to suggest how it can improve its own processes. For instance, by gathering hundreds of ideas from suppliers and employing the best ones, Honda reduced the cost of manufacturing the Accord by 21.3 percent.

Close partnership and collaboration does not mean that Honda doesn't strive for lower input prices. However, unlike some other car producers, Honda does not squeeze suppliers to achieve this.[11] It seeks a balance between cost control and supplier well-being through what it terms *target costing*. This requires knowing exactly how much it should cost to produce a particular component. In the U.S. alone, 15–20 people form the cost target study team. The team knows the true cost of everything purchased and from that knowledge develops tables that set cost targets.[12] Supplier price negotiations are based on these cost targets. However, Honda does not simply force less efficient suppliers to operate at these pricing levels regardless of profitability. Instead, it works with each supplier to identify inefficiencies that might be preventing it from meeting target cost. Thus, Honda's cost for a part falls as the supplier gains in efficiency.

Honda's Best Partner (BP) program underpins its supply chain optimization initiative. The name itself reinforces Honda's view of suppliers as partners. The globally renowned BP program combines quality analysis and problem-solving techniques to target five strategic improvement areas:[13]

- Best Position
- Best Productivity
- Best Product
- Best Price
- Best Partners

Success in the auto business depends on far more than styling, horsepower, price, and buyer incentives. The car companies we've researched in developing this book have superior supplier relationships—and, we might add, superior union relationships. Perhaps therein lies a clue to survival of the U.S. auto industry. Managerial and operational strategies based on relationships, not numbers, can produce the numbers that U.S. car makers need to make to survive. We've seen strong connections between the quality of stakeholder relationships and the top and bottom lines in industry after industry. There really is no mystery to this. Most of us accomplish more when working with people we like and respect than with people we don't like and respect. Clearly, collaborating with suppliers in a partnership manner is more profitable than exploiting them.

The Art of Ironic Management

FoEs want to make the world a better place. But that doesn't mean they are run by wooly-headed do-gooders. FoE leaders practice the art of "ironic management." Because the word *ironic* is so often misused, we want to make clear what we mean by it. We mean an incongruous or unexpected result that does not seem to be the natural outcome of the activity or condition that produced the result. Some might call an ironic result a counterintuitive outcome. In any event, FoEs frequently take actions that produce results quite different from what conventional management logic would indicate. Here is a sampling:

- FoEs decentralize decision making, but do so in ways that increase rather than decrease top executive influence at all levels of a company.

- FoEs typically pay frontline staff above norms in their category. Rather than increasing cost of sales, this often reduces the percentage of a revenue dollar that goes to wages.

- FoEs typically depend little or not at all on conventional marketing practices, yet often experience robust growth due to the affectionate regard that stakeholders have for them and the word-of-mouth promotion that results.

- Publicly traded FoEs tend to be less influenced by expectations of Wall Street analysts but typically achieve higher price/earnings ratios.

- FoEs operate with greater transparency than most companies but are involved in less litigation.

We might also aptly deem as ironic the FoE premise that dedicating company resources to making the world a better place is an effective wealth-building strategy. Of course there still are many antagonists to this idea. A typical article in *The Economist* argued "...corporate philanthropy is charity with other people's money."[14] We can only feel charity for executives such as T.J. Rodgers, CEO of Cypress Semiconductor, who see corporate good works in that light. We also feel sympathetic toward shareholders in companies that are headed by executives with such a narrow view, especially Cypress Semiconductor's shareholders for reasons that will shortly be disclosed.

In 2006, Rodgers issued an astonishingly scornful rebuke of John Mackey's commitment to use Whole Foods Market as a vehicle for making the world a better place. Writing in a point-counterpoint debate on Corporate Social Responsibility in *Reason* magazine, Rodgers said, "Mackey's subordination of his profession to altruistic ideals shows up as he attempts to negate the empirically demonstrated social benefit of 'self-interest' by defining it narrowly as 'increasing short-term profits.'" That is a perversion of Mackey's perspective as it showed up in his part of the debate. After charging Mackey with harboring Marxist beliefs, Rodgers complained, "I resent the fact that Mackey's philosophy demeans me as an egocentric child because I have refused on moral grounds to embrace the philosophies of collectivism and altruism that have caused so much human misery, however tempting the sales pitch sounds."[15]

Rodgers' mental frames prevent him from seeing the Whole Foods Market business model as a valid one. Instead, he demeans it as an unconscionable compromise of shareholders' interests. Curiously, amid his assault on John Mackey, Rodgers overlooked Cypress Semiconductor's long and fruitless struggle to be profitable. Its balance sheet shows negative retained earnings of $408 million. "This means that in its entire 23 years of history, Cypress has lost far more money for its investors than it has made," wrote Mackey in his decidedly more temperate rebuttal.

As to how well Mackey's business philosophy has served shareholders, listen to John Mackey in the *Reason* point-counterpoint:

> "Of all the food retailers in the *Fortune 500* (including Walmart), we have the highest profits as a percentage of sales, as well as the highest return on invested capital, sales per square foot, same-store sales, and growth rate. We are currently doubling in size every three and a half years. The bottom line is that Whole Foods' stakeholder business philosophy works and has produced tremendous value for all our stakeholders, including our investors."[16]

The Whole Foods Market business model is not based on vague, idealistic notions of corporate social responsibility. Bringing suppliers as well as other outside stakeholders into its five-year development plan helps in building trust capital. Who could argue that building trust with everyone you do business with is a wooly-headed idea?

Swedish FoE IKEA is the world's largest furniture company, with $35 billion in annual revenues in 2013. The company imposes stringent environmental standards on its suppliers. It also turns down low bidders to sign on suppliers with stronger commitment to mitigating environmental impacts. Some might say that IKEA has achieved its colossal size "in spite of those practices." However, others would say it is, in part, *because* of those practices.

IKEA requires lumber suppliers to support the global standards it has set for itself. These standards are applied to all suppliers, regardless of relaxed local policies on irresponsible foresting. Requirements imposed on suppliers include approved wood sourcing, elimination of harmful chemicals in wood products, and using environmentally appropriate packaging. IKEA's diligent and strict adherence to environmental standards at first surprises many suppliers but they quickly learn that they must come into line to remain a supplier.

Outfitter Patagonia places high demands on its suppliers to meet specified quality, environmental compliance, and social responsibility standards. In fact, of all the FoEs we studied, none places heavier demands on suppliers for social and environmental responsibility. Suppliers that decide to partner with Patagonia often take significant risks by retooling factories, training employees on new production methods, and incurring additional capital equipment costs. However, many of these companies have experienced higher productivity and improved profits, while securing a substantial competitive advantage over their competition, who are slugging it out on lower-priced commodities.

Why would a supplier submit to Patagonia's moral construct when there are many other companies they could supply that make no such demands? First, Patagonia is seen as a prized customer with whom there can be a long-term relationship. Second, Patagonia's criteria for selecting a supplier is not based on price, but on quality, responsiveness, and social conscience. Third, a business association with Patagonia enhances a supplier's prestige. One supplier crowed, "Banks compete to finance us—Patagonia is viewed as a trophy credit."[17]

Patagonia is unremittingly committed to mitigating environmental impact all along the value chain. This commitment is carried out in product design, manufacturing, and distribution. In working with suppliers in furtherance of this commitment, Patagonia does not so much demand certain behavior as it "co-ventures" with suppliers to make the world a better place.[18]

What we are seeing is nothing less than the emergence of a form of moral evangelism in the corporate world. This is a big event. It signals the social transformation of capitalism on a major scale. This book may disturb traditionalists, but the increasingly clear reality is that there is no going back to the Friedman model of capitalism. A growing number of companies—big, medium, and small—are no longer content to confine their purpose just to lawful profit making. Leaders in many such companies are no longer satisfied with confining the exercise of their social conscience within their own operations. They are using their buying power to raise the moral bar of their suppliers and even their customers. During the more than two-century history of modern capitalism, relationships between procurers and suppliers have routinely been adversarial. It still is that way in many companies. But suppliers to FoEs find them not only better to work with, but also valuable partners in their own enterprises, helping them become more productive and financially more successful. Beyond that, partnerships to make the world a better place that are formed between FoEs and their suppliers and other stakeholders, such as we've described in this chapter, create added value for suppliers and all other stakeholder groups. Customer loyalty becomes more pervasive and stronger. Employee turnover drops while productivity rises. Suppliers function as eager partners, not as beleaguered and embittered indentured servants. Communities benefit in countless ways from companies that bring their objectives and operations into alignment with the needs of the community. And shareholders get wealthier.

Who can argue with a business model that does all that? Yet, there are those who will. After all, *belief follows need*. Some people still need to believe the world is flat (if you don't believe us, Google "flat earth society"). Some people need to believe that capitalism is perfect as conceived and that there is no profit in changing. Their economic fundamentalism binds them to the belief that what was good in the past is good for the present and for the future. But invoking Bob Dylan's words once again, *the times they are a-changin'*.

Endnotes

1. Jenn Abelson, "Nervous Rivals Gird for IKEA Opening; Stores Seek Ways to Compete on Selection and Price," *The Boston Globe*, November 4, 2005; Jenn Abelson, "Devotees, the Curious Flock to IKEA's Opening," *The Boston Globe*, November 10, 2005.

2. Tim Sanders, *Love Is the Killer App: How to Win Business and Influence Friends*, Crown Business, 2002.

3. Kevin Roberts, *Lovemarks: The Future Beyond Brands*, PowerHouse Books, New York, 2004, pg. 49.

4. Bernie de Grote, "Companies In Crisis: Money, Relationships Aid In Recovery," *The University Record Online*, University of Michigan, Nov. 1, 2004.

5. http://seekingalpha.com/article/1312991-southwest-airlines-40-consecutive-years-of-profits.

6. Jody Hoffer Gittell, *The Southwest Airlines Way: Using the Power of Relationships to Achieve High Performance*, McGraw-Hill, 2002, pg. 5.

7. Martha Peak, "Harley-Davidson: Going Whole Hog to Provide Stakeholder Satisfaction," *Management Review*. June 1993.

8. "Like-Minded Soles," *The Boston Globe*, July 4, 1994, Sect. 1 pg. 18.

9. John Yuva, "Leveraging Value From Supplier Relationships," *Inside Supply Management*, August 2005, pg. 20.

10. Lisa H. Harrington, "Buying Better," *Industry Week*, July 21, 1997, pg. 74.

11. Jerry Flint, "Until the Pips Squeak," *Forbes*, Dec. 22, 2003, pg. 96.

12. Harrington, *op. cit.*

13. Dave Nelson, Patricia E. Moody, and Rick Mayo, *Powered by Honda: Developing Excellence in the Global Enterprise*, John Wiley & Sons, 1998.

14. *The Economist*, "The Union of Concerned Executives," Jan. 22, 2005, pg. 8.

15. Milton Friedman, T.J. Rodgers, and John Mackey, "Rethinking the Social Responsibility of Business," *Reason*, Oct. 2005, pp. 29–37.

16. Ibid.

17. Lorinda R. Rowledge, Russell S. Barton, and Kevin S. Brady, "Patagonia—First Ascents: Finding the Way Toward Quality of Life and Work," *Mapping the Journey, Case Studies in Strategy and Action Toward Sustainable Development*, Greenleaf Publishing, 1999.

18. Ibid.

8

Society: The Ultimate Stakeholder

In recent years, Panera has emerged as a great success story, by some measures the best performing restaurant chain in the country after Chipotle. Panera has $1.8 billion in revenue and $3.4 billion in system-wide sales, including franchisees. It is the market leader in a new category: the fast casual restaurant, with healthier offerings than other fast-food restaurants. Panera was the first to voluntarily provide calorie information at all of its restaurants. *Health* magazine judged it the healthiest fast casual restaurant in the U.S. in 2008. Zagat recognized it as #1 for best healthy option, best salad, and best facilities in 2009. Panera has the highest level of customer loyalty in its category, and was named the casual dining brand of the year in a 2012 Harris Equitrend poll.

Founder and CEO Ron Shaich describes what led up to launching the company's new initiative: Panera Cares, a café that operates on a "pay what you can afford" basis: "Panera has always had a commitment to community. We give $100 million a year in cash and product, but I got this feeling that it was disconnected from us. One day I'm watching NBC News, and it's the height of the recession. I hear about a pay-what-you-can café in Denver. They spent years trying to get this thing open. We open a café every 75 hours. We decided to do the full Panera experience, open a bakery-café identical to any other Panera, and list a suggested donation. We opened our first Panera Cares café in 2010, and just opened our fourth. They'll serve about one million people this year."[1] Estimates are that about 60 percent of customers pay the full amount and 15 to 20 percent pay more, so that Panera nets on average about 75 percent of the regular full price. Given the lower cost of food in these cafes, they are quite viable as ongoing businesses, and show the power of creative caring in developing viable business models that meet key societal needs.

Business Values vs. Human Values

Several years ago, an audience member asked a renowned spiritual teacher for his views on a sensational murder case in California that had gripped the nation's attention. This spiritual teacher travels the world teaching people how to lower their stress level by achieving inner harmony and peace of mind. His answer, "I feel responsible," stunned the audience. Asked to explain, he said that all human beings have a responsibility toward each other. "Acts of extreme violence result from extreme levels of stress," he continued. "I am responsible because if I had worked harder to reach more people, I might have been able to help this individual learn how to reduce his stress and gain control over his emotions. This tragedy could have been averted."

Ask anyone the question, "What do you take responsibility for?" You likely will get a carefully calibrated, narrow response: "I am responsible for my family, my job, my neighborhood, etc." But, as FoE leaders see it, our responsibilities extend well beyond our immediate worlds. Every person routinely touches many lives beyond his or her personal sphere. According to the spiritual leader in the story above, this imposes on us all, to one degree or another, a responsibility beyond the compass of our daily lives.

The same is true for business organizations. The larger the company, the greater its moral imperative to take full responsibility for all of its impact on the world. This view, of course, does not comport with the sentiments of many corporate leaders, possibly most economists, and almost certainly the majority of stock analysts. Economists have coined a term—*negative externalities*—to describe many of the consequences of a firm's actions on the world beyond its bottom line. These are deemed as external and thus beyond the scope of things the firm need concern itself with.

British economist John Kay has pointed out, "Since the time of Aristotle, and perhaps before... the critics of business have argued that business, and the people who engage in it, are *selfish in their motivation, narrow in their interests*, and *instrumental in their behavior*. The values of business are different from, and inferior to, those of other human activities."[2] (Italics added.)

In the past few decades, many business leaders came to accept this view, even revel in it. In so doing, they relieved themselves of guilt or misgivings over their rejection of any responsibility to society. As Kay points out, such claims became in the minds of many "not only morally admissible, but even morally required." It is an echo from the past of industrialist William Henry Vanderbilt's words, "The public be damned. I am working for my stockholders."[3]

But the world is changing. Recall our earlier discussion about how growing numbers of people at higher levels of personal development than ever before are changing the bedrock foundations of culture. This is changing expectations of companies across a broad sweep of society. The values of business cannot continue to be fundamentally divergent from the more humanistic values held by a more mature and increasingly conscious population. A wide chasm between business and human values is dangerous. It gives rise to a deep-seated tension between people's work and personal lives. It lowers productivity in the workplace and elevates ennui and stress. But it also invites heightened regulatory scrutiny and makes lawsuits by all stakeholders far more likely. Finally, a case can be made that a wide gap between business and human values can reduce the life expectancy of companies, along with the life expectancy of the humans that work there (it is a documented fact that heart attacks go up by 20% on Monday mornings).

The infamous Al Dunlap (nicknamed "Chainsaw Al" and "Rambo in Pinstripes" for his employee-decimating track record at Scott Paper, Sunbeam, and other companies) vehemently opposes a broader view of a company's responsibilities. Listen to his harsh words: "The most ridiculous word you hear in boardrooms these days is *stakeholders*.... The current theory is that a CEO has to take all these people into account in making decisions. Stakeholders! Whenever I hear that word, I ask 'How much did they pay for their stake?' Stakeholders don't pay for their stake. Shareholders do."[4]

Fortunately, this selfish, instrumental, and narrow view of business (which fortuitously can be converted into the acronym SIN) is crumbling. Bringing it down is the weight of accumulating evidence that this approach simply does not work well for anyone, shareholders included. Corporations may be virtual people in the eyes of the law, but the personas of growing numbers of these entities are materially evolving toward a higher degree of humanness. Reflect on this in the context of Abraham Maslow's words:

> "Every falling-away from species virtue, every crime against one's own nature, every evil act, every one without exception records itself in our unconscious, and makes us despise ourselves."[5]

The SIN approach to life or business is out of harmony with the verities of the Age of Transcendence. John Kay puts the SIN viewpoint in sharp relief in a business context:

> "How would we react on being told that the word *fair* was never mentioned in meetings of the Cabinet, in family life, in the deliberations of boards of examiners, in the decisions of the committee of a sports club; that all of these bodies came to their conclusions on the basis of naked assertions of self-interest by the participants? What would we think of a motorist who said that, while he had relations with other road users, his responsibility was to get to his destination as quickly as possible? What would be our response if the dean of the Chicago Medical School declared that the social responsibility of doctors was to maximize their incomes? Or imagine an extract from the Al Dunlap manual of parenthood: 'The current theory is that parents have responsibilities to their children. Parental responsibilities indeed! Whenever I hear that phrase, I ask, how much do children pay their parents? Children don't pay for their upkeep; parents do.'"[6]

Pirate or Great Humanitarian?

"At Cipla, it's not about making medicines; it's about making a difference."
—Cipla 2012 Annual Report

Cipla is a pharmaceutical company based in India. It was established in 1935 with a vision of making India self-reliant and self-sufficient in healthcare. In 1939, Mahatma Gandhi visited Cipla and inspired the founder Dr. K.A. Hamied to make essential medicines, those that would have a positive impact on the lives of ordinary people. Today, Cipla is among the world's largest generic pharmaceutical companies, with presence in more than 170 countries, and is led by Dr. Yusif Hamied, the son of the founder. The company produces around 2,000 products in 65 therapeutic categories and more than 40 dosage forms at 34 state-of-the-art manufacturing facilities.

Cipla is one of the few companies that produces medicines for rare diseases such as Idiopathic Pulmonary Fibrosis, Pulmonary Arterial Hypertension, and Multiple Sclerosis. It also established the Cipla Palliative Care Center in Pune, India, which provides care to terminally ill cancer patients free of cost.

In 2001, Cipla revolutionized HIV treatment. The medicine—a complex cocktail of multiple drugs—was priced by Western drug companies at between $10,000 and $15,000 per person annually. Millions of people in Africa and elsewhere simply could not afford this price and died. In stepped Cipla into this humanitarian crisis. It shook the world by developing and offering Triomune, a single tablet to be taken twice a day, priced at less than one dollar per day. This was literally a lifeline for millions of poor patients. Here is a telling statistic from the National Institutes of Health: India produces 92 percent of all AIDS drugs that are sold in the world and sells them for $1 billion. The other 8 percent generate revenues of $16 billion! In other words, each dose sold by non-Indian companies is priced 184 times higher than a dose produced in India.

Dr. Hamied said, "We are being humanitarian. But we are not doing charity. We are not making money, but we are not going to lose money either.... I'm not against patents, but against monopolies. We are dividing the people of the world into those who can afford life-saving drugs and those who cannot. This amounts to a systematic denial of people's right to life and health in the poorer parts of the world."

Ajit Dangi, the former head of Johnson & Johnson India, says, "In Africa, Cipla is a temple and Dr. Hamied is God." Hamied is revered by millions for his humane approach to medicine (including the establishment of several company-funded health centers) but has been branded a pirate by some global pharmaceutical companies that consider Cipla's products a direct rip-off of patented drugs. Whether you consider him a pirate or a caring leader, he is a revered figure for millions of people in the poorest parts of the world. Without him, they simply would not be alive today. Dr. Hamied believes that running a healthcare business is not about profit alone; it is equally about fulfilling the company's deeper purpose of healing human beings. In 2012, he was recognized as a "Conscious Capitalist of the Year" at the Forbes India Leadership Awards, awarded the CNN-IBN Indian of the Year Award, and given the Business Standard Lifetime Achievement Award.

FoEs and Society

FoEs view the well-being of each stakeholder as an end in itself rather than merely a way to maximize shareholder wealth. They operate with a broad view of their impact on the world, considering society and the environment to be key stakeholders. The following are some of the ways in which FoEs fulfill their keenly felt societal obligations.

Encourage Employee Involvement

Employees play a central role in helping FoEs support the communities in which they operate. For example, REI employees nominate organizations for the company's support. Grants are limited to conservation organizations that focus on environmental issues and recreational organizations that promote outdoor activities such as hiking, climbing, and biking. Solicitations for grants are not accepted. The Harley-Davidson Foundation, which started in 1993, has contributed more than $25 million to nonprofit organizations. Approximately 50 employees help review grants and guide company giving. The foundation targets the most under-served areas of communities. The bulk of its grants are in the areas of education and community revitalization.[7]

FoEs encourage and reward employees for volunteering their time and talents to support initiatives that benefit the local communities in which they operate. James Austin, a professor at the Harvard Business School, has written, "Community service is a form of job enrichment. Studies confirm that volunteer programs significantly increase employee morale, loyalty, and productivity, all of which contribute to enhanced business performance."[8]

Being an active and responsible member of the community is integral to the Honda philosophy. The company created the Honda Community Action Team (CAT) to help its associates participate in corporate community projects that impact the community and serve those in need.

At each of its five New England factory locations, New Balance has established enduring relationships with community organizations. Through its Community Connection Program, coordinators at each New Balance facility organize volunteer opportunities each month for employees. In its mission statement for the program, the company states the following:

> "Our corporate volunteer program encourages associates to make a hands-on difference in the lives of others for the betterment of our children and our communities. The program aims to demonstrate that New Balance is committed to the community, enable associates to fulfill their sense of civic duty, and help satisfy the many needs of the community."[9]

Employee interest in volunteer opportunities often exceeds the number of people needed. Drawings are held to pick participants. The company makes certain that participants are recognized for their contributions. Volunteers receive a Community Connection t-shirt prior to an event and a thank-you card afterward. The company also records each person's volunteer hours, hands out milestone awards when certain hours are completed, and holds annual volunteer appreciation events. In addition to the Community Connection Program, the company recently instituted a Personal Volunteer Time benefit. It provides full-time employees eight paid hours per year to volunteer for a nonprofit or not-for-profit organization. Part-time employees are allotted hours as well. By organizing, encouraging, and recognizing employee volunteerism, New Balance makes community service a corporate priority.

Patagonia has an Environmental Internship Program that gives employees up to eight weeks of paid leave to volunteer for an environmental organization of their choice. Individual stores of outdoor outfitter REI coordinate local service projects to which they draw other local businesses. Boot maker Timberland started its Path of Service program in the 1990s. It provides employees paid hours to encourage them to participate in community services. Through this program and its Service Sabbaticals and Earth Watch Sabbaticals, the company challenges employees to invest their skills and energy to create lasting change with nonprofit organizations. One of these projects, called the Serv-a-palooza, is an annual tradition. Timberland employees worldwide take a day off to work with neighborhoods to create "a better world." By 2012, employees had served more than 845,000 hours in more than 20 countries over a 20-year period.

Nurture Local Communities

FoEs strive to have a strong positive impact on their local communities. For example, communities generally welcome a Costco warehouse because it is recognized as a good corporate citizen that provides excellent job opportunities and tax revenues. But there can be a downside to a new Costco warehouse. It can cause traffic congestion, take away business from local stores, and may change the culture of the community. Working with the community, Costco tries to address all these concerns. Before moving into a neighborhood, Costco representatives sit down with the local stakeholders and ask them to voice their concerns about the proposed new warehouse. For example, Costco's plan to build a warehouse in Cuernavaca, Mexico in 2002 caused a protest from residents, community activists, and environmental groups. Construction of the warehouse would involve tearing down an old casino that housed murals by Mexican artists. The protesting groups were also concerned about the loss of trees in building the new warehouse. Costco took the concerns seriously. It spent previously unbudgeted money to preserve and restore the murals, relocate older trees, and donate 30,000 trees to the city.

FoEs demonstrate their commitment to the local community in highly tangible ways. For instance, Toyota has a 15-year marine terminal lease partnership with the Port of Portland in Oregon. It redeveloped the facility with better storm water runoff management and riverbank restoration that safeguards several wildlife habitats. A two-year $40 million redevelopment project in the port was 75 percent funded by Toyota.

Cultivate Global Community

FoEs strive to be exemplary global citizens, usually going well beyond local requirements. IKEA is a case in point. It uses uniformly high environmental and safety standards worldwide even when local regulations are less stringent. If stricter laws concerning chemicals and other substances are imposed in a country where IKEA does business, IKEA requires suppliers in *all* countries to conform to such laws. However, the company understands that different circumstances may make it more difficult for suppliers in certain countries to comply with its standards. For example, IKEA makes demands on waste disposal, but in countries that do not have an infrastructure for that, such as Romania, IKEA instead insists that suppliers store waste safely and not dump hazardous waste in the landfills with other non-hazardous waste.

IDEO is an investor in the Acumen Fund, a nonprofit fund whose purpose is to decrease global poverty. The fund attempts to bring basic services such as healthcare and water at affordable prices to poor communities in a way that can be sustained by the people who receive them. In addition to being an investor in the fund, IDEO also volunteered its design services in the creation of an irrigation pump to assist farmers in Africa. This device was introduced in Kenya and led to more than a tenfold increase in income for the farmers who use it.

Enhance Competitiveness

Milton Friedman's main argument against companies spending resources on social initiatives presumes that social and economic objectives are separate and distinct, so that spending on one comes at the expense of the other. Friedman also argues that corporations cannot achieve a greater impact than individuals making the same contributions can. However, Michael Porter and Mark Kramer, in an influential essay in *Harvard Business Review,* suggested that corporations could use their charitable efforts to actually improve their "competitive context" and thus align their economic and social goals. They define competitive context as "the quality of the business environment in the location or locations where they operate."[10] Corporations can also use their distinctive competencies—the things they do especially well—to provide societal services that in turn help them better compete in the marketplace.

Many FoEs have proven quite adept at aligning social and economic goals in this manner. For example, IDEO excels at incorporating ecological and societal concerns into its product designs. It is a leader in setting industry-wide guidelines and practices for such "sustainable industrial design." Because most of its products are made of wood, IKEA is deeply concerned with forestry. It has taken the lead in the home furnishings industry in ensuring that forests are responsibly managed. The company has developed a four-step process for suppliers to support its efforts. Suppliers must obtain timber from responsibly managed forests certified by the Forest Stewardship Council. IKEA employs its own forest managers to randomly check logging companies to ensure that the timber is coming from properly managed forests. The company tries to set an example for other corporations to follow. To this end, IKEA is active in several organizations that deal with environmental and social issues. This includes the Business Leaders' Initiative on Climate Change (BLICC), whose aim is to teach companies to measure, report, and reduce emissions of carbon dioxide. IKEA has an agreement with the International Federation of Building and Wood Workers (IFBWW) based on the IKEA code of conduct. It is also a member of several different networks that deal with transportation and the environment, through which it hopes to influence the development of environmentally friendly transportation solutions.

Focus on Sustainability

FoEs strive to operate in environmentally friendly ways. Their philosophy is encapsulated in a statement attributed to a U.S. athlete: "If you run in the forest, plant a tree."[11] Many FoEs invest resources to ensure they have a neutral or positive impact on the environment. They do so not because it may be a legal requirement (it often is not), but because it is the right thing to do. Just as IKEA does, they apply uniformly high standards across the world, regardless of local requirements that may be considerably more lax.

Surprisingly, this way of doing business often adds to the profitability of FoEs. Consider the experience of BMW. It views reducing the environmental impact of its manufacturing plants not just as a compliance issue, but also as an integral part of its corporate culture. BMW's Greer, South Carolina plant is recognized by state and federal environmental agencies as one of the most environmentally friendly plants in the industry. It has been hailed by many in the automobile industry as forward thinking in its utilization of "green power." In 2002, the Greer plant completed a pipeline that funnels methane from a local landfill to generate 25 percent of the electricity for the plant. This earned it the EPA's Green Power Leadership Award of 2003.

BMW does an outstanding job of extending environmental responsibility beyond factory walls. German law requires firms to be responsible for their products over their full lifetime. BMW has turned this law into a profit opportunity. It has learned how to disassemble cars in an economical and environmentally sound way that gives it a sizable advantage over other automakers subject to the same law.

Honda is also deeply committed to sustainable business practices. It has been a leader in balancing customer and environmental needs for more than two decades. Its compound vortex controlled combustion (CVCC) engine made Honda the first company to meet the emission standards of the Clean Air Act enacted by Congress. The engine not only met the Act's strict emission standards, it did so without degrading performance. Honda produced the cleanest gasoline powered vehicle in the world, available well ahead of California's strict regulations.

In another environmental achievement, Honda became the first automaker to use solvent-free waterborne paint in mass production. In 1996, the company manufactured a two-passenger solar car that broke the world solar challenge record. In 1997, Honda announced a zero-level-emission vehicle, driven by a virtually pollution-free, gasoline-powered internal combustion engine. In 1999, the company launched a fuel-efficient, low-emission hybrid engine with a gasoline engine and an electric motor.

Honda strives to produce environmentally friendly products in other areas as well. For example, the four-stroke outboard motors produced by Honda are about 90 percent cleaner, 50 percent more fuel-efficient, and 50 percent quieter than typical two-stroke outboard motors that release oil directly into the water. Honda also became the first company to meet the Environmental Protection Agency's year 2006 emission standards in the year 1998 and released a full line of high-performance outboard motors.

Honda has not only made its products environmentally friendlier, it has made the places where these products are made more environmentally friendly. Honda auto plants in the U.S. cut emissions by more than 65 percent in just five years. The Green Factory program helped every Honda facility reduce emissions and energy use, reuse more raw materials, and recycle manufacturing materials such as paper and plastic. Honda plants worldwide comply with the toughest international environmental management standards. The company has drastically reduced waste generated in manufacturing; for example, in 2000 it succeeded in completely eliminating landfill disposal of manufacturing waste in Japan.

The design firm IDEO is an active partner in The Natural Step, a nonprofit organization focused on environmentally safe design. The Natural Step was created in 1989 as a reaction against health concerns over increasing amounts of toxins in the environment. The organization helps corporations and governments design products and systems in a sustainable and environmentally safe way. IDEO's role as a partner in the organization is to help set guidelines and methods for environmentally safe industrial design. According to Tim Brown, CEO of IDEO, his company's reason for partnering with The Natural Step is to "lead to a new generation of products and services that demonstrate the economic, social, and environmental viability of sustainable design."[12]

Patagonia was the first company in California to commit to using only renewable energy through wind power. The company's Reno, Nevada Service Center was constructed with only recycled or reclaimed materials. It used rooftop mirrors that track the sun to provide light in the workspace in lieu of electrically powered lighting.[13] Patagonia refuses to use conventionally grown cotton because high quantities of chemicals are used in the growing process. In fact, ten percent of all agricultural chemicals in the United States are used in the production of cotton. Organically grown cotton yields the same as conventionally grown cotton but without toxic chemicals. Patagonia's entire Sportswear line is manufactured using organic cotton. Even though it costs more, Patagonia feels it has no choice to do otherwise because of its commitment to protect the environment and contribute to the well-being of communities in which its stakeholders live.[14]

Many FoEs have special environmental mission statements to guide their operations. For example, Starbucks lists seven principles in its environmental mission statement:

- Understanding environmental issues and sharing information with our partners.
- Developing innovative and flexible solutions to bring about change.
- Striving to buy, sell, and use environmentally friendly products.
- Recognizing that fiscal responsibility is essential to our environmental future.
- Instilling environmental responsibility as a corporate value.
- Measuring and monitoring our progress for each project.
- Encouraging all partners to share in our mission.

Timberland gives high priority to environmental concerns in three areas: energy, chemicals, and resources. It has partnered with Clean Air–Cool Planet, an organization that creates partnerships in the Northeast U.S. to implement solutions to climate change and build constituencies to generate and support effective climate policies and programs.

Timberland realizes that many of the chemicals it uses to produce its footwear are toxic. To address this, it has begun eliminating chemicals by minimizing solvents used to assemble the footwear. Timberland is a founding member of Organic Exchange, an organization focused on the expansion of an organic culture. In its own operations, it has developed new ways to use organic cotton in its products. Finally, Timberland uses recycled materials in the packaging department and in designing its stores. It prints its annual reports with soy ink on recycled paper.

Cooperate with Governments

The idea of corporations taking on a social agenda is not new. The first corporations were not-for-profit entities created in Europe prior to the seventeenth century. King Magnus Eriksson granted the earliest corporate charter on record to the Stora Kopparberg mining community in Falun, Sweden in 1347.[15] The East India Company was granted a Royal Charter by Queen Elizabeth I in 1600. Corporations were chartered by the State for public purposes such as building hospitals, bridges, roads, and universities. Generally, corporations undertook tasks deemed too risky or too expensive for individuals or governments to accomplish. The government closely oversaw them, and charters could be revoked if the corporations failed to fulfill their public purpose. Shareholders were beneficiaries, but were not regarded as the primary reason for the company's existence.

The modern form of corporations traces its origins to an 1844 act in Britain that allowed them to define their own purpose. This largely shifted control of corporations from the government to the courts.[16] But this did not wholly extinguish corporate involvement with social concerns. In the early decades of the Industrial Revolution, large companies, especially those located in remote areas, commonly operated company towns, providing employees with housing, schools, roads, public transportation, electricity, water, recreational facilities, and the like. Thus, companies became adept at providing public services, most of which later came within the purview of government.

As public infrastructures expanded, companies withdrew from these privately operated worker welfare activities to focus on their core business. In time, as companies and governments each grew more powerful, the relationship between them became more adversarial. We are now at the cusp of a new era that could be marked by greater cooperation between governments and corporations. As companies start to recognize the impact they can have on communities, and vice versa, they have come to better appreciate the role of governments as a proxy for society. FoEs, especially, view governments as important partners in creating a better world for everyone.

Honoring the spirit of laws is on a higher plane than merely following the letter of the law. Ponder for a moment how Toyota expresses this idea. The first clause of the company's Guiding Principles is "Honor the language and spirit of the law of every nation and undertake open and fair corporate activities to be a good corporate citizen around the world." Toyota has made legal and ethical compliance a top priority. It spells out its policies and expectations to local governments wherever it conducts business. It aligns its operation to suit a local government's regulations.

The pressure on companies to play larger roles in addressing social concerns will mount as we become less of a "having" society and more of a "being" society. Everywhere in the world, governments are maxed out. Funding the social agenda is becoming increasingly difficult. Ebbing materialism due to the overall greater psychological maturity in an aging society is slowing consumer spending in most developed countries, in turn slowing growth in government revenues. Add to this the rising costs of old-age entitlements, and the picture of governments' economic future becomes clearer: increasingly less money for other social needs. Lower tax revenues from a slower growing economy and rising entitlement payouts will leave national, regional, and local governments short on social welfare budgets. Governments must find new ways of promoting the general welfare. Increasingly, they must rely on business enterprises to fulfill their social agendas.

This is not just speculation; it's already beginning to happen. Across the U.S., for the first time since the very early 1800s, roads are being built and operated by private companies. A growing number of Department of Defense tasks are being outsourced to private firms. Private companies are now operating schools and prisons in dozens of locations around the country.

As the proportion of people focused on "giving back" grows through the maturation of boomers, social welfare needs will get more attention from individuals and corporations than ever before. Citizens will look less to government to solve social problems and more to the companies that they regularly deal with. Consumers and institutional investors will demand annual social balance sheets that detail what a company has done for the good of society. The 2005 disaster in the U.S. called Hurricane Katrina brought into clear focus the ability of private enterprises to outshine the government in meeting needs of the social agenda. Several companies played key roles in preparing for the disaster and coping with its aftermath, which included the flooding of 80 percent of the city of New Orleans:

- Walmart greatly enhanced its public reputation by leveraging its wide reach and sophisticated logistic capabilities to deliver relief supplies to hurricane victims. The company moved generators, dry ice, and fuel to strategic locations close to the disaster area ahead of time. It anticipated the course of the hurricane shifting toward New Orleans 12 hours before the National Weather Service did. Walmart used its stores to provide temporary housing for police officers and supplied National Guardsmen with ammunition.[17]

- Home Depot mobilized four days before Katrina hit. It moved electrical generators and a thousand extra workers into place on both sides of the hurricane's path. Stores were battened down ahead of time, allowing most to reopen a day after the storm. Based on past experience, the company stocked stores with extra supplies of products such as insecticides, water, and diapers.

- Valero, an oil refiner with operations near New Orleans, was able to get its refinery up and running eight days after the hurricane. This was much sooner than other companies managed. Valero's employee-first philosophy led to extraordinary results in the wake of Katrina. A maintenance supervisor used his own credit card to buy supplies. He then stayed up all night cooking gumbo for his crew as they coped with the fallout from the Category 4 hurricane. The company dispatched trucks from its San Antonio headquarters laden with food, water, chain saws, shovels, Nextel phones, and small generators to help its employees carry out their efforts to recover from the worst storm to land on U.S. soil in more than 70 years. Valero provided 60 mobile homes for employees whose own homes were uninhabitable. It gave free gasoline and diesel to employees as well as to law enforcement officials.[18]

Canon and the Path of Kyosei

The late Ryuzaburo Kaku, visionary President and later Chairman of Canon, introduced the concept of *kyosei* to the company in 1987. *Kyosei* means "spirit of cooperation," which reaches its strongest state at the highest level of corporate maturity. Just as humans evolve and mature over their lifespans, Kaku believed that companies also evolve toward maturity. *Kyosei* embodies five stages that unfold with a gradual shifting of corporate worldview from inner-directed to outer-directed.

Kaku described his philosophy of *kyosei* and how he applied it in an essay that appeared in *Harvard Business Review* in its July-August 1997 issue.[19] Figure 8.1 depicts the five stages of *kyosei*. They parallel the five levels of basic human needs in Abraham Maslow's famous hierarchy.

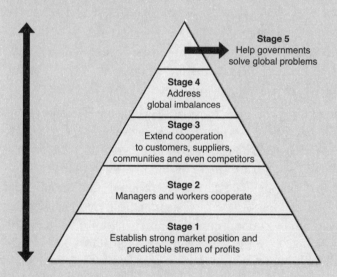

Stage 5
Help governments
solve global problems

Stage 4
Address
global imbalances

Stage 3
Extend cooperation
to customers, suppliers,
communities and even competitors

Stage 2
Managers and workers cooperate

Stage 1
Establish strong market position and
predictable stream of profits

Figure 8.1 The path of *kyosei*

Stage 1 is basic: Before a company can aspire to do good in the world, it must get its business in order. This is akin to the first level in Maslow's Hierarchy: *basic physiological needs*. In the business context, this first stage means putting together a sound strategy, developing superior products, investing in the right capabilities, and having the right organizational structure. Companies need profits to remain viable. However, Kaku cautioned that even in the self-centered Stage 1 of *kyosei*, they must never exploit their workers. He was highly critical of U.S. companies that "take the profit motive too far when they lay off workers to increase profits and at the same time pay large bonuses to their CEOs."

Stage 2 is roughly equivalent to the second level in Maslow's Hierarchy, *basic safety and security needs*. It is characterized by a spirit of cooperation and oneness between management and employees. Both management and employees view themselves as being in the same boat. For this reason, Kaku dissolved distinctions between salaried and hourly workers. On his watch, Canon became the first Japanese company to move to a five-day week. Ironically, it experienced unanticipated increases in productivity. In Stage 2, a company can afford to be more generous in its salaries and benefits policies. Not only were Canon's employees' basic safety and security needs better served at this stage, its complete avoidance of layoffs and strikes contributed to employees' psychological safety and security. However, despite the more humanistic bent of a company in Stage 2, it still remains primarily inwardly focused.

Stage 3 bears similarities to Maslow's third level of basic human needs: *love and belonging needs*. In Kaku's model of corporate maturation processes, Stage 3 is when companies start turning their focus outward toward their community. Kaku defined "community" broadly to include suppliers, customers, and members of the public. Canon closely monitors customer satisfaction and works with suppliers to help them improve quality and productivity. Instead of just donating money, the company contributes technological expertise to community causes. For example, it has developed and distributed products for the sight and speech impaired on a not-for-profit basis. It was at this stage that Canon began to extend the spirit of cooperation embodied in the *kyosei* model to competitors. It was a pioneer in forging partnerships with competitors. Early beneficiaries of the *kyosei* spirit of cooperation include Texas Instruments, Hewlett-Packard, and Eastman Kodak. Each company remained a robust competitor of Canon's in some ways, but enjoyed a profitable partnership with it in other ways—*a classic example of ironic management.*

Stage 4 is the rough equivalent of Maslow's fourth level of basic human needs: *self-esteem and esteem of others.* A company enters this stage when it achieves a broad global presence. It can devote time and resources to figuring out how it can contribute more broadly to the well being of people around the world and helping to solve larger problems. Canon expresses this disposition in concerning itself with three kinds of imbalances:

- Trade imbalances (by moving more manufacturing to countries struggling with trade deficits).

- Income imbalances (by building plants in developing countries, creating employment and export growth, increasing the tax base, reinvesting profits, and transferring technology).

- Environmental imbalances (by becoming heavily involved in recycling its own products and investing in environmentally friendly technologies such as solar panels and bioremediation). Canon has a large department dedicated to looking at ways of minimizing damage to the ecosystem. Its largest American plant reprocesses photocopiers for resale and recycles more than 90 percent of its solid waste. Through its actions in each of these areas, Canon achieves a win-win outcome: It addresses pressing global concerns while increasing its own profits.

Stage 5 is clearly the corporate equivalent of self-actualization in Maslow's model of human development. Kaku believed that few companies ever reach this stage. Maslow said the same about people; many get close to a state of self-actualization, but few reach the goal posts. Kaku said this stage of corporate maturation involves only large companies. He considers Canon to be one of the few companies to reach Stage 5. It has demonstrated this by taking on responsibility for solving problems that governments cannot solve, at least on their own. Kaku observed, "Too few politicians in Japan today are capable of solving global problems. The mantle of leadership has fallen onto the shoulders of corporations such as Canon."

For instance, it works on urging government to take actions to correct the kinds of global imbalances described previously. Companies and government should work together to create regulations that would reduce pollution, or abolish trade barriers that work against less advantaged nations. Such cooperation between business and government is vastly different from much of what we've seen in the past. More often, large companies focus on getting as much from government as possible with the least possible amount of reciprocal responsibility. Companies lobby for special subsidies, protective tariffs, tax breaks, and other benefits from government without any concern for participating in solving major social problems.

In concluding his inspiring message in the *HBR* essay quoted from in the accompanying sidebar, Ryuzaburo Kaku challenged the leaders of large global corporations with this thought:

> "Because multibillion-dollar corporations control vast resources around the globe, employ millions of people, and create and own incredible wealth, they hold the future of the planet in their hands. Although governments and individuals need to do their part, they do not possess the same degree of wealth and power.... If corporations run their businesses with the sole aim of gaining more market share or earning more profits, they may well lead the world into economic, environmental, and social ruin.... It is our obligation as business leaders to join together to build a foundation for world peace and prosperity."[20]

There is not a loftier thought on which we could close this chapter on society as the ultimate stakeholder. For reasons we stated earlier in this chapter, we see an urgent need for corporations to return to the role of serving as a vehicle to help facilitate public purpose. We challenge those who would disagree to come up with a better solution to the problems all nations face as their populations get older and slowed tax revenues and entitlements for the elderly progressively restrict governments' ability to process the public agenda. The idea of the welfare state may have lost much of its viability, but the needs that gave rise to welfare state ideas have not gone away. More and more it seems as though the well being of civilization depends on the cultures and actions of business enterprise.

Endnotes

1. http://money.cnn.com/2012/07/17/smallbusiness/panera-ron-shaich.fortune/index.htm.

2. John Kay, "The Role of Business in Society," February 3 1998 (www.johnkay.com).

3. William Henry Vanderbilt. Quoted in Letter from A.W. Cole (*The New York Times*; August 25, 1918).

4. Albert J. Dunlap and Bob Andelman, *Mean Business: How I Save Bad Companies and Make Good Companies Great*, Fireside, 1997.

5. Abraham Maslow, *Toward a Psychology of Being*, New York: John Wiley & Sons, 1968.

6. Kay, op. cit.

7. "Harley-Davidson Foundation." http://www.harley-davidson.com/CO/FOU/en/foundation.asp?locale=en_US&bmLocale=en_US. (April 2005).

8. James E. Austin, "The Invisible Side of Leadership," *Leader to Leader*, No. 8 Spring 1998.

9. *New Balance Community Connection Program Associate Handbook*.

10. Michael E. Porter and Mark R. Kramer, "The Competitive Advantage of Corporate Philanthropy," *Harvard Business Review*, Vol. 80 (December 2002), pp. 56–68.

11. Arturo Barrios, U.S. athlete. Quoted in *Running With the Legends* (Michael Sandrock), 1996.

12. http://www.naturalstep.org/about/partners.php.

13. Patagonia. Harvard Business School Case Study, pg. 15.

14. http://www.patagonia.com/enviro/organic_cotton.shtml, (April 14, 2004).

15. http://en.wikipedia.org/wiki/Corporation.

16. *New Internationalist*, "A Short History of Corporations," July 2002.

17. Jessica Lewis, "The Only Lifeline was the Walmart," *Fortune*, October 3, 2005, pp. 74–80.

18. Janet Guyon, "The Soul of a Moneymaking Machine," *Fortune*, October 3, 2005, pp. 113–120.

19. Ryuzaburo Kaku, "The Path of *Kyosei*," *Harvard Business Review*, July-August 1997.

20. Ibid, pg. 122.

9

Culture: The Secret Ingredient

This chapter is about FoEs' strongest competitive difference: their corporate cultures. The topic is one that has been written about extensively; what new can be said about it? Googling "corporate culture" brings up millions of entries. Amazon lists more than 1,200 titles devoted to corporate culture. Thousands of articles have mulled over the subject. Therefore, it is not our purpose here to cover ground well trod by others. Instead, our time is more profitably spent identifying and describing attributes of FoEs' corporate cultures that play a decisive role in their success.

The Greatest Place to Work?

As far as we know, there are no perfect human beings on this planet and no perfect companies either. But some come pretty darn close. One of those is SAS Institute, an analytics software company based in North Carolina. In November 2012, SAS (pronounced *sass*) was named the world's best multinational workplace by the Great Places to Work Institute. Think about how many companies there are in the world, and now think about what it takes to be recognized as the best place to work among all of them.

What makes SAS so special? It meets just about all of the criteria that we have for a highly conscious company, or a firm of endearment. First, some numbers: SAS has enjoyed 37 consecutive years of record revenues and earnings, and generated $2.8 billion in revenue in 2012. It employs about 13,000 people worldwide. Only two percent of its employees voluntarily leave in a given year (compared to 22 percent on average in its industry). And get this: Last year it had 65,040 applicants for 433 jobs—that's 150 applicants per job! Forty-four percent of its employees are women, who make up 32 percent of executive and senior management positions.

The company was cofounded in 1976 by Dr. Jim Goodnight, a faculty member at North Carolina State University. He has now come to be recognized as one of the great business leaders in the world. His leadership philosophy is really quite simple: It is all about the people. If you can focus on creating a great environment for employees to feel engaged, connected, respected, challenged, and rewarded, they will do extraordinary things for customers; that in turn will lead to sustained business success. Of course, that sounds easy, but it's really difficult to pull off.

SAS does everything it can to reduce distractions at the workplace, so that employees can focus unfettered on their work. It provides on-site amenities such as healthcare, a fitness center, subsidized childcare, and a long list of wellness programs. But this is not just about providing generous perks. The company understands that the feelings and emotions of its employees are extremely important, even critical. It has sought to create a benevolent organization in which every human being is individually valued. The company's philosophy is, "If you treat employees as if they make a difference to the company, they *will* make a difference."

Author Mark Crowley went to visit the SAS campus recently and concluded that its success was founded on four pillars:[1]

- Value people as much as possible.
- To give is to get.
- Trust above all things.
- Ensure that employees understand the significance of their work.

Value People as Much as Possible

When the great recession of 2008 started, sales of the company's products slowed dramatically. The analytic software industry was unusually affected, and many companies initiated mass layoffs. At SAS, Jim Goodnight announced over a global webcast to employees in January 2009 that none of the 13,000 employees would lose their jobs. He asked them to be careful with their spending and to look for ways to help the firm get through the tough times. As he explained, "By making it very clear that no one was going to be laid off, suddenly we cut out huge amounts of chatter, concern, and worry—and people got back to work." Astonishingly, SAS generated record profits that year even though it was fully prepared to absorb a loss if it had to for the first time in 33 years.

To Give Is to Get

SAS started the tradition of providing great employee perks before Google made it famous. All employees as well as their families enjoy free access to a state-of-the-art gym (with tennis and basketball courts, weight room, and a heated pool). There is a free on-site health-care facility that includes physicians, nutritionists, physical therapists, and psychologists. On-site childcare is deeply discounted, and work life counseling to help employees manage everyday stressors is free. All work areas are stocked with snacks. The company invests in all of these perks as much for their symbolic value as for their tangible worth. They think of them as a signal of how much they value their people. All of this has led to extraordinary levels of engagement and miniscule levels of turnover, generating huge gains in creativity and large savings in training and recruiting. As one long-time employee puts it, "People want a life with money, not money without a life."

Trust above All Things

Goodnight believes that the greatest factor in employee happiness at SAS is its culture of trust. The key elements of trust are open communication, respect between employees, fair access to career paths, and "being treated as a human being." SAS invests a great deal in constantly tracking the sentiments of its employees, as well as assessing how well its leadership team is fulfilling its responsibilities. The company completely trusts its employees to do their work without monitoring their hours or whereabouts.

Critically, the company has made it clear that for any employee to be promoted to management, he or she must demonstrate an inclination to support and help others. Leaders are judged on how well they facilitate the success of others, rather than their own. Those who advocate consistently for others are rewarded and promoted.

Ensure That Employees Understand the Significance of Their Work

Knowing that your work has inherent value and will positively impact the lives of others is extremely important to all employees. SAS goes to great lengths to ensure that its employees realize this and feel connected to the impact of their work. Programmers "own" their work, and even landscapers are encouraged to take ownership of the acreage they tend to. This gives them a higher purpose than just doing a job.

The leadership model at SAS is one that is based on the idea of abundance rather than scarcity. Employees are well rewarded and have a deep sense of satisfaction with their work. Customers are delighted with exceptional products and consistently outstanding service. And the business and its owners thrive as well. Consider the startling fact that Prof. Goodnight has become one of the wealthiest people in America, with a net worth of more than $7 billion! Richly deserved, and we have no doubt he will put that fortune to good use.

The Primacy of Culture

Earlier in the book we raised the question, "Which stakeholder matters the most?" The prevalent view in the past was that investors are the most important, as the stakeholder whose interests come first. In the last chapter, we made the case that society be viewed as the "ultimate" stakeholder. Others would put either the employees (The Container Store) or customers (Whole Foods Market) first.

However, to transcend the debate over *who* matters most, we should first ponder *what* matters most for FoEs. That "what" is corporate culture. This is what most sets FoEs apart from the crowd and enables them to create greater value for *all* their stakeholder groups. The executive leadership of the internationally prominent industrial design firm IDEO believes that it is more important to preserve the company's culture than it is to pursue money. Southwest Airlines considers its culture so crucial to its performance that it established a standing "Culture Committee" consisting of 96 employees nominated by their peers from all echelons of the company. The Culture Committee is responsible for "doing whatever it takes to create, enhance, and enrich the special Southwest spirit and culture that has made it such a wonderful company/family."[2] Southwest CEO James Parker (who succeeded Herb Kelleher) said, "We focus on corporate culture more than anything else we do. We are a big company now. We really focus on developing local leaders. We try to have people at every station that understand our corporate culture, who value it, and who can share it with other employees."[3] Who could plausibly argue with Parker? After all, Southwest Airlines is the most successful U.S. airline in the history of flying.

The passion, energy, dedication, generous spirit, and expansive creativity found in every FoE are all products of their culture. Like air, the culture is invisible but pervasive. It exerts a strong, transformational influence on all who experience it, especially employees. Employees pumped up about their company infect customers with their enthusiasm. Customers reciprocate with their own enthusiasm to round out an exquisitely symbiotic relationship whose significance is lost to those who gauge companies only through numbers.

An organization's culture is its *psychosocial infrastructure*. It embodies the shared set of values, assumptions, and perspectives that draws members of the organization together into a tight-knit, smoothly operating team dedicated to a common purpose. A company's culture shapes its worldview. This in turn predisposes its behavior. A strong, cohesive, and highly motivating culture is the hallmark of FoEs. We have concluded that investment analysts give far too little attention to the role of corporate culture in predicting future performance. The fact that FoE leaders, employees, investors, and suppliers all "hear the same music" adds enormously to a company's prospects for future success.

Research shows a link between corporate culture and employees' work styles. In one study, employees of the same company were found to be more likely to have similar leadership competencies than those with the same job at other companies. In other words, the leadership style of a female American engineer working for Toyota in the U.S. is more similar to that of a male Japanese accountant at Toyota in Japan than to another female American engineer at Ford.[4]

There are three primary elements to organizational culture:

- **Organizational vision**—This is about creating and implementing a winning game plan. It is like a road map, intended to answer the question, "Where we are going and how do we intend to get there?" Although the range of competitive strategies followed by FoEs is as varied as those of companies in general, a common element found in every FoE is dedication to optimizing the creation of value for all stakeholders. Whether it is Patagonia and The Container Store with their distinctive high-margin products or Costco and Southwest with their low prices and low margins, a superior value creation model is a constant.

- **Organizational values**—This is the aligning force that keeps an organization centered and balanced. Managing an organization's values is like steering a car, essential to staying on the path and reaching the desired goal. Values are the answer to the questions "Who are we, and what makes us tick?"

- **Organizational energy**—Like the engine of a car, this is the force that propels the organization forward at a steady speed.[5] All FoEs are high-energy organizations. They reflect the passion, joy, and commitment of their employees and other stakeholders.

We will examine vision and values in more detail later in the chapter. But let's first look at the issue of organizational energy—where it comes from, how to harness it in a productive way, and how to sustain it.

Unleashing Organizational Energy

Organizational energy is created and released when an organization's people are emotionally and intellectually excited by the firm's vision and values. One of the most important tasks of a leader is to mobilize this energy and focus it on the achievement of meaningful goals. Organizational energy is a force like a sailor's good wind, invisible but holding the power to move the sailing vessel forward. It is measured by the dynamism and urgency with which a company operates.

The two main dimensions of organizational energy are its *intensity* and its *quality*. The intensity of organizational energy is reflected in the amount of activity, interactions, alertness, and emotional arousal. Organizations that have low energy intensity are characterized by apathy, inertia, rigidity, and cynicism. The quality of organizational energy can be positive (reflecting emotions such as love, enthusiasm, joy, and satisfaction) or negative (associated with feelings such as fear, frustration, and sorrow).[6]

The most desirable energy state is the "passion zone," which is characterized by high levels of positive energy. Employees of companies working out of this zone are full of enthusiasm and excitement, and take palpable pride and joy in their work. These companies are alert to problems as well as opportunities, and mobilize quickly to address both. Among FoEs, this positive life force spills over into society, as their employees participate in numerous community-improvement initiatives. In turn, serving others in the community recharges the emotional batteries of employees, reinvigorating them for their workplace challenges.

Setting Organizational Vision: Seeing the Larger Picture

FoEs share four primary elements in their corporate visions:

- A broader purpose than wealth generation
- Dedication to servant leadership

- Commitment to exemplary citizenship
- Recognition that they are part of an economic ecosystem with many interdependent participants

A Broader Purpose

The ever thoughtful and inspiring Charles Handy, in a brilliant *Harvard Business Review* essay, asked a rather basic but crucial question: "What's a Business For?"[7] The nature of companies and their assets has changed dramatically in recent years. Companies remain at one level an assemblage of material assets that can be bought and sold like any other property. However, the greatest component of value of most companies today lies in their people and their intellectual property, not in hard assets—in their intangible assets, in other words.

The International Accounting Standards Board defines intangible assets as "identifiable non-monetary assets without physical substance that an entity holds for its own use or for rental to others."[8] Officially, examples of intangible assets include computer software, licenses, patents and copyrights. However, stepping outside the world of accounting to draw on a broader meaning of *asset,* we understand it as referring to a "useful or valuable quality, person, or thing; an advantage or resource."[9]

Ask FoE executives to list their company's most valuable assets and they will likely put "our people" and "our culture" at the top of the list. They see their employees as sources of competitive advantage that translate into real economic value. The problem here is that the accounting profession has yet to come up with a way of assigning economic value to employees and corporate cultures. And yet, when assessing prospects for future earnings, how can the talent of employees and their level of passionate dedication to a company's vision, mission, and financial objectives be ignored?

We believe that employee discretionary effort and corporate culture can and should be quantifiably assessed to give investors and others better insight into a company's future prospects. This can be done with as much validity as attends the assessment of the economic value of computer software, licenses, patents, and copyrights.

Ample evidence exists to assert that corporate cultures stressing humanistic values produce higher levels of employee productivity, stronger customer loyalty, and higher margins. Providing shareholders a good return on their investment remains an important objective, but the idea is spreading that investment returns can be greater when wealth creation for shareholders is not the sole or even main purpose for which a company exists. The well-worn metaphor "We need to eat to live, but we do not live to eat" is apt here. Satisfying shareholders is the means to the "real" end, which is to add qualitatively to peoples' lives and the world at large. Here is how Konosuke Matsushita, founder of the giant Japanese electronic products bearing his name, saw the purpose or mission of his company: "The mission of a manufacturer should be to overcome poverty, to relieve society as a whole from misery, and bring it wealth."[10] David Packard, cofounder of Hewlett-Packard, put a similar thought this way:

> "I think many people assume, wrongly, that a company exists simply to make money. While this is an important result of a company's existence, we have to go deeper and find the real reasons for our being. As we investigate this, we inevitably come to the conclusion that a group of people get together and exist as an institution that we call a company so that they are able to accomplish something collectively that they could not accomplish separately—they make a contribution to society, a phrase which sounds trite but is fundamental."[11]

As befits one of the world's largest and most important companies, Toyota has put forward an ambitious and expansive "Global Vision 2010." Described as "A Passion to Create a Better Society," Toyota's vision is to help create a more prosperous society by following these precepts:

> Be a driving force in global regeneration by implementing the most advanced environmental technologies; create automobiles and a motorized society in which people can live safely, securely and comfortably; promote the appeal of cars throughout the world and realize a large increase in the number of Toyota fans; and be a truly global company that is trusted and respected by all peoples around the world.[12]

Servant Leadership

Individuals with uncompromising integrity, a strong sense of self, and a long track record within the company lead FoEs. They are exemplars of what has come to be known as "servant leadership." They are humble, self-effacing, and modest in their lifestyles. Here is how C. William Pollard, Chairman of ServiceMaster, describes such leaders:

> "The real leader is not the person with the most distinguished title, the highest pay, or the longest tenure. The real leader is the role model, the risk-taker. The real leader is not the person with the largest car or the biggest home, but the servant; not the person who promotes himself or herself, but the promoter of others; not the administrator, but the initiator; not the taker, but the giver; not the talker, but the listener. Servant leaders believe in the people they lead and are always ready to be surprised by their potential. Servant leaders make themselves available. Servant leaders are committed—they are not simply holders of position. They love and care for the people they lead. Leadership is both an art and a science. Everyone is a leader and everyone can also be a servant."[13]

Peter Drucker famously argued in an essay he wrote in 1984 that CEO compensation should add up to no more than 20 times rank and file wages. He said this at a time when CEOs began reaping massive earnings while firing workers by the thousands. He said, "This is morally and socially unforgivable and we will pay a heavy price for it." Executive compensation reaching well into the millions is incompatible with the notion of servant leadership.

CEO compensation in FoEs is modest in comparison with the executive compensation of most of their peers. Many of the companies have ratios of highest pay to average pay that they will not exceed (the ratio is 19-to-1 at Whole Foods Market). Some FoE CEOs have even refused additional compensation when offered to them by their boards. In 2006, Whole Foods Market CEO John Mackey took his commitment to the company's purpose to the ultimate limit, deciding to forego his already modest salary, bonus, and stock options for the rest of his career. Here is the full text of the letter he wrote in November of that year:

To All Team Members,

The tremendous success of Whole Foods has provided me with far more money than I ever dreamed I would have, and far more than is necessary for either my financial security or my personal happiness. I continue to work for Whole Foods not because of the money I can make, but because of the pleasure I get from leading such a great company, and the ongoing passion I have to help make the world a better place, which Whole Foods is continuing to do.

I am now 53 years old and I have reached a place in my life where I no longer want to work for money, but simply for the joy of the work itself and to better answer the call to service that I feel so clearly in my own heart.

Beginning January 1, 2007, my salary will be reduced to $1 per year and I will no longer take any other cash compensation at all. I will continue to receive the same benefits that all other team members receive, including the food discount card and health insurance. The intention of the Board of Directors is for Whole Foods to donate all of the future stock options I would be eligible to receive to our two company foundations: the Whole Planet Foundation and the Animal Compassion Foundation.

One other important item to communicate to you is, in light of my decision to forego any future additional cash compensation, our Board of Directors has decided that Whole Foods Market will contribute $100,000 annually to a new Global Team Member Emergency Fund. This money will be distributed to team members throughout the Company based on need when disasters occur (such as Hurricane Katrina last year).

With much love,

John Mackey

We believe that there is quantifiable value to shareholders in companies whose CEOs voluntarily choose levels of remuneration that meet the Drucker Remuneration Test. Employees in companies headed by such CEOs are more strongly motivated to work in pursuit of company objectives. Employees view these CEOs as approachable, hard-working individuals, willing to get their hands dirty in working with the entire staff, not just with other managers or executives. These CEOs are not driven by the actions of their competitors or personal ego-driven agendas but by service to all of their stakeholders, and they are guided by their moral compass instead of by their egos.

Emotionally Intelligent Leadership

Emotional intelligence (EI) is one of the key attributes that sets apart great business leaders, including the CEOs of firms of endearment, from the pack. One of the times when this is most evident is when companies need to go through a strategic transformation. Any change is difficult, and resistance to change is the most common emotional reaction. There is growing interest in understanding how the EI of corporate leaders facilitates strategic transformation.[14]

Many studies have looked at the relationship between EI and transformational leadership, and found a strong connection between the two. This was clearly found to be true in an investigation of a UK-based retailing organization.[15] Another study demonstrated clear differences between leaders with transformational versus transactional leadership styles; the former exhibited a much higher level of EI.[16]

Leaders with a high level of EI display and help spread positive emotions such as enthusiasm and cheerfulness. Both negative and positive emotions are highly contagious among a leader's followers because followers tend to develop similar emotions through empathy. A leader's positive emotions lead directly to elevating employees' emotional state and inspiring more enthusiastic performance.[17] Effective leaders use techniques such as stories, inspirational speeches, and rituals to motivate employees to reflect company values and pursue common goals.[18] We see this very clearly in FoEs; for example, Herb Kelleher's infectious personality and well-known antics have become deeply engrained in the Southwest Airlines culture. The fun-loving personalities of company co-leaders Barry and Elliot Tatelman are clearly reflected in the culture of Jordan's Furniture; some employees even strive to look like one of the brothers!

Goleman and his coauthors have found that EI becomes more important in a leader as he or she progresses up an organization, and other research has generally confirmed this. For example, one study found the EI was considered to be "extremely important" among members of companies' Board of Directors.[19]

Daniel Goleman defines *primal leadership* as the "emotional dimension of leadership." Here is how he puts it:

> "A leader's primal task is an emotional one—to articulate a message that resonates with their followers' emotional reality, with their sense of purpose—and so to move people in a positive direction. Leadership, after all, is the art of getting work done through other people.... In a climate of uncertainty, primal leadership becomes more important than ever, because people need a leader who lends an air of certainty, or at least conviction, a sense of "this is where we're heading these days," at a time when fears and anxieties can overtake them. All of this is particularly important because of the relationship—which is neurologically based—between emotions and attention and cognition."[20]

Goleman emphasizes the importance of resonance, which he defines as

> "...a reservoir of positivity that unleashes the best in people. (To build it) first, you have to reach within yourself to find out your own truth, because you can't be resonant if you're clueless, if you're pretending, or if you're just trying to manipulate people. You have to speak from your heart, and you have to do it in a way that speaks to other people's hearts. So it takes authenticity."[21]

Exemplary Citizenship

FoEs do not reflexively regard governments as antagonists and all regulation as bad. They recognize that governments at all levels have legitimate and important objectives that must be met for society to function smoothly and to promote wider flourishing. FoE management genuinely appreciates the fact that they depend heavily on taxpayer-funded infrastructure. They recognize the need for well-thought-out regulations that promote fair competition, protection from unscrupulous practices, and further the public welfare.

FoEs project a sense of purpose that conveys to their stakeholders that they want to make the world a better place. FoE leaders are as serious about achieving economic success as the most avaricious executives are. However, they refuse to pursue their economic goals at the expense of their resolve to make the world a better place. Toyota's guiding principles can serve as an example for any global corporation:

- Honor the language and spirit of the law of every nation and undertake open and fair corporate activities to be a good corporate citizen of the world.

- Respect the culture and customs of every nation and contribute to economic and social development through corporate activities in the communities.

- Dedicate ourselves to providing clean and safe products and to enhancing the quality of life everywhere through all our activities.

- Create and develop advanced technologies and provide outstanding products and services that fulfill the needs of customers worldwide.

- Foster a corporate culture that enhances individual creativity and teamwork value, while honoring mutual trust and respect between labor and management.

- Pursue growth in harmony with the global community through innovative management.

- Work with business partners in research and creation to achieve stable, long-term growth and mutual benefits, while keeping ourselves open to new partnerships.[22]

The Organization as a Living Organism

Organizations, whether structured as partnerships, corporations, or governmental entities, are living organisms. Strange idea you say? Hear what Kevin Kelly, founding editor of *Wired* says in *Out of Control*, a book that everyone who wants his or her company to be an FoE should read:

> We (and by this I mean scientists first) are beginning to see that those organizations once called metaphorically alive, are truly alive, but animated by a life of larger scope and wider definition. I call this greater life "hyperlife."[23]

Viewing business organizations as inanimate, impersonal mechanisms obscures their true organic natures. As with all biological organisms, companies grow and develop from the inside out, and evolve over time.[24] They go through developmental stages that are remarkably like those that people go through. Upstart companies are like teens in many regards: challenging tradition, seeking and shaping an identity, and supremely confident. Companies, like people, tend to begin life with a primary focus on self, evolving over time to serve purposes that transcend mere survival and self-interest. This is how nature's organisms secure their species' future. This is how FoEs secure their future.

Biological organisms can only be understood in the context of their relationships in their ecosystems. It is the same with business organizations. Their true nature is revealed only in the dynamic relationships they have with members of all stakeholder groups. FoEs recognize that they are part of a complex web of mutually reinforcing relationships between various stakeholders. For example, Costco acknowledges that it is defined by its stakeholder relationships when it proclaims its mission is "to continually provide our members with quality goods and services at the lowest prices. In order to achieve our mission, we will conduct our business with the following code of ethics: Obey the law; Take care of our customers; Take care of our employees; Respect our suppliers; Reward our shareholders."[25]

Nurturing Organizational Values by Building Endearing Cultures

FoEs are not reticent when it comes to explicitly communicating their values. Their values are integral to who they are and how they operate, and these companies take every opportunity to reinforce their values with their employees and other stakeholders. These are not just words; every one of these companies visibly lives by these commitments and takes them very seriously. In the vernacular, they "walk the talk." As Herb Kelleher of Southwest says, "Southwest is not a typical modern American corporation. There's a lot of altruism, an 'everybody-pitches-in' attitude, a sense that life should be enjoyed. There's a lot of tolerance, but the one area where there's no compromise is values. An employee who compromises on those is out."[26] When asked about building manufacturing facilities in North America, Toyota President Fuji Cho replied, "To export quality, first export company values."[27]

While the specific values that FoEs identify with vary, there are important common threads: treating all people with respect and dignity, eliminating waste while spending on things that matter, uncompromising integrity, having fun, and continuous improvement. Jordan's Furniture lists its values as teamwork, trust, respect, appreciation, fun, entertainment, customer delight, and philanthropy. Trader Joe's seven values are as follows:

- Integrity—act like your customer is looking over your shoulder.
- Product-driven company—focus on great products.
- Produce "wow" customer experiences.
- Hate bureaucracy—have few layers, place the customer at the top of the pyramid.
- Kaizen—an attitude of teamwork for continuous improvement.
- No elaborate budgeting.
- Treat the store as a brand, and fulfill the covenant between company and customer.

Costco is all about eliminating frills and keeping costs down, so it can pass the savings on to members and pay its employees well. Former CEO Jim Sinegal said, "Costco is able to offer lower prices and better values by eliminating virtually all the frills and costs historically associated with conventional wholesalers and retailers, including salespeople, fancy buildings, delivery, billing, and accounts receivable. We run a tight operation with extremely low overhead, which enables us to pass on dramatic savings to our members."[28]

FoE Cultural Characteristics

One term sums up the rich and varied cultures of FoEs: "people centered." These companies believe in dealing with all people, whether employees, customers, or any other stakeholders, as individuals, not as numbers or as objects for exploitation. Through the lens of their worldviews, they see and address the needs of the "whole person." This is reflected in the following tenets of FoE corporate cultures:

- Culture of Learning
- Culture of Trust
- Culture of Interconnectedness and Interdependence
- Culture of Integrity and Transparency
- Culture of Loyalty
- Culture of Respect
- Culture of Belonging and Oneness
- Culture of Caring
- Culture of Fun

Culture of Learning

FoEs are deeply dedicated to being "learning organizations." They make heavy investments in training new as well as experienced employees. The Container Store's commitment to training is truly extraordinary. Full-time employees get 241 hours of training in the first year and 160 hours every year thereafter. Contrast this with retailing in general: new employees get an average of seven hours of training and typically no continuing training.

Harley-Davidson created the Harley-Davidson Learning Center, dedicated to life-long learning. The Center serves employees with continuous training and learning opportunities within their jobs and cross-functionally throughout the organization. The company has a Vice President of Continuous Improvement.[29] Toyota's philosophy of *kaizen* (continuous improvement) keeps it at the cutting edge of productivity and performance.

Culture of Trust

Francis Fukuyama argues that a nation's prosperity and ability to compete depends heavily on one pervasive cultural characteristic: the level of trust or cooperative behavior based upon shared norms that prevail within it.[30] The same is true of companies. High-performance organizations are high-trust organizations. Trust is the lubricant that allows companies, employees, customers, and other stakeholders to work together with minimal friction and maximum harmony. Trust between rank-and-file employees and senior management enables companies to make short-term sacrifices for long-term prosperity. A high degree of trust goes hand-in-hand with open, inclusive cultures that waste little energy on monitoring and policing people's behavior.

At Toyota, openness is a prized virtue. Unfavorable information is conveyed to executive management when it is identified, rather than being concealed. This allows the company to act upon bad news constructively in a timely manner. BMW encourages its people to question the necessity of the jobs they are doing for the company. In most companies, employees would not do so for fear of losing their jobs. However, in BMW's culture of trust, employees know that they will not lose their jobs, but will be trained to fill another role in the company.

The value of trust extends beyond employees to include customers and suppliers as well. Jordan's Furniture does an outstanding job of developing customer trust by projecting an image of the company as "honest, reliable, and amusing." Because Jordan's uses a "no hassle," consultative sales approach, customers are more willing to visit its stores and trust the company is sincere about providing them an enjoyable in-store experience, regardless of whether they buy any furniture. Jordan's support for a large number of local and national charities and the fact that it donates proceeds from many of its entertainment attractions to these charities reinforces customer trust.

Culture of Interconnectedness and Interdependence

Interconnected, interdependent economic systems are considerably more powerful than those that consist of separate and independent parts. The parts of the former interconnect and mesh together to form a larger whole that transcends anything that its participants can achieve individually. FoEs are characterized by a strong degree of such synergistic interdependence between stakeholders. Instead of acting autonomously, or making demands on one another, the stakeholders of these companies are bound together in a cycle of interdependency.

The Japanese culture is built around the concept of interdependency. "Everything in Japanese culture depends upon everything else, and performance is the product of the interactions of the subsystems."[31] *Amae* is a term used to stand for this concept of dependency, which at first blush seems unattractive to the typical Western mind. "*Amae* refers, initially to the feelings that all normal infants at the breast harbor toward the mother—dependence, the desire to be passively loved, the unwillingness to be separated from the warm mother-child circle and cast into the world of objective 'reality.'"[32] The Western focus on self, on the ego, spurns such tight interdependence. Yet, if not in a true Japanese form, American and European FoEs do reflect something of the *amae* commonly seen in Japanese companies.

The Toyota Production System is rooted in the philosophy of *amae*. It has been a major driver behind Toyota's pursuit of excellence in the automobile industry. But we can see the marks of *amae*, for example, in Patagonia's worldview. It takes a similarly holistic approach in all aspects of its business. It incorporates its philosophy of "do no harm" into its manufacturing processes, supplier relationships, employee programs, and community relationships. Honda reflects a holistic, interdependent approach to managing its entire supply chain and building long-term, value-driven relationships with key suppliers.

Culture of Integrity and Transparency

Every company that we have classified as a firm of endearment places strong emphasis on maintaining the highest standards of integrity. In most cases, this is reflected directly in their mission statements or other formal documents.

Transparency goes hand-in-hand with integrity. Don Tapscott and David Ticoll write in *The Naked Corporation*, "If you have to be naked, you had better be buff." In today's information-rich world, it is virtually impossible for companies to keep important information hidden from employees, customers, suppliers, or anyone else. As Tapscott and Ticoll write, "We are entering an extraordinary age of transparency, where businesses must for the first time make themselves clearly visible to shareholders, customers, employees, partners, and society. Financial data, employee grievances, internal memos, environmental disasters, product weaknesses, international protests, scandals and policies, good news and bad; all can be seen by anyone who knows where to look."[33]

FoE leaders know that transparency works to a company's advantage if it consistently undertakes the "right" actions. Tapscott and Ticoll argue at length in *The Naked Corporation* that transparency enhances value. Transparency ensures that companies that engage in unsavory actions are quickly discovered and punished, while those that consistently try to do the right things for the right reasons are rewarded.

As discussed earlier, FoEs generally share more information with their employees than other companies. FoE management knows that liberally sharing financial and production information with employees develops a stronger bridge of trust between employee and management. Moreover, it helps to spur productivity by giving employees benchmarks to measure their efforts against. This has been key to New Balance keeping the productivity of its U.S. shoe-making employees at some of the highest levels in the world.

At The Container Store, financial statements have routinely been available to all employees, even though the company was privately owned until recently. At Southwest Airlines, Herb Kelleher and Colleen Barrett were known for communicating honestly and realistically under all circumstances. Former UPS CEO Michael Eskew said, "We place great value in the transparency of our business and the ways in which we hold ourselves accountable."[34]

Culture of Loyalty

Fred Reichheld has observed that the "major companies replace half their customers in five years, half their employees in four and a half, and their investors in less than one."[35] Such low levels of loyalty have many value-deflating repercussions. For one, it creates a "revolving door" cycle whereby profitable customers and capable employees exit and are replaced with unprofitable customers and novice employees, rapidly degrading the human capital of a company. It perpetuates short-term thinking and is enormously wasteful of resources.

Many companies expect their employees, suppliers, and customers to be loyal to them. However, most fail to reciprocate in kind. For example, after 9/11, American Airlines and Northwest Airlines used clauses in their labor contracts regarding national emergencies and extraordinary circumstances to make large layoffs without making severance payments. U.S. Airways took this practice to an extreme by invoking *force majeure* clauses (also known as "acts of God") in their union contracts. As a result they had the highest layoff count at 24 percent. Southwest, meanwhile, refused to lay off a single employee. Herb Kelleher's belief was that even though the company might lose money in the short term, this approach would protect Southwest's long-term health by maintaining job security and strengthening morale. In the grocery world, Wegmans believes that most grocery retailers are in such a "price cut" mode that they miss the opportunity of building relationships with their customers. Wegmans' customers are fanatically loyal. Many know their local store employees by name.

Culture of Respect

Toyota holds its policy to "respect all people" close to the heart. The purpose of its existence is to grow as a company together with its customers, shareholders, and employees, while seeking harmony with people, society, the global environment, and the world economy.[36]

Patagonia shows respect to its employees in part by aligning their interests with the corporate philosophy. By hiring employees who fit the culture and allowing them time to pursue outdoor and environmental passions, Patagonia is fostering an employee base that comes to work every day invigorated about their (and the company's) passions while continuing to drive the success of the company. Whole Foods Market regularly includes the opinions of its employees at every level in planning its future strategy.

Culture of Belonging and Oneness

FoEs excel at creating an atmosphere of belonging in which employees, customers, and other stakeholders feel a sense of ownership and belonging with the company. Employees of FoEs are not just team members; they are family. At Starbucks, the importance of treating people like family is core to what the company is all about. When Howard Schultz became CEO, he promised to leave no one behind. He believes that you "treat people like family and they will be loyal and give their all." Toyota uses company uniforms, songs, morning exercise, after-work social gatherings, and ceremonies to sustain and build its culture. This develops an individual sense of belonging not only to one's functional team but also to Toyota as a whole, creating oneness in the workforce. At UPS, 30,000 active management employees as well as full-time non-management employees hold much of the company's stock. This increases the likelihood that employees will go the extra mile and provide greater service to their customers.[37] For IKEA founder Ingvar Kamprad, the concept of "the firm as a family" is his greatest pride. He created a fellowship where his employees became members of one family (the Ikéans) and shared the values of "togetherness, enthusiasm, constant desire for renewal, humbleness, willpower, cost consciousness, simplicity, leadership and diversity."[38]

Culture of Caring

In addition to treating stakeholders as members of their extended family, FoEs also adopt a caring and nurturing attitude toward them. Lance Secretan, who built Manpower Limited into an international giant, says, "Everything that inspires us comes from love—without exception."[39] IKEA genuinely cares for its employees and wants them to be able to work without shortchanging what is important in their personal lives, such as families. This can be seen in its benefits package and by the amount of attention given to employee "quality of life" issues. Caring for its employees fosters loyalty, empowerment, confidence, and drive, all of which are very valuable to IKEA.[40]

Caring companies go beyond what is expected to surprise and delight their stakeholders. When the owners of Jordan's Furniture decided to sell the company to Warren Buffet, they showed their appreciation for their employees by paying each of them 50 cents for every hour they had worked for Jordan's Furniture, though they were under no legal obligation to do so.

The company best known for unabashedly embracing the idea of love and caring in the workplace is Southwest Airlines. Since it began operating at Houston's Love Field, the company has never given up on the theme of love. It promotes love for its employees and love for its customers. On how the company with the stock symbol of LUV treats customers and employees, Colleen Barrett, former President, once stated, "It is simple respect, decency, and friendliness. Southwest doesn't purport to be all things to all people, and we're very upfront about it. We tell our customers why we don't do this, that, and the other... and then we just kill them with kindness, caring, and attention."[41]

Culture of Fun

The last—but not least—cultural value is fun. Although FoEs vary in the degree to which they create a fun atmosphere within which to work and do business, they all believe that it is important. This is certainly the case with New Economy companies such as Amazon and Google. Jeff Bezos urges his employees to "work hard, have fun, and make history." Laughter is contagious, and Jordan's emphasizes that it "wants both its customers and its employees to have fun." Southwest has created a quirky, fun-loving image that connects with its customers. There is a huge emotional bond between the company and its customers. Analysts note, "It is the customer service and friendly employees that give the airline an edge. As the network carriers narrow the fare gap between themselves and Southwest, Southwest should be able to hold onto its customers because they really like flying Southwest."[42]

Culture = DNA

As many others have observed, a company's culture is like its DNA. What the DNA does for an organism, corporate culture does for an organization. A person's DNA carries genetic information that is copied when a cell divides. The function of the DNA that is contained in the nucleus of each cell is to provide information on how to build and operate the organism.

An organism's DNA needs to be genetically resistant and adaptive at the same time. Likewise, a corporate culture needs to be resistant to short-term incidental influences, but also have the ability to adapt as needed. If a company has strong DNA but goes off-track for a time, a new CEO can sometimes trigger the expression of its built-in DNA to bring it back. For example, GE has shown an amazing ability to adapt and reinvent itself, almost as though it were reflecting the DNA of its legendarily innovative founder, Thomas Edison. We see many encouraging signs that Walmart is reconnecting with its DNA, which was developed when Sam Walton built the company up from its small town roots with bedrock American values.

Toyota has shown a high degree of cultural adaptability over the years. For example, from its inception until the late 1970s, Toyota did not enjoy a good reputation for how it treated its assembly line workers. Its focus was on relentlessly increasing efficiency without much regard for the impact on workers. Many employees developed "shoulder-arm-neck" syndrome, due to the long hours spent in unnatural body positions. Absence from work was not tolerated, and suicides were quite frequent.[43] Toyota recognized that it had to change, and is now regarded as an exemplary employer.

So how can companies create such rich and productive cultures as FoEs have, and then protect and preserve those cultures for the long-term? First, by hiring people who "buy" and "live" the culture and the vision/mission of the company. This is especially important at "lifestyle" companies. L.L. Bean, Patagonia, and REI hire people with a strong interest in outdoor recreation, whereas Whole Foods Market, Trader Joe's, and Wegmans hire "foodies," people with a passionate (almost obsessive) interest in food.

Given the stellar performance that FoEs continuously turn in and the fact that most of them say their corporate culture is their most important asset, how can anyone argue with the evidence? It's not executive brilliance. It's not serendipitous markets. It's not clever marketing strategies. It's a corporate culture that motivates and inspires employees to do the very best they can and the respect that all other stakeholders have for a company's culture that makes it all work so well for FoEs.

Endnotes

1. Mark C. Crowley, "How SAS Became The World's Best Place To Work," *Fast Company*, January 22, 2013.

2. James L. Heskett, "Southwest Airlines 2002: An Industry under Siege," Harvard Business School Case 9-803-133, pg. 8.

3. James Parker quoted by Staff Writer, Philips Business Information, "Southwest May Not Be #1, But it Sure Looks Like The Leader," *Airline Financial News*, Potomac, Nov 24, 2003, pg. 3.

4. Thomas Kell and Gregory T. Carrott, "Culture Matters Most," *Harvard Business Review*, May 2005.

5. Heike Bruch and Sumantra Ghoshal, "Unleashing Organizational Energy," *Sloan Management Review*, Fall 2003, pp. 45–51.

6. Bruch and Ghoshal, *op. cit.*

7. Charles Handy, "What's a Business For?" *Harvard Business Review*, December 2002.

8. http://www.pwcglobal.com/Extweb/service.nsf/0/24F4F9C7A641894 680256C7D00586A48?opendocument#one.

9. http://www.thefreedictionary.com/asset.

10. Konosuke Matsushita, *Quest for Prosperity* (1988).

11. David Packard at an HP management training session in 1960; http://64.233.161.104/search?q=cache:rmc46F2vzfQJ:https://www. stanfordalumni.org/news/magazine/1998/julaug/articles/founding_ fathers/founding_fathers.html.

12. Toyota website.

13. C. William Pollard, "The Leader Who Serves," *Strategy & Leadership*, September/October 1997, Volume 25, Issue 5, pg. 49.

14. Ranjit Voola, Jamie Carlson, and Andrew West (2004), "Emotional Intelligence and Competitive Advantage: Examining the Relationship from a Resource-Based View," *Strategic Change,* Mar/ Apr, Volume 13, Issue 2, pp. 83–93.

15. Hilary Duckett and Elspeth Macfarlane (2003), "Emotional Intelligence and Transformational Leadership in Retailing," *Leadership & Organization Development,* Volume 24, Issue 5/6, pp. 309–317.

16. Benjamin Palmer, Melissa Walls, Zena Burgess, and Con Stough (2001), "Emotional Intelligence and Effective Leadership," *Leadership & Organization Development Journal,* Volume 22, Issue 1, pg. 5.

17. L. Melita Prati, Ceasar Douglas, Gerald R. Ferris, Anthony P. Ammeter, and M. Ronald Buckley (2003), "Emotional Intelligence, Leadership Effectiveness, and Team Outcomes," *International Journal of Organizational Analysis*, Volume 11, Issue 1, pp. 21–40; "elevates the team's emotional state": B.E. Ashforth and R.H. Humphrey (1995), "Emotion in the Workplace: A Reappraisal," *Human Relations*, Volume 48, Issue 2, pp. 97–125; "inspires members to perform with more enthusiasm": K.M. Lewis (2000), "When Leaders Display Emotion: How Followers Respond to Negative Emotional Expression of Male and Female Leaders," *Journal of Organizational Behavior*, Volume 21, pp. 221–234.

18. Ashforth and Humphrey (1995), *op. cit*.

19. Victor Dulewicz and Malcolm Higgs (2003), "Leadership at the Top: The Need for Emotional Intelligence in Organizations," *International Journal of Organizational Analysis*, Volume 11, Issue 3, pp. 193–210.

20. Stephen Bernhut (2002), "Primal Leadership, with Daniel Goleman," *Ivey Business Journal,* May/June, Volume 66, Issue 5, pp. 14–15.

21. Bernhut, *op. cit.*

22. Toyota website.

23. Kevin Kelly, *Out of Control,* Addison-Wesley Publishing Company, 1994, pg. 348.

24. William E. Schneider, "Why Good Management Ideas Fail: The Neglected Power of Organizational Culture," *Strategy & Leadership*, January/February 2000, Vol. 28, Issue 1, pg. 24.

25. Costco website.

26. "Southwest Airlines' Herb Kelleher: Unorthodoxy at Work." *Management Review*, June 1995, pg. 10.

27. Andrew Tilin, "The Smartest Company of the year: And the Winner is... Toyota," *Business 2.0*, January/February 2005, pp. 67–72.

28. Costco website, Investor section.

29. Martha Peak, "Harley-Davidson: Going Whole Hog to Provide Stakeholder Satisfaction," *Management Review*, June 1993.

30. Francis Fukuyama, *Trust: The Social Virtues and The Creation of Prosperity,* New York: The Free Press, 1996.

31. Samsong Fang and Brian H. Kleiner, *Management Research News*, 2003. Volume 26, Issue 2-4. pg. 116.

32. Takeo Doi, translated by John Bester, *The Anatomy of Dependence,"* Kodansha International, Tokyo and New York, 1990, pg. 7.

33. Don Tapscott and David Ticoll, *The Naked Corporation: How the Age of Transparency Will Revolutionize Business*, New York: Free Press, 2003.

34. UPS press release (Nov 14, 2003). "Sustainable Business Practices Crucial to Viable Economy, Says UPS."

35. Frederick F. Reichheld and Thomas Teal, *The Loyalty Effect: The Hidden Force Behind Growth, Profits, and Lasting Value*, Boston: Harvard Business School Press, 1996.

36. Toyota 2003 Environmental and Social Report.

37. 2004 UPS Annual Report, pg. 5.

38. http://www.IKEA-group.IKEA.com/corporate/work/why.html.

39. Lance Secretan, "Love and Truth," *Worthwhile,* Sep-Oct 2005, pg. 34.

40. IKEA USA website.

41. Frances X. Frei, "Rapid Rewards at Southwest Airlines," Harvard Business School Case 9-602-065, pg. 3.

42. Betsy Snyder as quoted by Staff Writer, Philips Business Information, "Southwest May Not Be #1, But it Sure Looks Like the Leader," *Airline Financial News*, Potomac, Nov 24, 2003, pg. 3.

43. S. Kamata, *Employee Welfare Takes a Back Seat at Toyota*, Pantheon Books, 1982.

10

What We Have Learned

A journey through the FoE universe presents formidable challenges to long-standing ideas about the place and purpose of corporations in society. But aside from the philosophical and ethical issues brought up by those challenges, and whether or not you have a narrower traditional view of a company's purpose, it seems to us that it's hard to argue with the success of FoE business models. That being the case, we devote this chapter to the most important lessons we learned in our research for this book.

Distinguishing Traits of Firms of Endearment

We identified seven traits that distinguish FoEs. At first blush, these traits do not appear to be all that unique to FoEs. Many companies can lay claim to the same traits. However, it is how FoEs express these traits and weave them through their culture and operations that give them unique standing.

- FoEs challenge industry dogma.
- FoEs create value by aligning stakeholders' interests.
- FoEs are willing to break traditional trade-offs.
- FoEs operate with a long-term perspective.
- FoEs favor organic growth to growing by mergers and acquisition.
- FoEs blend work and play.
- FoEs reject traditional marketing models.

Challenging Industry Dogma

Every industry promotes formulas for success that companies in the industry generally follow. Benchmarking studies glean what industry leaders do to give everyone in the industry a deeper understanding of the formulas for success. But not every successful company in an industry needs to follow such "best practices" formulas for success.

In Gary Hamel's view, each industry has Rule Makers (industry leaders), Rule Takers ("peasants who only keep what the Lord doesn't want"), and Rule Breakers ("revolutionaries who overturn the 'curse of incrementalism,' rewrite industry rules, and overthrow industry boundaries").[1] Rule Breakers don't follow the dictates of industry-sanctioned "best practices." They use resources sparingly, focus them more tightly, generate additional resources through partnerships, complement their resources by combining them in synergistic ways, and recover resources from the market more quickly.[2]

The sporting goods behemoth Nike is a Rule Maker. It wrote the rulebook for the athletic shoe industry. Its rules stress product styling, endorsements by popular athletes, outsourcing of all manufacturing to low-wage countries, and a huge marketing budget. Reebok replicated much of this formula to become the second-largest company in the industry. Adidas reached third place doing much the same. However, the fastest growing company in the sneaker industry (and for a brief while the #2 company before the Reebok-Adidas merger in 2005) in recent years has been New Balance. New Balance is a Rule Breaker. It challenged industry dogma with a different business philosophy and strategy. The company places greater emphasis on fit and function than on styling. It rejects marquis name endorsements. It spends far less on marketing as a percentage of sales than do Nike, Reebok, and Adidas. Finally, New Balance's stakeholder-grounded management has given it enviable standing with the retailers who sell its products, its suppliers, and its highly engaged workforce.[3]

FoEs' willingness to challenge industry dogma means that they don't fit into the norms that Wall Street is most comfortable with. This leads many analysts to criticize FoEs that pay wages and benefits above industry standards. They would surely take Jim Davis to task for continuing to manufacture in the U.S. if New Balance were a public company.

Southwest Airlines' readiness to override industry dogma is legendary. It defied conventional industry wisdom in identifying its biggest competitors as cars, buses, and trains. It acted accordingly by focusing on short-haul segments in its earlier days. It also rejected the "hub-and-spoke" method in favor of "point-to-point" flights, and offered a single class of service instead of economy, business, and first class.

Wegmans Food Markets defied industry dogma by not following the industry practice of paying low wages and benefits. Many grocery retailers contend publicly that retailing is not a long-term "career" option, and use this position to defend their low wages and poor benefits. Wegmans belies those claims. The company is known for great benefits, above-average wages, an extremely low employee turnover rate, and an extraordinarily loyal customer base. CEO Danny Wegman is convinced beyond all questioning that Wegmans' outsized customer loyalty rests on a foundation of greatly satisfied employees.

Aligning Stakeholders' Interests

The foundation of the FoE business model is alignment of stakeholders' interests. Nothing else so decisively sets FoEs apart from the rest of the business world than their active promotion of every stakeholder's interests.

FoEs view stakeholders not as competing claimants on a fixed pool of value but as active contributors to it. We think of this as "corporate alchemy." Alchemy, of course, is the medieval practice of trying to transform base metals into gold. We use the term to describe the ability of FoEs to transmute stakeholder groups from separate, sometimes competing groups into a cohesive whole in which the value of the whole is far greater than the sum of the parts.

Stakeholder participation in value creation is basic in FoE management. Whole Foods Market demonstrates this when it brings all of its stakeholders together to develop its five-year plans, as part of a multi-day process called "Future Search." We observed earlier that Harley-Davidson and Southwest Airlines enlist the participation of unions in planning for the future because they view unions as partners rather than as adversaries.

UPS pursues value-creating synergy with stakeholders by paying attention to its "triple bottom line." This refers to the economic, environmental, and social dimensions of UPS operations. Former CEO Michael Eskew says balancing these three responsibilities "is a formula that has served UPS well since our inception in 1907, and will remain a guiding imperative as we enter our second century."[4] To monitor its progress, UPS established Key Performance Indicators with the help of the Global Reporting Initiative. These include three main categories:

- Economic (return on equity)
- Social (retention rate, "Employer of Choice" index, automotive accident frequency [per 100,000 driver hours], philanthropy as a percentage of profit, and total charitable contributions)
- Environmental (fines as a percentage of environmental agency inspections, ground network fuel efficiency, global aircraft emissions/maximum payload capacity, and percent of fleet that meets stringent noise reduction requirements)

Jordan's Furniture approaches the task of stakeholder alignment quite simply: It views each of its stakeholders as customers. By paying detailed attention to the needs of each group, Jordan's succeeds where many other retailers have failed. It succeeds because of a three-fold philosophy: "creating prosperity, improving productivity, and generating fulfillment." This triumvirate of concerns helps to develop value-creation synergy between all stakeholder groups, and sets Jordan's apart from its competitors.[5]

Jordan's fun approach to work ensures that employees will find personal fulfillment on the job. It infuses employees with the confidence that they are working for the best interest of customers. By investing in its employees, soliciting their feedback, and rewarding them accordingly, Jordan's creates a "culture of creativity, hard work, and loyalty." Customers benefit because they reap the rewards of dealing with enthusiastic, motivated, and fun-loving employees. The "Jordan's bug" has spread throughout its six locations and results in record volumes of sales year after year. Manufacturers and distributors continue to see their relationships with Jordan's thrive, and stockholders, including Warren Buffet, are delighted to invest in such a dynamic company. They can feel good about supporting a company that cares about people, gives back to the community, and still succeeds at making money. Jordan's management works smartly to create a domino effect of positive outcomes for each stakeholder. "Customers, employees, and communities first, and the rest will all fall in line."[6] That simple synopsis results from wise business leadership and a tireless commitment to strong stakeholder relationship management.

How Honda Balances, Aligns, and Integrates Stakeholders

Honda is heavily committed to deeply satisfying the needs of every one of its stakeholder groups. It delivers leading-edge quality and satisfaction to its customers, motivates and leverages its people, creates mutually beneficial relationships with suppliers, and consistently delivers superior value for shareholders. At the same time, it remains engaged with surrounding communities and generally stays on the right side of governments and regulators. How does Honda do it?[7]

The key is that the company is able to create synergies between these different groups. Beyond simply maintaining a controlled balance between stakeholders, Honda has actually implemented many practices and programs that create synergies between these groups. These include executive compensation plans, employee motivation tactics, the REACH (Recognizing Efforts of Associates Contributing at Honda) program of rewards, the Best Partner initiative, as well as the company's corporate structure.

To avoid employees benefiting at the expense of investors—or vice versa—Honda has implemented many performance-based pay initiatives for its staff. Using these practices, the company rewards results and innovation without excessive pay packages or overly generous benefits. Honda's top management makes less money than those of many of Honda's competitors. By closely tying executive compensation to the company's performance, Honda ensures greater transparency and fairness for investors and sends the right message to the rest of its workforce. If Honda is doing well and customers are happy, then employees benefit (through bonuses) along with investors.

The Honda culture rewards good ideas and continually empowers employees to look for more efficient ways to work. The REACH program is a good example of a financial reward mechanism that helps to get the best ideas from employees for continually improving quality, innovation, and efficiency. Under the program, the company gives individuals "kaizen awards" for their successful ideas. Honda also offers awards for detecting defects in product quality and safety hazards in the plants. The company has given many cars to participants in the REACH program over the years as rewards, as well as cash awards.

Because Honda relies heavily on vendors to supply most of the components of its products, it has rightly recognized that suppliers—when treated as partners—can enable positive synergies across the enterprise. Collaborating with suppliers helps improve quality and ensures that costs are tightly controlled—both of which relate directly to Honda's customer value proposition. High-quality reliable products at affordable prices are only possible and sustainable if the whole supply chain is efficient. In working with its supply chain, Honda successfully balances partnership with demanding standards on price and quality.

An important component in Honda's supplier strategy is the BP (Best Partner) program. A dedicated team of people works with suppliers to help them to achieve the high standards and target costs that Honda Manufacturing demands. This creates a collaborative and synergistic relationship that benefits both the supplier and Honda. Surveys of suppliers have shown that Toyota and Honda rate the highest in terms of which automakers enable suppliers to earn acceptable profit margins, far ahead of U.S. manufacturers.

Breaking Traditional Trade-Offs

Thinking in terms of trade-offs is a mainstay mindset in business. It derives from the disposition of the scientifically grounded Western mind to value "if/then" and "either/or" constructs over "both/and" constructs. This style of thinking leads to absolutist black-and-white renderings of reality that restrict options. The alternative style of thinking—"both/and"—opens up the mind to accommodate seemingly contradictory conditions (for example, high wages and high profit margins) and avoids the limitations of trade-off computations (for example, there is only one *best way* to accomplish something).

FoEs generally occupy the "best value" position in their industry. They offer customers superior products or services, frequently at remarkably competitive prices. Costco carries only high-quality products, but offers them to the marketplace with uncommonly low markups. Amazon offers an exceptional service experience with low prices, often with free shipping. Toyota generally offers more quality, reliability, and fuel efficiency for the money than its competitors. Trader Joe's specializes in inexpensive but exotic (even gourmet) food products from around the world.

Some FoEs, such as Whole Foods Market, Starbucks, Patagonia, and The Container Store, are on the higher end of pricing, but give customers experiences and unique products that keep them coming back. Though customers could easily find lower prices elsewhere, they are more than willing to pay higher prices for these companies' offerings because they perceive both products and experiences as attractively unique.

One trade-off that FoEs consistently break is between employee wages and value to customers. Costco, Wegmans, and Trader Joe's give proof of this. They offer outstanding wages to their employees and competitive prices to their customers—and make healthy profits to boot. Higher wages and benefits paid by these companies do not show up in the prices consumers pay. The greater productivity of higher caliber employees and lower employee turnover in part explain this. Also, employee-generated process improvements continuously show up because employees care enough to strive for making the company more profitable. Finally, the link between satisfied employees and customer loyalty is beyond question. These companies generate a high share of wallet by focusing on share of heart. Talk about alchemy—higher wages and benefits transmuted into lower operating costs!

A Long-Term Perspective

Perhaps no single factor robs shareholders of more value than relentless pressure on management from Wall Street analysts to think short term. This may be good for day traders and other speculators, but can do great harm to the interests of longer-term investors.

Unfortunately, many CEOs all too gladly adopt the short-term perspective for reasons of quick personal gains via stock options. The result is that management can be richly rewarded, short-term investors have more opportunities to gain from shorting and churning of shares, but long-term investors may ultimately come out losing because opportunities for greater gains were ignored.

It is worth noting that a number of companies we studied are privately owned, and thus shielded from Wall Street pressures. But even publicly traded FoEs tend to be relatively impervious to such short-term pressures. Google's founders, for example, have clearly stated that they believe "shareholders are better off in the long run when the company is doing good things for the world even though they might have to let go of some profits in the short run."[8] In their "Letter From the Founders: 'An Owner's Manual' for Google's Shareholders" within their IPO SEC filing, the founders also warned potential investors that they would not make operational decisions based on projected or actual quarterly earnings. "We will optimize for the long term rather than trying to produce smooth earnings for each quarter."[9]

We'll close this section with this thought: Wall Street is inherently biased against the long-term investor because most people and companies working in the Wall Street environment make their money through trading, not by building value. In the aggregate, the more trading that is done, the more money most companies working in equity markets make. The irony in this from Wall Street's perspective is that FoEs' long-term approach appears to be a major factor in their generally superior returns over the long term. In the final analysis, equity markets view FoEs' long-term perspective as making them more attractive investments.

Organic Growth

Most FoEs could grow much faster than they have chosen to. Take Wegmans, for example. It receives thousands of letters every year begging it to open stores in locations close to where the letter writers live. However, the company chooses to only add two to three stores a year. This slow rate of expansion builds tremendous anticipation for new stores in the market. It ensures that every new store opening is a community event. Wegmans' pace of growth is influenced by its insistence that its employees be fully trained before opening a new store. Also, it deploys some of its "best and brightest" employees from existing stores when opening a new store. This also limits the pace of growth because only so many "best and brightest" can be taken from their regular jobs. In February 2004, Wegmans opened a store near Dulles airport in the Washington DC area. It drew 15,500 shoppers on its first day, more than shop at most supermarkets in a week. All the managers of the store came from different Wegmans locations, and dozens of other employees flew in to help get the store off the ground smoothly. The company spent approximately $5 million on training for this one store. It could have opened months earlier (in time for the holiday season), but Wegmans insisted on waiting until it was completely prepared.[10] (Another example of FoE patience in taking the long-term view.)

Blending Work and Play

Marketers like to talk about brands as archetypal personalities, such as the Jester and the Rebel. Lee Lynch, who is the second half of Harley-Davidson's ad agency Carmichael and Lynch, once impishly told an audience one of us were in, "There's a bit of Harley-Davidson in each of us." Wink, wink. Nearly everyone likes to experience the thrill of breaking a rule now and then. There's a bit of Harley in CEOs of FoEs, for sure. Rule breaking regularly occurs in FoEs, with management's enthusiastic encouragement.

The aura of the Rebel that makes it fun for employees to build Harley-Davidsons makes it fun to own them, as well. It is no mere curiosity that the average age of a new Harley owner is 47! A signature characteristic of the midlife course is blending work with play and experiencing growing autonomy with a little bit of "legal" rule breaking from time to time. With the largest block of adults now in midlife, it only makes sense that the Harley-Davidson brand has become a midlife icon signifying the freedom of the open road with a little bit of the Rebel thrown in.

Tough-talking, bourbon-swilling, chain-smoking Southwest Airlines cofounder Herb Kelleher chose the Jester as the archetypal personality for his airline. But it is a loving, caring Jester, as Southwest's stock symbol LUV suggests. Kelleher's antics (like having a flight attendant hide in an overhead bin on a plane) are legendary, but he has infused healthy levity into work styles of the Southwest family. But let it not be overlooked that Southwest's fun persona also has a serious side. Flying is stressful for many people. Kelleher's antidote is humor. So Southwest's employees are introduced to the positive contribution that humor can make to easing customer's anxieties as well as to making work more fun. Imagine customers' reaction when one Southwest pilot announced on the intercom, "We've reached our cruising altitude now, and I'm turning off the seat belt sign. I'm switching to autopilot, too, so I can come back there and visit with all of you for the rest of the flight." Another incident helped anxious flyers breathe a sigh of relief upon landing when a voice came from the cabin, "Whoa, big fella... WHOA!"

Another classic brand archetype is the Caregiver. That personality fits the personalities of many FoEs, especially from the perspective of employees. For instance, Google's caring nature is reflected in the around-the-clock free meals that bring employees closer together to discuss projects and have fun over a hamburger or full course. Indeed, Google's mantra "Do no evil" brings to mind the caregiver motto of the medical profession, "First, do no harm," expressed in the Hippocratic Oath.

Industrial design firm IDEO thrives on play. Founder David Kelly and his brother Tom created a culture that allows employees to sometimes feel as though they are not at work at all. It is acceptable to take an afternoon off with your team to see a movie or ballgame. Unplanned breaks are daily affairs. Wacky diversions and silly pranks spice the relationships employees have with each other.[11] Visitors are often a bit taken aback when they see employees playing miniature golf and throwing Nerf balls in the hallways of a company recognized by *The Wall Street Journal, Fortune, Business Week* and other publications as among the premier design companies in the world.[12] Clearly, David Kelly believes it when he says, "play ignites the innovative spirit."[13]

Rejecting Traditional Marketing Models

One of the more important bonuses of being an FoE is lower marketing costs. FoEs are sustained by direct experience and great word-of-mouth. Delighted customers, employees, and suppliers tell others about these companies, reducing the need to advertise to create awareness. Consider that Google became one of the most valuable brands in the world—without any advertising. Starbucks became an international brand with virtually no advertising. Costco and Harley-Davidson built powerful brands without advertising. FoEs generally do not rely on frequent sales and other promotions. This is a huge cost saver as well as a source of comfort for customers, who do not have to wait for a sale to buy what they need now. This has been a core attribute of Jordan's marketing model. Whereas the typical furniture retailer spends approximately seven percent of gross revenue on marketing and advertising, Jordan's spends only two percent. Yet, Jordan's leads the industry with annual sales of nearly $1,000 per square foot, while the average store sells between $150 and $200 per square foot.[14]

Conclusion

FoEs offer a cornucopia of valuable lessons for the rest of the business world. In this chapter, we highlighted just seven lessons regarding what we view as among the most distinguishing traits of FoEs. In our estimation, FoEs represent the architectural template for a new genre of business models that companies will need to adopt to thrive in the long run in the Age of Transcendence. Business models based on stakeholder relationship management will increasingly be essential to business survival and growth. Call it a new form of social Darwinism in the business world.

Like the fundamentalists of capitalism, we too believe in applying social Darwinism in a business context. However, we don't construe the term to represent competitors figuratively long in tooth and red in claw battling it out to the finish in the Coliseums of the marketplace. Instead, the "fittest" who survive in the long run will be those who can best adapt to changing conditions in their environments. In addition to the shifting value system (or psychological center of gravity) caused by the rise of the median age in virtually every society, nothing has ever changed the environment in which companies must work in so short a time and in such great magnitude as the Internet. With the Internet as a resource for learning about what goes on in corporations, companies have lost the power to manipulate customers, workers, and other stakeholders by controlling information flow. Companies are now challenged to adapt to the growing demands of their stakeholders for transparency and collaborative behavior or else go the way of the dinosaur. FoE leaders know this in their bones. They know that the most effective way to compete in today's business world is by operating in the open and adding to their core asset base the value that all stakeholders bring to the table. This then generates the augmented value that the company can leverage for the benefit of all.

Endnotes

1. Gary Hamel, "Strategy as Revolution," *Harvard Business Review*, Vol. 74; Issue 4; July-August 1996, pg. 69.

2. Ibid.

3. Personal interview by coauthor David Wolfe in 2003 for another book he was writing.

4. http://sustainability.ups.com/overview/letter.

5. http://www.business-wisdom.com/articles/pdfs/BusinessesDemonstrate.pdf.

6. www.business-wisdom.com/artilces/pdfs/businessdemonstrate.pdf.

7. This section is based on a paper by Bentley College MBA students Joanne Girdlestone, Mehmet Agyuz, and Sameer Mundhra.

8. M. Lewis, "The Irresponsible Investor," *The New York Times Magazine*, June 6, 2004.

9. SEC 8/13/04, File 333-114984, Accession Number 1193125-4-139655, pg. 32.

10. Matthew Boyle and Ellen Florian Kratz, "The Wegmans Way," *Fortune*, January 24, 2005, pg. 62.

11. Tom Kelley and Jonathan Littman, *The Art of Innovation* (New York: Double Day 2001) pg. 95.

12. Tom Kelley and Jonathan Littman, *The Art of Innovation* (New York: Double Day 2001), pg. 4.

13. "Seriously Silly" (interview with David M. Kelley, CEO and founder of IDEO) *Business Week*, Sept. 13, 1999, pg. 14.

14. Arthur Lubow, "Wowing Warren," *Inc. Magazine*, March 2000.

11

The Other Side of Complexity

We are nearing the end of our journey through the humanistically flourishing fields of the FoE landscape. In writing this book, we were struck by the fact that no one had taken on this topic quite as we have. It's not as though FoEs represent a new, radical *avant-garde* business model. A slew of companies have been around for many decades endearing themselves to all their stakeholders. One exemplar that became a household name started doing business as an FoE in the back woods of Maine in 1912. Tired of trudging through snow and mud with poorly made footwear, hunting enthusiast Leon Leonwood Bean started making better boots in 1912. From its founding, L.L. Bean employed a stakeholder relationship management business model that sets FoEs apart from the corporate herd. Through good times and bad, L.L. Bean has stayed true to Leon Leonwood's business ethos for nearly a century. But L.L. Bean was not the first FoE.

A few years earlier, in 1907, teenager James Casey and his friend Claude Ryan founded the American Messenger Company in San Francisco. AMC, now UPS, was an FoE from its first days. Casey and Ryan believed that overarching dedication to customer service and generosity toward employees (along with high expectations of them) when combined with sound management would make profitability a virtual certainty. They intuitively felt no need to overly focus on the bottom line when the human side of a company's life is well tended.

Even UPS is not the oldest FoE in the book. The venerable Tata Group of India dates back to 1868. At that time, India was still a British colony, and the country had huge infrastructural and other developmental needs. In deciding what businesses to invest in, founder Jamshedji Tata always asked the question, "What does India need?" This led him to lay the groundwork for the first steel plant and the first hydroelectric plant in India. After he was denied admission to a hotel in his own country that was "for British only," Jamshedji resolved to build the finest hotel in the world, one that would proudly serve Indians as well as anyone else. The Taj Mahal Hotel opened in 1903 in what is now called Mumbai. It was the first building in India with electricity and featured the finest of furnishings and amenities from all over the world. Since these proud beginnings, the Tata Group has grown to become one of the most beloved and reputable organizations in the world. The group now has 100 operating companies (including 32 that are publicly traded) in 80 countries, with revenues over $100 billion and nearly half a million employees. Its activities span across an extraordinary range of businesses, including steel, electric power, cars, trucks, tea, chemicals, software, and much more. Through it all, the Tatas have maintained a deeply caring and humane culture, an impeccable reputation for integrity, a tradition of true servant leadership, and extraordinary contributions in the community. The group holding company Tata Sons owns a controlling interest in all of the group's public companies, and is in turn two-thirds owned by a number of philanthropic trusts dedicated to a broad range of educational, health, research, and community enrichment activities.

We have not presented this book as this triad of authors' theory of postmodern management. Rather, we set out to report on the common sense ideas of a select group of entrepreneurs who over the past century have shared a view of what it takes to be a good businessperson without compromising what it takes to be a good human being. Bring on the violins if you want, but this *is* a human interest story of a great moment—and momentum. It undergirds the social transformation of capitalism in the Age of Transcendence. You are either one with this development and vitally animated by a sense of excitement over being part of a new order or you will increasingly feel left behind by a whole new world. Once again, we recall the wide-eyed wonderment of Valentine in Tom Stoppard's play *Arcadia*, when he marvels at the scale of change taking place and exclaims, "It's the best possible time to be alive when almost everything you thought you knew is wrong." One of the things we thought we knew about doing business that is now wrong is that business should not concern itself with social benevolence.

Of course, social benevolence at the hands of business leaders is not new. Its most dramatic expressions in the past have been in the form of hugely funded foundations, institutional endowments, and grants of considerable sums to various causes by very rich old men, usually after decades of callous business behavior. We all know the names of many of these men whom we have come to call "robber barons." They include John D. Rockefeller, J. P. Morgan, Cornelius and William Vanderbilt, Andrew Carnegie, and Jay Gould. In their twilight years these old-style capitalists underwent a metamorphosis like plant-destroying caterpillars turning into benign butterflies, and left the world's stage as men of goodwill and great generosity. Philanthropic largesse was the coin they used to buy wide social acceptance and self-forgiveness before drawing their last breaths.

Companies that begin as FoEs are started by men and women who wish to express their own sense of social benevolence. Patagonia, Costco, and Whole Foods Market are such companies. Some companies that began corporate life as opportunistic enterprises bent on exploiting whatever was exploitable for their ends have somewhere along the line undergone a social transformation. Toyota is such a company. It was once so beholden to an ethos of exploitation that it penalized workers on the assembly line for taking toilet breaks.

Boot maker Timberland is another firm changed by an epiphany in the executive ranks that turned it into an FoE after decades of an insular self-serving existence. In 1989, third-generation Timberland executive Jeffery Swartz (his grandfather founded the firm) had a life-altering experience in a conversation with a troubled teen in a halfway house. The teen asked Swartz what he did.

"I'm the COO."

"What do you really do?"

"I'm responsible for the global execution of strategy. So what do you do?"

"I work at getting well."[1]

Swartz later said with genuine humility, "That was an answer that sort of trumped mine." So moved was he by the experience he resolved to turn his company into an instrument for social good, and sold the idea to his employees that Timberland had taken on a mission to change the world.

The fundamentalists of capitalism may rail against Swartz's conversion to social activism. They might view what they consider to be the subordination of this publicly traded company to Swartz's private social agenda as an unforgivable sin against the dogma of Milton Friedman and the richly honored traditions of classic capitalism. But such fundamentalists ought to give rapt attention to what Don Tapscott and David Ticoll say in their book *The Naked Corporation* when they remind us that "values-oriented consumers have agendas that go beyond personal benefit. They probe deep into a company's supply chain to expose environmental and human rights practices, then demand and force change."[2] Timberland's performance on behalf of its stakeholders has been nothing less than outstanding since Swartz's "conversion." In the Age of Transcendence, an elevated corporate social consciousness is a big plus, and appears less and less to be optional.

Capitalist fundamentalists fixated on the bottom line need to come to terms with the reality that the idea of building and protecting shareholder wealth is no longer sustainable as the sole rationale for business. Yes, shareholder gain remains a crucially important factor in business, but shareholder gain is no longer the supreme factor in running companies. It is just one of a number of factors, all of which must be taken into account to secure the best prospects for the highest levels of business flourishing.

As we see it, the biggest winners from here on will generally be companies with a strong sense of social purpose that value the well-being of all their stakeholders rather than treating some as means and others as ends. Of all the ideas we've touched on, none surpass in importance the idea that with sound management in place, focus on service to *all* stakeholders gives a company a competitive advantage over companies that focus primarily on shareholders and profits. *This is the crucial cultural difference* between FoEs and non-FoE companies. And as we've shown throughout this book, the payoff to shareholders from this way of being has generally been extraordinary. So if this is such a winning approach to business, why have we not seen a raft of writings on this phenomenon?

Oliver Wendell Holmes offers us a clue in his famous statement, "I would not give a fig for the simplicity this side of complexity but I would give my life for the simplicity on the other side of complexity." In his book *The Executive's Compass: Business and the Good Society,* James O'Toole elaborates on Holmes' wisdom:

> To move beyond the confusion of complexity, executives must abandon their constant search for the immediately practical and, paradoxically, seek to understand the underlying ideas and values that have shaped the world they work in. Managers who clamor for how-to instruction are, by definition, stuck on the near side of complexity.[3]

When it comes to business, the simplicity on this side of complexity can devolve into a *simplistic* understanding of the nature and purpose of business: that the sole purpose of business is to maximize profits. Everyone knows that profits equal revenue minus costs. To maximize profits, the company must therefore maximize revenues and minimize costs. To maximize revenue, it must sell as much as possible to as many people as possible, charging as high a price as possible. To minimize costs, it must pay its suppliers and employees as little as possible, and externalize whatever costs it can onto society. But such a business is no blessing to the world. It might create financial value for some while destroying many other kinds of value for all its other stakeholders. Such a business is not a net value creator; rather, it is a parasite that destroys far more than it generates. Human societies can no longer afford and will not much longer tolerate businesses that operate in this manner.

There hasn't previously been a book of the sort you now hold in your hands because most business scholars, practitioners, and observers have been stuck on the near side of complexity where the pros and cons of stakeholder relationship management are debated in rationally derived quantitative terms. Left on the sidelines is the qualitative emotive side of SRM that gives this book its title. What is more complex in the affairs of humans than the emotional dimensions of their lives? Yet, rather than pursuing deeper understanding of this dimension in a business context, most students and practitioners of business have seemed to prefer staying on the seemingly rational near side of complexity.

To get a sense of the importance of the emotional dimensions of life as they relate to company performance, try talking to ardently loyal customers of an FoE about their experiences with the company. Most will tell you how the company makes them feel, what an episode of shopping is like in subjective terms. Talk to the employees of FoEs, as we often do, when shopping in an FoE outlet. None has ever told us that the company is great to work for because it pays more than its competitors. To tell us why they like being an employee, they say things like, "I'm part of a family," "They respect me," "It's a fun place to work," and "They make me feel important." Talk to any other stakeholder and you will likely hear such words as *trust, responsible, generous,* and *dependable* when they describe why they enjoy their relationship with a firm of endearment. In short, the emotional right brain rules in matters of relationship in business contexts as well as in personal contexts.

Of course, we must make allowances for investors—especially day traders and other speculators—who view their connections with a company strictly as no more than a financial investment. Suggesting that they have an emotional investment in a stock is an insult to many investors. Nevertheless, emotional factors are more at play in investment decisions than commonly admitted. How else could it be when analysts often attribute wide swings in the stock market to emotional factors? In a worldview drawn from simplicity on the near side of complexity, meeting the needs of multiple stakeholders seems impossible to do without a cost to owners of a company's stock. After all, *everyone* can't win—or so the thinking goes in a worldview constrained by a rational simplistic win-lose perspective on corporate operations. But FoEs fervently believe in a world in which it is possible for everyone to win, not by making someone else lose but by creating a harmonious concinnity of interests.

People whose thoughts center on the simple perspectives this side of complexity may churlishly dismiss much of what we have said as being just words, or perhaps worse, *just a theory.* Gravity is a theory, too, but improving our understanding of it has done much to give us the modern world we live in. Our claim throughout this book has been that the multiple stakeholder business model will contribute to the betterment of the capitalistic system, and by extension the betterment of society.

The Big Challenge of the Times: Transcending a Zero Sum Mindset

There are few absolutes in the Age of Transcendence. This means a profusion of opportunities. Absolutes, which by definition are limiting, are found everywhere on the near side of complexity. They emerge from people's perennial quest for pat solutions, or "silver bullets," as they are sometimes described. The next time you go into a bookstore, take a look at the titles in the business stacks. Particularly look at books under the headings of marketing and sales. Most titles in that category are grounded in the near side of complexity. Many such books promise readers great results if they follow the enumerated steps around which the book is structured. Publishers and authors have learned that titles such as *"Ten Steps to..."* and *"Eight Minutes to..."* can increase book sales.

Thinking that is grounded in the seductive but shallow simplicity found in abundance on the near side of complexity stifles innovation and creative solutions to problems. Near-sided thinking blinds the mind's eye to infinite possibilities. Near-sided thinking is the foundation of the *zero sum* thinking that undergirds the rationale for shareholder-biased business models.

A zero sum mindset leads to the conclusion that one stakeholder can only benefit at the expense of other stakeholders—or as the rephrasing of a hoary cliché has it, "Peter must be robbed to pay Paul." But opportunities increase by an order of magnitude when the mind breaks free of zero sum thinking.

The adherents of a zero sum view of business tend to be devout believers in social Darwinism. However, these capitalist fundamentalists hold a distorted version of Darwin's message. Darwin talked about "survival of the fittest," not "survival of the winner." Among human beings, the "fittest" are not necessarily those who subdue, conquer, and control others. In the long run, the fittest tend to be those who know how to cooperate. However, the competitive spirit in business is often so dominant that most stakeholders come to be dealt with as adversaries to be subdued. Suppliers become objects of exploitation rather than partners. Employees become burdensome expenses that can be eliminated at will when income and profits are down. Communities and governments are considered monkeys on the backs of business. Customers are objects of prey to be conquered, seduced, manipulated, and controlled. In the fundamentalist view of social Darwinism, business is a no-holds-barred rough-and-tumble contact sport.

A zero sum view of business is becoming unsustainable. For a value-creation system to thrive, each participant must make a profit—that is, each must ultimately get back more value than they originally invested. If they consistently fail to make a reasonable profit, they will inevitably drop out of the system.

FoEs operate from a *positive sum* worldview. This triggers imaginative processes that bring into focus new ways to harness the energies and resources of all stakeholders. This is how FoEs are able to generate greater value for all than is possible when the primary concern is maximizing short-term value for shareholders.

The ability to transcend ruthless competition and embrace the fruits of cooperation is the essence of evolved humanness. Robert Wright, in a book called *Nonzero*, shows how human beings have greatly benefited by moving away from barbaric no-holds-barred competition and toward civilized cooperation. His research found that early human societies tended to have little trust in one another and many were constantly engaged in fighting, treachery, slaughter, and war. Any victories they achieved were short-lived, and over time, every aggressively competitive society was decimated through non-stop killing. Gradually, human societies learned the benefits of cooperation. Wright writes about early hunter-gatherers, the Shoshone, sharing food: "You give someone food when his cupboard is bare and yours is overflowing, he reciprocates down the road when your cupboard is bare, and you both profit, because food is more valuable when you're hungry than when you're full."[4]

The world is becoming ever more hospitable to positive sum thinking. New technologies, especially those that deal with information, are inherently positive sum in nature. They bring to mind Thomas Jefferson's statement, "Knowledge is like a candle. When I light your candle from mine, my light is not diminished."

In the business world, forward-thinking companies over the past few decades have started to benefit greatly from cooperation with all their stakeholders—even with direct competitors, in many cases. For example, competitors in the information technology space have cooperated in developing many standards and notably have worked diligently together in efforts to curb spam. Going further, companies that vigorously compete with one another are recognizing that they can still be business partners. For example, Samsung has emerged as a key supplier of components such as memory chips and LCD panels to its competitors, such as Apple and Sony.

Companies are finding that the more they are willing to do for their stakeholders, the more they tend to get back. The remarkable thing about the FoE idea of striving to create value for all stakeholders is that building value in this fashion is often done with little or no additional expense to the company. Rather than worrying about how to slice the pie, FoEs seek to bake the largest possible pie.

All of this may sound utopian and idyllic—and even Marxist, as Cypress Semiconductor CEO T.J. Rodgers seems to think. But we're not promoting fantasy or radical economic and social theory. FoEs treat their employees better, have profitable suppliers, offer superior value to customers, and invest heavily in their communities. They do all this while delivering exceptional results to investors.

Don Tapscott and David Ticoll tell us in *The Naked Corporation* that, "'Good' firms that optimize the needs of all stakeholders are more likely to be good for investors."[5] No company better exemplifies this idea than Whole Foods Market does in its "Declaration of Interdependence," which was drafted in 1997 by 60 team members. Today, the Declaration is prominently displayed in each store location, and serves to unite stakeholders and highlight the importance of each. As stated on the company website, balancing the interests, desires, and needs of stakeholders "...requires participation and communication by all of our stakeholders. It requires listening compassionately, thinking carefully and acting with integrity. Any conflicts must be mediated and win-win solutions found. Creating and nurturing this community of stakeholders is critical to the long-term success of our company."

Recall from Chapter 8, "Society: The Ultimate Stakeholder," the spirited debate on the merits of a shareholder versus stakeholder perspective that Whole Foods Market's visionary founder and CEO John

Mackey found himself in that was carried by *Reason* magazine.[6] His rhetorical adversaries were Nobel laureate economist Milton Friedman and T.J. Rodgers, founder and CEO of Cypress Semiconductor. An ardent libertarian, Mackey has run Whole Foods for 33 years with impressive success. Starting with $45,000 in capital, he has built a business with 72,000 employees, nearly $13 billion in annual revenues, and a market capitalization of more than $22 billion. Of all food retailers in the *Fortune 500,* Whole Foods Market has the highest profits as a percentage of sales, the highest return on invested capital, the highest sales per square foot, and the highest sustained growth rate. So, who could fault John Mackey for his success? Cypress Semiconductor's T.J. Rodgers does.

In the *Reason* debate, Rodgers drips sarcasm about Mackey's "collectivism and altruism" and his alleged "subordination of his profession as a businessman to altruistic ideals." Rodgers reveals himself as a dyed-in-the-wool capitalist fundamentalist when he fulminates, "I balk at the proposition that a company's 'stakeholders' (a term often used by collectivists to justify unreasonable demands) should be allowed to control the property of the shareholders."

Rodgers' bombast continues as he suggests that Mackey's business philosophy is little different from that of Karl Marx, but how well has Rodgers done with his business philosophy? In case you slid by the answer in Chapter 8, Cypress has been unprofitable over much of its 23-year history. Its balance sheet reflects negative retained earnings of $408 million. The company has lost far more money for its shareholders than it has made. We suspect that Mackey's shareholders are a bit happier than Rodgers' shareholders are. Rodgers appears to regard keeping the intellectual purity of his capitalistic fundamentalism intact as more important than building value for his shareholders.

Mackey's worldview is less insular, to say the least. Mackey draws inspiration from Adam Smith himself—not just from *The Wealth of Nations*, but also from Smith's less well known *The Theory of Moral Sentiments*. In that work, which preceded *The Wealth of Nations*, Smith made clear that human nature is not only or even primarily about self-interest. Motives such as sympathy, empathy, friendship, love, and the desire for social approval are, for many people, even stronger than self-interest, especially as they achieve a higher level of psychological maturity.

Adam Smith separated human nature from corporate nature. But in conscious capitalism, such a schism need not—and should not—exist. It is no longer the case, if it ever was, that people must place their humanity in a blind trust in order to be successful at business. Clearly Mackey and the other leaders of firms of endearment harbor no such beliefs. He concluded the *Reason* debate with these words:

> "At Whole Foods, we measure our success by how much value we can create for all six of our most important stakeholders: customers, team members (employees), investors, vendors, communities, and the environment.... This is our potential as human beings, to take joy in the flourishing of people everywhere. Whole Foods gives money to our communities because we care about them and feel a responsibility to help them flourish as well as possible.... To extend our love and care beyond our narrow self-interest is antithetical to neither our human nature nor our financial success. Rather, it leads to the better fulfillment of both.... Like medicine, law, and education, business has noble purposes: to provide goods and services that improve its customers' lives, to provide jobs and meaningful work for employees, to create wealth and prosperity for its investors and to be a responsible and caring citizen.... The ideas I'm articulating result in a more robust business model than the profit maximization model that it competes against, because they encourage and tap into more powerful motivations than self-interest alone. These ideas will triumph over time, not by persuading intellectuals and economists through argument but by winning the competitive test of the marketplace. Someday, businesses like Whole Foods, which adhere to a stakeholder model of deeper business purpose, will dominate the economic landscape. Wait and see."[7]

FoE Management Requires Holistic Thinking

After people get past the barrier of zero sum either/or thinking (for example, choosing between satisfying investors or employees), they may still remain caught up in a "Who's on first?" debate.

Generally, companies talk about customers, investors, or employees coming first. As we noted earlier, such debates miss the point. They *all* come first, and they all come last. The reality is that all have to be satisfied, and each stakeholder has its moments of ascendance in the FoE universe.

John Mackey considers the satisfaction of each stakeholder as an end itself, not a means to an ultimate end. Any other position can mark a company as an opportunistic manipulator. Mackey says, "In the profit-centered business, customer happiness is merely a means to an end. In the customer-centered business, customer happiness is an end in itself, and will be pursued with greater interest, passion, and empathy than the profit-centered business is capable of." He feels similarly vis-à-vis each stakeholder.

Another reason why a holistic approach to stakeholders has become essential is that the walls that used to separate different classes of stakeholders are melting away. More and more customers want to actively support companies that they can feel good about in every way. Many customers today are also active investors (through mutual funds, stocks, retirement funds) who make their own decisions about where to invest. This is very different from the "old" days when investors relied heavily on stockbrokers for recommendations. A second important development is heightened environmental sensitivity. Many people view the environment as a limited resource that "belongs" to them. This makes a company's actions with respect to the environment and other societal issues much more personal to them. Citizens can readily gain access to information on how a company behaves and in turn can also affect the behavior of companies through blogs, selling shares, and so on.[8]

With their holistic bent for seeing the world—or perhaps more graphically, seeing the forest and not just the trees—FoE leaders take a systemic view of their opportunities, challenges, policies, and operations. Artificial barriers (for example, "silos") between functions and departments are not tolerated. The integration of technology, culture, and physical work environment is more evident than in most organizations that are not FoEs. *Alignment* has become a much-overused term in business literature, but it probably best describes how these firms endear themselves to all stakeholders. They have aligned their strategies with the needs and desires of multiple stakeholders.

Getting to the "Other Side of Complexity"

Becoming an FoE depends on the development of a kind of mindset that reaches fullest development on the far side of complexity. What did Oliver Wendell Holmes mean by the "far side of complexity," the place that he said he'd be willing to give his life to get to? We'll answer that question this way: None of the authors of this book have any medical training. To us, stuck in the near side of medical complexity, a heart transplant seems almost unbelievably complex. Yet, to the seasoned heart surgeon who has traversed through complexity to gain a deep understanding of the body, heart transplant operations are quite simple—just intense and tedious.

A full understanding of FoEs cannot be developed standing in the zone of simplicity on the near side of complexity. Transforming a company into an FoE is a journey through complexity that involves much new learning. There are no shortcuts. Above all, a company can't go around complexity and fake its way into becoming a firm of endearment like a college student paying someone else to attend class and write papers. Authenticity pulses through an FoE's veins either because the founders (true believers) are still at the helm or because thoughtful measures have been taken to preserve the culture after their departure (for example, Southwest Airlines' Culture Committee).

Remember, people don't rally around fake flags. After hearing a discussion of the authentic leadership that exists within FoEs, a mid-level executive who works for one of the largest U.S. financial services firms said, "We'd never make the FoE cut. We've been going through culture change workshops for almost a year and everybody knows it's a bunch of crap. You sit through a workshop in the morning about open and honest communication and then witness power jockeying and data 'massaging' to alter the true picture that same afternoon. Everybody gives politically correct lip service to culture in the workshops, but we all know our dog-eat-dog culture is here to stay and everybody behaves accordingly."

The person who told us that story said his friend's company is financially quite successful despite its hypocritical course. He then posed the question, "If making money is all that really matters, who cares what the culture is like? As it turns out, my friend does. He's leaving the company and it's a real loss because he's real good at what he does."

To get to the simplicity on the other side of complexity requires the intellectual investment and full moral commitment of company leadership, starting at the top. The CEO must double as the CTO— chief transformational officer—and becomes the personification of the new corporate vision. He or she must play an active, ongoing role in guiding the social transformation of the company, much as Ricardo Semler did in his impressive remaking of Semco (Chapter 4, "Employees: From Resource to Source") and Jeff Swartz did in the social transformation of Timberland (discussed earlier in this chapter).

The process of becoming an FoE starts with a self-assessment that compares the present culture of an FoE-wannabe company with the signature attributes of FoE corporate cultures (discussed in Chapter 9, "Culture: The Secret Ingredient"). No step toward getting to the other side of complexity outranks this one in importance. Without self-assessment (as both Semler and Swartz did, for example), there is no way to become an FoE.

Above all, remember this: *culture rules*. Every FoE CEO knows this. Members of the executive staff of FoEs don't cite "product superiority," "value," "service," or any other mundane reason when asked about their company's chief competitive advantage. They almost invariably say it is the company culture. Rick Frazier, who resides in and works from Niantic, Connecticut, has advised a number of *Fortune 500* companies on reinventing themselves through changes in corporate culture over the years. After reading our manuscript, Frazier summed up the power of culture in lifting a company to the lofty heights of uncommon success through its employees when he said, "Many employees of FoEs feel that they are as much volunteering for a cause as showing up to work for a paycheck." Imagine building your company with people who love their jobs and come to work because they feel they are contributing to making the world a better place. Clearly, levels of productivity and customer satisfaction will reach higher levels than in companies where most people report to work every day with less than consummate enthusiasm.

Once a company reaches the other side of complexity and begins to blossom as an FoE, all is changed. Clarity replaces the faux simplicity that the venerable chief justice Oliver Wendell Holmes said he would not give a fig for. Reflect for a moment about how we indulgently smile when children strip away the complexity of a matter to describe it to us in simplified fashion. We find these reductions of complexity to simplicity charming, even though we know them to be distortions of reality. We do much the same in the adult world. Often to our enduring regret we embrace the unauthentic simplicity of the sort that Holmes deplored. Our world is filled with self-styled gurus in dieting methods, love matters, moneymaking, and other dimensions of personal need and desire who seduce us with hollow promises of simplicities that corrupt legitimate complexity. The self-help book industry benefits greatly from this (as does, we must admit, the business book industry).

Once we have made it to the "simplicity on the other side of complexity," little of what is being left behind fits our more clarified view of the world. Thomas Jefferson set down a thought that can be aptly applied to what happens to old ways once we reach the far side of complexity:

> "I am not an advocate for frequent changes in laws and constitutions, but laws and institutions must go hand in hand with the progress of the human mind. As that becomes more developed, more enlightened, as new discoveries are made, new truths discovered and manners and opinions change, with the change of circumstances, institutions must advance also to keep pace with the times. We might as well require a man to wear still the coat which fitted him when a boy as civilized society to remain ever under the regimen of their barbarous ancestors."[9]

And so it is in the Age of Transcendence when we as a society, indeed as a species, have become "more developed, more enlightened." We must renounce "the regimen of our ancestors," for the worldviews and many of the ways that served them well no longer have relevance to the conditions that define our lives and the world in which we live today.

Conclusion

We have come to the end of our journey. It's a good time to recall a few words by Jonathan Rowe that appeared in *The Washington Monthly* years ago. The article began with a reflection on Aaron Feuerstein's textile mill in Lawrence, Massachusetts. The mill had just burned to the ground. Feuerstein made national headlines with his pledge to rebuild the mill rather than truck his operations off to Mexico or some other cheaper locale. Moreover, he would pay his employees for one month through the end of the Christmas season. Feuerstein didn't know what to make of all the fuss over his actions. "What?" he asked. "For doing the decent thing?"[10]

As we discussed earlier, the first corporations were pointedly established for public purposes. It was not until well into the nineteenth century that they became the self-serving vehicles of commerce they have become in recent years. Today, we could fill a sizable library with all the books and articles that defend the insular belief that a business enterprise's only social obligation is the lawful making of profits for its owners. We ask, "Who laid down that law? Whence comes its legitimacy?" To the extent it has any, its legitimacy must come from society, not from the men and women running corporations or from their lawyers. Because business corporations benefit from government and a plentitude of public and quasi-public institutions, and because society's members support companies by buying their products and services, there is no moral defense for the idea that corporate isolation from social concerns is a valid tenet of capitalism.

When he asserted in 1970 that the only social responsibility of business is to legally maximize its profit, Milton Friedman lacked the evidence that we have today. Perhaps there were too few companies with a strong sense of stakeholder responsibility to encourage serious examination of the relationship that might exist between broader concerns and corporate bottom lines. Or, perhaps a more enlightened view of corporate purpose and operation had to await the *collective* maturation of society today that is linked to the aging population and rapidly advancing human consciousness. This has played an incalculable role in the emergence of the Age of Transcendence. Remember, in midlife and beyond—where most of the adult population now is—people tend to concern themselves more with matters beyond their own skins. Mirroring this disposition is the growing list of companies that are concerned with matters not directly connected with their bottom lines. These companies know that they have a mandate to secure healthy bottom lines for their owners, but they have learned that their bottom lines grow richer by their embrace of this new stakeholder business model that is not bottom line driven. When Friedman made his famous statement about corporate purpose in 1970, no one had fully articulated the strategic system of stakeholder relationship management that FoEs practice. Ed Freeman's groundbreaking book on the subject was still 14 years in the future.

Friedman's position suggested that you should set out to "Make money or be socially conscious; you shouldn't try to do both." On the other hand, advocates for a broader perspective say, "You don't need to beat the Street, or even do as well as the Street if you are also shepherding your stakeholder responsibilities." We say "No" to both sides of this debate. Instead, we advocate the business model described in this book, which enables "self-actualized" companies to do both.

Let's assume for a minute that we agree with Friedman that the only social responsibility of business is to make a profit (we don't, but let us stipulate for the moment). It would follow that as a company you'd want to be as good at that as possible. We have shown that the FoE stakeholder model generally outperforms the shareholder-biased business model. This being the case, if you are a rational "Friedmanist" (is there any other kind?), your best choice as a company is to embrace the FoE business model. If you feel a strong duty to shareholders to increase value for them, do you have any other rational choice?

Recall once more the spirited debate on this issue between Milton Friedman, John Mackey of Whole Foods Market, and T.J. Rodgers of Cypress Semiconductors. In a subsequent issue, *Reason* published a number of letters from readers weighing in passionately on both sides of the issue. In one of the letters, the author says, "Businesses like Starbucks, REI, and Whole Foods engage in overt social responsibility *because it gives them a Darwinian advantage.* This only reaffirms the rules of capitalism; it does not supersede them."[11] (Italics added.) In our view, however, this is *not* a reaffirmation of the classical rules of capitalism. Rather, it's strong evidence that the rules of capitalism that give a company Darwinian advantage have changed. If you want to be among the survivors, you'll improve your prospects for survival by acting more like FoE leaders do.

A new era has dawned. Fundamentalists of capitalistic theory can no longer hide with impunity behind arguments that champion corporate insulation from social concerns, contrived in the name of shareholders' rights. It's not a matter of morality, but of sound corporate management in the twenty-first century. Defenders of the argument for shareholder-biased business models deprive themselves and their organizations of richer opportunities than they might have dreamed possible. Leading companies of the future will almost always be those that have crossed over to the other side of complexity to transform their organizations into *firms of endearment*.

Endnotes

1. Jennifer Reingold, "Walking the Walk," *Fast Company*, Nov. 2005, pg. 83.

2. Don Tapscott and David Ticoll, *The Naked Corporation*, Free Press, 2003, pg. xii.

3. James O'Toole, *The Executive's Compass: Business and the Good Society*, Oxford University Press 1995.

4. Robert Wright, *Nonzero: The Logic of Human Destiny*, Vintage 2001.

5. Ibid, pg. 19.

6. John Mackey, Milton Friedman, and T.J. Rodgers, "Rethinking the Social Responsibility of Business," *Reason*, October 2005, pp. 79–87.

7. Mackey, *op. cit.*

8. We are indebted to Bentley College MBA student Diane M. Hartung for these observations.

9. Quotation on the Jefferson Memorial, Washington D.C.

10. Jonathan Rowe, "Reinventing The Corporation—Corporate Responsibility," *The Washington Monthly*, April 1996.

11. *Reason*, January 2006.

Appendix A———

Brief Company Profiles

U.S. Public Firms of Endearment

3M

3M is an American multinational manufacturing leader, with $30 billion in sales and 88,000 employees. It has operations in 65 countries. The company is heavily focused on innovation, producing 55,000 different products. The leadership and culture emphasize innovation and seek to drive it throughout the firm. The company is also greatly concerned with its environmental impact. It launched its "Pollution Prevention Pays" program in 1975, much earlier than most companies became conscious of their impact on the environment. Through this program, 3M has engaged in numerous innovations that have reduced pollution while also saving money and/or adding value to products. The company has long been famous for its 15 percent rule, whereby all employees are encouraged to use 15 percent of their time to develop ideas for new products or improve existing ones.

Adobe Systems

One of the many offshoots of Xerox's Palo Alto Research Center, Adobe was established in 1982 to develop and sell the PostScript page description language. Today, it focuses on multimedia and creativity-enhancing products. Adobe is a company built on innovation. Its mission is to be the premier provider of products and services for professional publishing solutions, business publishing solutions, document solutions, and digital imaging solutions. It expresses its values and commitment to stakeholders with the statement "by operating with integrity and transparency, we build and deepen credibility and trust with our employees, customers, vendors, partners, stockholders, and the community." The company is ranked highly in the areas of sustainability, ethics, and employee satisfaction. It consistently ranks very highly as a place to work. The company has abolished annual performance reviews, instead giving employees continuous feedback. Employees have personalized Individual Development Plans, and have flexibility in choosing how they want to learn and grow.

Amazon.com

Founded in 1994, Amazon.com has become the world's top online retailing company, with revenues over $60 billion, tens of millions of customers, and a huge selection of every kind of product imaginable. Amazon describes itself as an intently customer-centric company, and this approach is seen clearly in its values statement, which highlights principles such as "Customer Obsession," "Innovation," and "Bias for Action." Amazon also helps empower content creators through endeavors such as Amazon Publishing, Amazon Studios, and CreateSpace; developers, meanwhile, are given access to technology programs offered by Amazon Web Services. This spirit of innovation and helping people move forward is at the heart of Amazon.com as a company.

Autodesk

Autodesk, Inc., is a global leader in 3D design, engineering, and entertainment software. It enables customers to design, visualize, and simulate ideas before they are built or created. It has more than ten million customers, including every company in the *Fortune 100*. The company's dominance is indicated by the fact that its software has powered the last 17 Academy Award winners for Best Visual Effects. Autodesk defines its purpose as helping people imagine, design, and create a better world.

Boston Beer Company

Boston Beer Company was founded in 1984 by Jim Koch, a sixth-generation brew master and former Bain consultant. Two months after it was first offered, Samuel Adams lager was picked the best beer in America at the Great American Beer Festival in Denver. Boston Beer's purpose is also its big selling point: crafting the best beers, pursuing brewing as craft and art, not as an industrial process. Furthermore, the company wants to change the way Americans think about the quality of their own beer. This means educating customers to appreciate good beer.[1] Samuel Adams has won more awards in international beer-tasting competitions than any other brewery worldwide since 2000.[2] The company is also recognized as an excellent place to work, investing heavily in training to enable its employees to continually grow and develop.

CarMax

Named "America's Most Admired Company in Automotive Retailing," CarMax has been on *Fortune*'s "100 Best Companies to Work For" list eight years running. From 2008 to 2012, it was a top 125 company for training in *Training Magazine* and scored highly on the Corporate Equality Index. The company was launched with the idea of transforming the used-car buying experience, based on high levels of integrity and trust. It delivers a no-hassle, no-haggle experience with a wide selection of reliable cars that have undergone a 125-point inspection and 12 hours of renewing. It offers customers a five-day money-back guarantee.

Chipotle

Chipotle is the only national restaurant chain in the U.S. serving food made with ingredients from sustainable sources, local and organic produce, and milk from cows not treated with synthetic hormones. It is known for offering products made from sustainable, organic ingredients, while remaining price competitive with other fast food chains. Chipotle owns and operates more than 1,200 quick-casual eateries popular for their burritos and other Mexican food items. Chipotle's operations value all stakeholders. For customers, it seeks to provide the "Chipotle Experience," changing the perceptions associated with fast food. Chipotle cares for the environment by using sustainably grown products and incorporating programs into its food sourcing to help support farmers who grow sustainable food.

Chubb

Chubb Corporation is a global property and casualty insurance company. Founded in 1882, Chubb consistently pushes the envelope to provide the best experience for all its stakeholders. This includes going to great lengths to meet its commitments to customers by consistently trying to find ways to help beyond its legal obligation. Chubb's leadership has always demonstrated a commitment to doing the right thing, instead of just focusing on the bottom line. Hendon Chubb once said, "We are the company that goes beyond the four corners of the contract to find ways to pay claims." In 1906, one of the first leaders of the company, Percy Chubb, traveled across the country with a briefcase full of cash to pay claimants who were affected by the devastating earthquake and ensuing fire in San Francisco. This depleted the company's reserves near to the point of bankruptcy, but it was the only company that paid all the claims resulting from that disaster. The CEO John Finnegan has said, "We take particular pride in knowing that our financial success has been achieved at the same time we have been widely recognized by others as a company that consistently treats its employees, customers, and investors with dignity, fairness, and respect."

Cognizant

Cognizant was founded in 1994 as an in-house technological unit of Dun & Bradstreet and started serving external clients in 1996. The company's purpose is to make clients' businesses stronger by leveraging its business processes, technological know-how, deep industry expertise, and worldwide resources. Cognizant has the highest level of client satisfaction in its industry. In 2011, 97 percent of revenues came from existing customer relationships, and for the fourth straight year, more than 85 percent of clients expressed high satisfaction.

Cognizant's culture emphasizes empowerment and ongoing personal development. Employees are encouraged to pursue paths that fulfill their personal and professional goals, instead of just leveraging their talent to meet company objectives. Cognizant aims to have a positive impact on humanity through free education and the use of technology.

Colgate-Palmolive

Colgate-Palmolive markets a host of well-known and iconic brands in product categories such as oral health, personal care, and pet food. The company articulates five priorities: promoting healthier lives, contributing to its communities, delivering products that delight consumers and respect the planet, making every drop of water count, and reducing its impact on the environment. Each of these is reflected in multiple initiatives. For example, in 1991, Colgate-Palmolive started the "Bright Smiles, Bright Futures" program that has reached more than 650 million children with free dental screenings and education programs. From 2005 to 2012, it reduced water use per ton of product by 31 percent. It has introduced concentrated products that require less packaging, less water, and less transportation fuel. The company subscribes to a philosophy of "Leadership with Respect" and is very highly regarded for the work-life balance its employees enjoy.

Costco

The leading warehouse-style retailer in the world, with annual revenues over $100 billion, Costco provides some of the best wages and working conditions in its industry. It enjoys very high customer trust and loyalty, with a no-questions-asked return policy and a policy of limiting its markup on all products. Costco's warehouse stores—more than 600 worldwide—are stocked with a huge variety of products, from appliances to food to apparel to sporting goods, available to its 68 million members at prices consistently lower than other retailers. Before coming into a local community, Costco representatives sit down with various community stakeholders to address any concerns. Costco treats suppliers with respect and seeks to provide equal opportunities for women and minority-owned businesses.

FedEx

The world's first overnight express delivery company, FedEx today serves in more than 220 countries and territories. The company's "integrated air/ground network"—using trucks and planes at the same time—helped revolutionize the shipping world.[3] It is committed to providing customers with high-quality service and developing mutually beneficial relationships with all stakeholders. Founder and CEO Fred Smith says that the company tries "to make every FedEx experience outstanding," or what it calls its "Purple Promise."[4] The company promotes a "culture of safety" that manifests itself in measures such as comprehensive safe workplace education for employees, teams that propose improvements to safety measures, and first-rate equipment and technology designed to keep workers safe.[5] According to CEO Smith, FedEx's success depends on constant improvement: "There isn't a year that's gone by where we haven't invested an enormous amount into trying to make the service better."[6]

Google

Fortune magazine has twice named Google as the best company to work for in the United States. Its employees enjoy an open, communicative culture "designed to encourage interactions... and to spark conversation about work as well as play," and benefits such as flexible work hours and child care centers.[7] Google users are offered dozens of technological services and products, from a search engine to Gmail to a social networking service Google+, all dedicated to making customers' lives easier and more efficient. The company's list of "Ten things we know to be true" shows the basic principles it operates by, including "Focus on the user and all else will follow" and "You can make money without doing evil."

Harley-Davidson

More than a hundred years old, Harley-Davidson has survived multiple upheavals, ownership changes, quality problems, and intense global competition to establish itself as a uniquely American company with a range of classically designed motorcycles. The company's stated purpose is, "We fulfill dreams of personal freedom." It has cultivated a large and fanatically loyal customer following. The company offers new riders training classes that last 25 hours for a very reasonable fee. Harley-Davidson has become such an iconic brand that the company generates more than $40 million a year from licensing the brand to other companies. Seeking to expand beyond its traditional base of customers, the company is targeting young adults, women, Hispanics, and African-Americans for growth.

IBM

IBM manufactures and sells computer hardware and software, and offers infrastructure, hosting, and consulting services. It has nearly half a million employees in more than 170 countries. Its employees have earned Nobel Prizes, National Medals of Technology, National Medals of Science, and many other honors. IBM holds more patents than any other U.S. company, topping the list every year for the last 15 years. IBM's purpose is to use technology to help make the planet work better in areas such as healthcare, education, environmental causes, economic development, and other important areas. Employee satisfaction at IBM is very high, and the company is very well known for its emphasis on diversity. Over its long history, the company has proved not only its power and financial success, but also its continued service to purpose, people, and the planet.

J.M. Smucker

For more than 115 years, the J.M. Smucker Company has provided consumers with quality products that bring families together over meals. The Parents Television Council has repeatedly recognized the company for being the most responsible advertiser in the country. In 2004, it was ranked #1 on the "100 Best Companies to Work For" list by *Fortune* magazine. The strong ethical values of the company's founder are now the standards of the company. These include honesty, respect, trust, responsibility, and fairness. The company's commitment to all its stakeholders is articulated very clearly: "Our commitment to each other and to our constituents—consumers, customers, employees, suppliers, communities, and shareholders—has been a driving force behind our success in sustaining this purpose for more than a century."[8]

Marriott International

Marriott began in 1927 as a root beer stand, and today it is a globally successful company with more than 3,700 hotels in 74 countries. It aims to be the number-one hospitality company in the world. To achieve this goal, the company focuses on its core values: "putting people first, pursuing excellence, embracing change, acting with integrity, and serving our world."[9] It has received extensive recognition for its culture and treatment of employees. Former CEO J.W. "Bill" Marriott, Jr., believes that the four most important words a leader can say to employees are, "What do you think?" The company's "people-first" philosophy is summed up by Bill Marriott thusly: "Take good care of the employees, and they will in turn take good care of the customers who will return again and again... [this] leads to profit and market share gains and ultimately a successful business."[10]

MasterCard Worldwide

MasterCard is about money but knows that money is not everything. With its highly successful "Priceless" campaign ("There are some things that money can't buy. For everything else, there is MasterCard"), MasterCard acknowledges that the most important things in life cannot be bought. For everything else, the company works toward "A World Beyond Cash." It is recognized as an excellent place to work, ranks very highly in diversity and training, and scored 100 percent in 2012 on the Corporate Equality Index. With its values-driven approach to business, MasterCard has been steadily moving toward a leadership position in its industry.

Nordstrom

Nordstrom was founded as a small Seattle shoe store in 1901. Today, it is one of the largest and most successful upscale apparel retailers in the U.S., with 257 stores in 35 states, as well as a website with global reach. Its stated goals are "to provide outstanding service every day, one customer at a time," as well as to "work hard to make decisions in the best interest of our customers and those serving them."[11] Nordstrom has a reputation for strong customer service, including an easy return policy, and has an empowered and diverse workforce. It has a program called Nordstrom Cares, which seeks to support veterans and provide wellness programs for its employees.

Panera

The key ingredient to Panera Bread's company culture is caring: It cares about success, community, individuals, and its employees' futures. The company's care for employees is seen in the competitive compensation and benefits it offers. Panera's 1,708 bakery-cafes in 44 states and Ontario, Canada are all devoted to "delivering fresh, authentic artisan bread served in a warm environment by engaging associates."[12] Panera has the highest level of customer loyalty among quick-casual restaurants and is consistently at the top of rankings for best casual dining brand and customer service. Panera donates its entire stock of unsold bread and baked goods to local hunger relief agencies and charities. Its Panera Cares cafes aim to fight hunger by allowing customers to pay what they can.

Qualcomm

Founded in 1985, Qualcomm is a global semiconductor company that is a world leader in designing, manufacturing, and marketing digital telecommunications products. Qualcomm's goal is "to deliver the world's most innovative wireless solutions." According to Qualcomm, "innovation is more than something we do, it's who we are." Its efforts have allowed the wireless industry to grow at an extraordinary rate and make it one of the fastest growing industries in the world, transforming billions of lives in the process. Qualcomm is described as a "diverse, inclusive, safe and inspiring place to work."

Schlumberger

Oil services and equipment company Schlumberger has been named as one of the most innovative companies in the world by *Forbes*.[13] Its success can be partly credited to the quality of its services and technologies compared to its competitors as well as its strong global presence (more than two-thirds of its sales come from international markets).[14] The company is committed to providing customers with the highest quality service possible, as well as maintaining its strong reputation for integrity and fairness. The Schlumberger Foundation Faculty for the Future provides fellowships to women from developing countries to pursue graduate study in science and engineering.[15]

Southwest Airlines

Southwest seeks to do things differently from other airlines. The Southwest experience is built on simplicity and fun, from self-serve kiosks for flight check in to picking your own seat on the flight, to enjoying complimentary snacks and nonalcoholic drinks. Flight attendants and other employees are committed to providing top-quality customer service and unite around that goal, thus creating a fun environment for all. Employees can attend its University for People, which serves the mission of delivering personal, professional, and leadership development while also offering customized training.

Starbucks

Starbucks is the largest coffeehouse company in the world, with nearly 21,000 stores in 62 countries, including 13,279 in the United States. From its founding in 1971 as a Seattle coffee bean roaster and retailer, the company has expanded rapidly. Since 1987, Starbucks has opened on average two new stores every day. It has revenues over $13 billion and employs more than 150,000 people. Starbucks is more than just coffee, tea, and pastries; it is a gathering place. All Starbucks coffee is ethically sourced, and the company seeks to promote sustainably grown coffee through programs such as C.A.F.E. The company is considered an excellent place to work, with a culture of caring and respect for all employees regardless of their position. It enjoys tremendous loyalty from its customers.

T. Rowe Price

T. Rowe Price is a highly trusted name in the financial services/mutual fund industry. Its founder, T. Rowe Price, is considered the father of growth investing. He believed deeply that if clients flourished, the firm would also thrive. As a result of that belief, Price considered the clients' interests to be the most important aspect of his business. The company believes that social responsibility in the investment world means giving people the knowledge and skills toward making sound financial decisions for themselves and their families. It has developed online games for children to learn about savings and money. T. Rowe Price sees its purpose as providing its clients and ordinary people sound financial advice to help them attain a prosperous future.

United Parcel Service

UPS was founded in 1907 as a messenger company and is today the world's largest package delivery company and a leading provider of transportation and logistics services in more than 200 countries. The company is legendary for the efficiency of its operations and is recognized as an excellent place to work. It has a deep commitment to sustainability, with numerous innovations and accomplishments to its credit, and is listed on the Dow Jones Sustainability Index. Even as it grows, it has reduced its emission of greenhouse gases. It has an initiative to plant a million trees by the end of 2013. Its employees and their families donated 1.8 million volunteer hours in 2012, and the company's charitable contributions totaled nearly $100 million. The company has received numerous awards and recognitions, such as *Training Magazine* Top 125 for training, Harris Interactive Top 10 in Reputation, and #1 in the Delivery category of *Fortune*'s World's Most Admired Companies.

Walt Disney

Disney's basic core purpose is to make people happy. Its primary way of achieving this goal is through exceptional customer care and by creating content that has a positive message. The company keeps its parks spotless so that they're always "show-ready." Every customer is treated in a way that makes them feel important with "assertive friendliness" (actively approaching customers who look in need of help instead of waiting to be asked).[16] Its unique organizational culture is focused on four values: innovation, organizational support, education, and entertainment.[17] Every new park employee is sent to the "Disney Institute," which is well known for educating people about how to deliver exceptional service. This kind of investment in its employees pays off both in terms of the level of service provided and the feeling of community and pride inspired in employees.

Whole Foods Market

Founded in 1978 as "Safer Way," Whole Foods Market is committed to providing its customers with "the highest quality natural and organic products available." The company supports organic farming, uses diverse energy sources, and contributes at least five percent of its profits to charitable organizations. It has been on *Fortune* magazine's list of 100 Best Companies to Work For every year since 1998 (when the list was started). The company's core values include satisfying customers, supporting team members, creating wealth through profits and growth, supporting local and global communities, practicing environmental stewardship, and creating win-win partnerships with suppliers and stakeholders. Whole Foods Market has self-managed teams in each store that have the authority to make decisions regarding the day-to-day operations of the store. Its "Declaration of Interdependence" delineates the importance of all stakeholders in the operations of Whole Foods.

U.S. Private Firms of Endearment

Barry-Wehmiller

Barry-Wehmiller is a Midwestern industrial conglomerate with more than $1.5 billion in annual revenues. The company is notable for its unique focus on people-centric leadership and its emphasis on pursuing "disciplined operational strategies and purpose-driven growth."[18] It has developed a philosophy called "people-centric leadership" that it believes enables businesses and organizations to be a powerful force to change the world for the better. Barry-Wehmiller's Guiding Principles of Leadership focus on creating an environment based on trust, pride, positive communication, and fair treatment for employees.[19] CEO Robert Chapman's vision is to provide fulfillment and bring out the potential of the people in the company: "The purpose for which we come together is to build great people."[20]

Bon Appetit Management Co.

Bon Appetit Management Co. provides cafes and catering services to companies, universities, and other venues. It is known for its culinary expertise and its deep commitment to socially responsible practices. It offers healthy and nutritious food that is prepared from scratch using fresh, authentic, seasonal ingredients. The company was founded in 1987 with the idea of catering to the new breed of companies that are looking to offer better quality food to their employees. In 1999, the company embraced the idea of local sourcing for food that not only looked good but also tasted much better. This was the beginning of its "Farm to Fork" initiative and its commitment to a myriad of food-related sustainability issues. The company has received numerous awards and recognitions for its pioneering efforts in these directions. It has been named by the Princeton Review as the "No. 1 College Food Service in the Country" for several years. Bon Appetit Management Co. is owned by Compass Group plc, a publicly traded British multinational contract foodservice and support services company.

Clif Bar

Clif Bar produces high-energy food bars for athletes, hikers, and other active people. The company has steadily increased its use of organic ingredients and undertaken significant initiatives toward environmental sustainability. It follows a "five bottom lines" model: Sustaining our Business, our Brands, our People, our Community and the Planet. The company encourages its employees to engage in extensive community service, and provides great benefits to its employees, such as trainers, massages, and haircuts at work. Clif Bar has five core personal communication values: Create, Inspire, Connect, Own It, and Be Yourself. Over ten years, the company has grown at a compounded 17 percent, with employee turnover below one percent.[21]

Driscoll's

Driscoll's is committed to providing its customers the "freshest, best tasting, highest quality berries year-round."[22] To achieve this, it uses natural growing methods such as cross-pollination in order to ensure that its berries are "flavorful, attractive, resistant to disease, and hardy."[23] The company's Global Food Safety program, founded on the principles of Good Agriculture Practices laid down by the Food and Drug Administration, ensures that everything it grows is safe and nontoxic.[24] Driscoll's CEO J. Miles Reiter says that the company's mission is to "continually delight berry consumers through alignment with our customers and our berry growers."[25]

GSD&M Idea City

Advertising agency GSD&M has worked with clients such as Southwest Airlines, AT&T, and L.L. Bean. GSD&M believes in "Purpose-based branding." It views its own purpose as doing "whatever it takes to grow our clients' business so that they can fulfill their purpose." This purpose statement is supported by its six core values: freedom and responsibility, curiosity, winning, community, integrity, and restlessness. GSD&M has also helped make a difference through public service advertisements such as "I Am an American," after 9-11, and "Hope Is Stronger than a Hurricane," after Katrina. Its 1986 anti-littering slogan "Don't Mess with Texas" has become iconic, with a place in the Advertising Hall of Fame.[26] The company has also established a "Purpose Institute" to help client companies discover their own sense of higher purpose.

Honest Tea

Honest Tea strives to create tea that is pure, natural, and healthy. Its mission is to "create and promote great-tasting, truly healthy, organic beverages" and "to grow our business with the same honesty and integrity we use to craft our products, with sustainability and great taste for all" (from the Honest Tea "Mission Statement"). The company is committed to exemplary corporate citizenship, which it defines as living up to the ideals of honesty and integrity and maintaining strong relationships with its workers, suppliers, customers, and communities. In 2010, *The Huffington Post* named Honest Tea as one of eight "Revolutionary Socially Responsible Companies." Honest Tea donates to cancer research and has partnered with organizations such as Green America, the Organic Trade Association, and City Year.[27]

IDEO

With locations around the globe, design firm IDEO is considered one of the most innovative companies in the world. IDEO describes its approach as "human centered" and "design based." The company searches for ways to help people and companies by "uncovering latent needs, behaviors, and desires" and by helping to design "products, services, spaces, and interactive experiences." President and CEO Tim Brown describes the firm's approach of "design thinking" as "a human-centered approach to innovation" that integrates "the needs of people, the possibilities of technology, and the requirements for business success."[28]

Interstate Batteries

Interstate Batteries is a 62-year-old Dallas-based company that sells batteries but has a sense of purpose rooted in biblical principles such as servant leadership, empathy and compassion for all stakeholders, and embodying the Golden Rule. It is known for its commitment to providing "Outrageously Dependable" service to customers. The company has a very strong culture of service to its communities, largely grounded in the religious faith of its employees. It conducts extensive research to understand what its stakeholders need and is intently focused on eliminating trade-off thinking in the way it deals with its stakeholders. The company provides an excellent working environment. Employees receive generous healthcare benefits and are intensely loyal, with 90 percent believing that the company operates with strong values and ethics. Interstate has a very strong commitment to the environment. It recycles one and a half times what it sells, and is recognized as a company with leading expertise in scrap battery recycling and transportation, collecting used batteries from every county in the U.S.

Jordan's Furniture

One of the most successful furniture retailers in the country, Boston-based Jordan's Furniture offers customers a unique blend of shopping and entertainment it dubs "shoppertainment." Each of its stores has entertaining features such as IMAX theaters, a motion odyssey ride, Mardi Gras parades, acrobats, and the like. Instead of following the industry's standard practice of frequent sales and heavy promotional activity, Jordan's offers everyday "Underprices" so that customers do not have to wait for a sale. The company spends far less than its industry peers on marketing but has sales per square foot that are several times higher. It takes great care of its employees, has mutually beneficial partnerships with its suppliers, and is very active in the community. When it was purchased by Berkshire Hathaway in 1999, every employee received a gift of 50 cents for every hour they had ever worked at the company.

L.L. Bean

L.L. Bean has been selling high-quality apparel and outdoor equipment since it was founded in 1912. Founder Leon Leonwood Bean ran the company by his golden rule: "Sell good merchandise at a reasonable profit, treat your customers like human beings, and they will always come back for more." According to current President and CEO Chris McCormick, the emphasis on great customer service is still central to the company's success. L.L. Bean is committed to conducting its business "in an environmentally responsible manner, using the best practices in our industry" by focusing on packaging reduction, a corporate recycling program, alternative fuel use for transportation, energy conservation, and sustainable management of natural resources such as paper. L.L. Bean also supports a number of charitable organizations involved in outdoor recreation, health and human services, education, and arts and culture.[29]

Method

Childhood friends Adam Lowry and Eric Ryan began Method, their company of eco-friendly soaps and cleaning supplies, after noticing the boringness and monotony—as well as environmental unfriendliness—of most cleaning products. They focused on innovation and a "commitment to trying new things," designing bottles and packaging that are as unique-looking as they are functional.[30] They also committed to creating nontoxic, biodegradable products, with a goal "to make sure that every product we send out into the world is a little agent of environmental change, using safe and sustainable materials and manufactured responsibly."[31] Method's system of "marrying high-end design with environmental science" has brought it great success: By 2012, it had estimated revenues of more than $100 million.[32]

Millennium Oncology

Millennium: The Takeda Oncology Company is a biopharmaceutical company that, according to president Anna Protopapas, aims to "extend the frontier of cancer treatment." To that end, the company works toward a "high-powered level of scientific endeavor" that requires "personal determination on the part of our scientists and an intolerance of conventional wisdom." *Fortune* has named Millennium one of the 100 Best Companies to Work For, citing its excellent pay and benefit packages. The company's culture is based on genuine passion: Its employees view their work as more than just a job and are "driven by [a] passion for progress and innovation." Millennium provides grants to educational and healthcare programs and patient advocacy groups.[33]

New Balance

New Balance Athletic Shoes believes in "responsible leadership," which to the company is based on "giving back, moving the environment forward and encouraging people to act as catalysts and coaches." This company that "runs on its everyman (and everywoman) appeal" is also committed to domestic manufacturing: 25 percent of its shoes are made in the U.S., making it the only major athletic shoe manufacturer to do so.[34] New Balance places a high value on the safety of its workers and only works with suppliers who agree to follow its Supplier Code of Conduct. The company also tries to reduce its carbon footprint by using "environmentally preferred materials" such as 100-percent recycled paper for its shoeboxes. With its New Balance Foundation, the company focuses on causes such as preventing childhood obesity.[35]

Patagonia

Patagonia was founded by Yvon Chouinard as a small company that made equipment for outdoor activities such as climbing. Today, the company is still motivated by a love of the great outdoors; it actively works to help the environment by donating "time, services, and at least 1% of [its] sales to hundreds of grassroots environmental groups all over the world." In manufacturing its clothing, Patagonia uses recycled polyester and organic cotton, following its mission statement of "Build the best product, cause no unnecessary harm, use business to inspire and implement solutions to the environmental crisis."[36]

prAna

Named after the Sanskrit word meaning "vitality and breath," prAna's roots are in rock climbing and yoga. The company is now a leader in the active apparel sector. It is particularly focused on greater consciousness and sustainability in manufacturing practices. The company is phasing out rayon fabrics and increasing its share of organic cottons. prAna brings in Buddhist meditation teachers to help employees embody mindfulness in their daily tasks. One practice: A gong is rung at 3 p.m. every day followed by all employees observing a minute of silence. In 2012, prAna was recognized by Free2Work as being in the top one percent of brands for working conditions, traceability, and overall supply chain health, and the Global Sourcing Council recently recognized prAna with a Sustainable and Socially Responsible Award as the most innovative company for sustainability.[37]

REI

REI is an outdoor retail consumer co-op. REI Gear and Apparel, its line of outdoor gear and clothing, combines "quality, performance, style, and functionality" for the outdoors. REI supports the community by promoting outdoor volunteer projects and giving funding to nonprofit organizations. It is also committed to helping the environment through its Sustainable Operations program—described as "a targeted approach to reducing our environmental impact"—which focuses on issues such as reducing greenhouse gas emissions, recycling, and energy use. REI has been on *Fortune*'s list of 100 Best Companies to Work For several times.[38]

SAS Institute

SAS Institute is consistently rated as one of the very best places to work in the world. Employees receive numerous benefits, such as subsidized childcare, unlimited sick days, and a free health care center at the company's campus. The business analytics firm helps organizations "anticipate business opportunities, empower action and drive impact" through "advanced analytics" that lead to "fact-based decisions for undeniable bottom line impact." SAS is committed to its customers and thus enjoys strong customer loyalty. Its software is used by nearly 80 percent of *Fortune 500* companies. By focusing on its values—"approachable; customer-driven; swift and agile; innovative; trustworthy"—SAS helps "drive innovation and improve performance" for organizations around the world.[39]

SC Johnson

Founded in 1886, SC Johnson's brands of cleaning supplies are sold in more than 110 countries. The company has always been committed to integrity in its business, as seen in its philosophy "This We Believe," which names "the five groups of stakeholders to whom we are responsible and whose trust we have to earn": employees, consumers, the general public, neighbors and hosts, and the world community. SC Johnson continuously works to improve its products to make them as eco-friendly as possible using its Greenlist process, which helps it select "the best earth-responsible raw materials that maintain high performance and are cost-effective." When it comes to ingredients, SC Johnson is committed to transparency—customers can go to whatsinsidescjohnson.com for detailed information on what goes into its products. From 2006 to 2011, the company reduced its global greenhouse gas emissions by 26 percent.[40]

Stonyfield Yogurt

Stonyfield Yogurt began as a "farming school that taught sustainable agricultural practices." Founders Samuel Kaymen and Gary Hirshberg initially sold yogurt in order to fund the school, but they soon realized that a yogurt company could make more of a difference than their school could. Today, their business helps "support hundreds of family farms" and is committed to making healthy, organic products with no pesticides or chemical fertilizers. In 2010, Stonyfield introduced the Grower Sustainability Toolkit, which sets a high standard by looking "at how our suppliers treat their workers, their energy and water use, [and] equity issues."[41] The company has won many awards, both for its yogurt and for its environmental work. Since 1993, its Profits for the Planet charity has donated $15 million to environmental organizations. Everything it does is focused on furthering their commitment of "healthy food, healthy people, a healthy planet, and healthy business."[42]

TDIndustries

One of the factors that sets TDIndustries apart from its competitors is its focus on its employees, or partners. This is one reason why the company has regularly been on *Fortune's* list of Best Companies to Work For; in 2011, the magazine wrote, "Most construction companies hire workers on a job-by-job basis. Not TDIndustries, an employee-owned company that retains its workers as full-time employees, offering a complete range of benefits."[43] In operating its business, TDIndustries abides by the following values: concern for and belief in individual human beings; valuing individual differences; honesty; building trusting relationships; fairness; responsible behavior; and high standards of business ethics.[44] The company believes that leaders and partners must listen to and respect each other in order for the company to run smoothly. TDIndustries' commitment to taking care of its employees has earned it one of the best safety records in the industry.

The Container Store

Hourly employees at The Container Store earn approximately double the industry standard, which is one of the reasons it is consistently listed as one of the best companies to work for. The company was founded on fundamental values—which it calls Foundation Principles—that focus on "treating employees, customers and vendors with respect and dignity." Other foundation principles include its philosophy that "1 great person = 3 good people," which leads the company to be highly selective in its hiring and to treat its employees very well, which in turn leads to commitment and loyalty to the company. The Container Store also believes that "Communication is leadership" and that its focus on "open, honest, transparent, and thorough" communication is key to running a successful business. When it comes to serving customers, The Container Store strives to provide the "best selection, service, and price." It seeks to maintain an "air of excitement" in its stores among both employees and customers.[45]

The Motley Fool

Financial services company The Motley Fool is "dedicated to building the world's greatest investment community." It does this by "[championing] shareholder value and [advocating] tirelessly for the individual investor." The company's core values include collaboration, innovation, fun, honesty, and competitiveness. The Motley Fool reaches out to customers through its syndicated weekly newspaper column, a national radio program, and books, several of which have been bestsellers. The culture at The Motley Fool is "as irreverent as our name," and it's one in which its employees "have the freedom to follow their passion every day." Its "Foolanthropy" provides support to charitable efforts in financial education and advocacy, so that they can "help people take control of their financial lives" and invest better.[46]

Timberland

Outdoor apparel and footwear company Timberland was founded on "a core belief that business can create positive impact in the world." The company believes in the importance of corporate citizenship and integrating "personal values and mission into the workday."[47] To this end, it focuses mainly on "people, value, purpose, and passion," which means making sure its employees are happy, engaged, and inspired. The company strives to treat every one of its employees as an individual—or as former CEO Jeffrey Swartz put it, "probing for the human inside the shell."[48] Timberland's employee volunteer program gives staff members an annual benefit of up to 20 (for part-time workers) to 40 (for full-time workers) hours of paid community service. Its Sustainable Living Environment program helps make sure the factory workers and managers manufacturing its supplies are able to meet their basic living needs.[49]

TOMS

When it was created in 2006, TOMS quickly became known for its inspired One for One program: Every time TOMS sells a pair of shoes, it donates a pair to a child in need. By spring 2013, the company had donated 10 million pairs of shoes in more than 60 countries. Every time it sells a pair of eyewear, part of the profit goes toward providing prescription glasses and medical treatments for people in developing countries. Since 2011, TOMS has helped restore sight to 150,000 people. Founder Blake Mycoskie says the company allows him to blend his passions of "travel, hands-on helping, and creative entrepreneurism."[50] TOMS "works hard to integrate sustainable and responsible practices into all that they do"; to this end, the company offers shoes made of sustainable and vegan materials (such as natural hemp, organic cotton, and recycled polyester) and shoeboxes made from 80 percent recycled material.[51]

Trader Joe's

Trader Joe's has elevated grocery shopping "from a chore to a cultural experience."[52] It stands out from other grocery stores by embracing a "non-conventional approach and attitude": unique product selections; clever, handmade signs; a funny, engaging monthly newsletter; and no sales—instead, it keeps prices consistently low by buying directly from suppliers when possible.[53] Perhaps most important, the company encourages and listens to feedback from customers. For suppliers, Trader Joe's is a "dream account: It pays on time and doesn't mess with extra charges... that traditional supermarkets charge suppliers."[54] According to the company, the real secret to its success is its workers, and it maintains an atmosphere in which employees feel respected and nurtured: "We cannot grow without providing our crew with an environment that allows them the freedom to be themselves so they have the ability to be their best."[55] As a result, Trader Joe's employees are friendly and seem to enjoy what they do, which customers pick up on. The company has high levels of employee loyalty and low levels of turnover.

Union Square Hospitality Group

Union Square Hospitality Group owns many popular, critically praised restaurants that together have won 25 James Beard awards (sometimes called the "Oscars of the food industry"). Its company philosophy is based on the concept of "Enlightened Hospitality," which it defines as a "virtuous cycle that perpetuates positive energy." The idea is that creating a "warm-and-fuzzy" energy within the company will then extend outward to "patrons, the community, suppliers, and, ultimately, [the] company's backers."[56] The idea of "employees first" is crucial to this method. In 2010, the company started Hospitality Quotient, a consulting business aimed at spreading the philosophies and methods that have made it so successful: "the art of making people feel important and cared for."[57] USHG has also "dedicated time and resources to supporting hunger relief initiatives and beautifying our urban environments, among many other causes."[58]

USAA

USAA is a provider of financial services for the military community. Its mission is to "facilitate the financial security of its members, associates, and their families." It was founded on the values of "service, loyalty, honesty and integrity." Its nonprofit organization, The USAA Educational Foundation, helps consumers by "providing information on financial management, safety concerns and significant life events." The company is also environmentally conscious and committed to issues such as energy conservation, recycling, paper reduction, and water consumption reduction. It donates to the charity United Way to support programs that provide services for children and families, veterans, and senior citizens.[59]

Wegmans

One of the most beloved food retailers in the U.S., Wegmans strives to create an atmosphere in which "caring about respecting our people is the priority." The company emphasizes high standards, making a difference, respect, and empowerment. It believes that in order to serve customers as well as it can, it must fulfill the needs of its employees first. It offers generous benefits to part-time and full-time employees and maintains an environment that supports all employees. Compared to most other supermarkets, Wegmans stores are larger and carry a much wider selection (more than 70,000 products versus the supermarket average of around 40,000). Wegmans gives back to the community through food bank donations, busing services for senior citizens, and healthy cooking classes for children.[60]

WL Gore

Technology and manufacturing company WL Gore has a uniquely egalitarian culture. There are very few traditional job titles and no "bosses" in the conventional sense.[61] Its culture is team based and encourages individual initiative and potential. Employees become shareholders after one year, giving them a sense of ownership and self-direction. The company is known for creating innovative, technological solutions in electronics, fabrics, industrial, and medical products. Gore has strong Standards of Ethical Conduct. It has used its technology to create products that help solve environmental issues such as alternative energy, waste management, and air filtration.[62]

Non-U.S. Companies

BMW (Germany)

One of the most admired and successful car companies in the world, BMW aspires to produce "the ultimate driving machines." The company is noteworthy for its industry-leading approach to environmental sustainability. In June 2012, BMW was named the #1 most reputable company in the world by Forbes.com based on factors such as "people's willingness to buy, recommend, work for, and invest in a company, driven 60 percent by their perceptions of the company and only 40 percent by their perceptions of their products."[63]

Cipla (India)

Cipla was established in 1935 with the vision of making India self-reliant and self-sufficient in healthcare. Today, it is one of the world's largest generic pharmaceutical companies, with a presence in more than 170 countries. Renowned for making affordable, world-class medicines that meet the needs of patients across therapies, Cipla also offers services such as consulting, commissioning, plant engineering, and technical know-how transfer and support. It is particularly known for its revolutionary impact on the treatment of AIDS patients in Africa and across the world, bringing much-needed affordability to prohibitively expensive drugs.

FabIndia (India)

FabIndia is an Indian retail company that specializes in cultivating traditional apparel and crafts. It has 137 stores in India and additional stores in 33 countries. The company was founded "with the strong belief that there was a need for a vehicle for marketing the vast and diverse craft traditions of India and thereby help fulfill the need to provide and sustain employment." The company combines contemporary designs with indigenous craft techniques to create attractive and affordable products that appeal to today's consumers.[64]

FEMSA (Mexico)

FEMSA is the largest beverage company in Mexico and in Latin America as well as the largest independent Coca-Cola bottler in the world. It also runs a large chain of convenience stores in Mexico. The company has long been recognized for its strong management and humanist culture that is "rooted in a humanist philosophy that recognizes that there is no economic consideration that stands above human dignity." It has created a structured human resources platform, called the "Internal Value Proposition for Employees," that has eight levels: financial security, health and welfare, secure environment, enablement, freedom to act, recognition, development, and transcendence.[65]

Gemalto (France)

Gemalto is a leading company in the domain of digital security, providing software applications, secure personal devices such as smart cards and tokens, as well as managed services. The company "brings trust and convenience to the digital world" giving people the "security to be free." As CEO Olivier Piou has stated, "Bringing trust and convenience to this new world is the contribution we've taken upon ourselves to deliver. It's a noble social role."[66]

Honda (Japan)

Honda is a leading car manufacturer and the world's leading maker of motorcycles. It is also the world's largest producer of internal combustion engines. The company has always been known for its strong engineering skills and tradition of innovation. Honda has an excellent track record of satisfying all its stakeholders. It is an excellent place to work with an open working culture, enjoys great customer satisfaction and loyalty, and is very highly regarded for its supplier relations.

IKEA (Sweden)

This Swedish company is the world's largest furniture retailer, with more than $38 billion in annual revenues and 332 stores in 38 countries. The company has revolutionized its industry, offering stylishly designed products at highly attractive prices. It offers a unique shopping experience, with onsite childcare and dining options. The company is considered a very good place to work, and has a strong record of environmental stewardship.

Inditex (Spain)

Inditex is a Spanish clothing manufacturing and retailing company with more than 6,000 stores worldwide, operating under brands such as Zara and Massimo Dutti. It designs and produces almost all of its products, and ships them directly to stores twice a week, thus keeping very current with fashion trends. In 2001, the company adopted a "social strategy" that includes dialogues with all key stakeholders, an internal code of conduct, and social audits of all suppliers.

Mahindra & Mahindra (India)

Mahindra & Mahindra has a range of businesses, from automobiles to vacation resorts. The businesses are united by a common purpose—to enable people to rise. Its motivation comes from its core purpose, expressed as "We will challenge conventional thinking and innovatively use all our resources to drive positive change in the lives of our stakeholders and communities across the world, to enable them to rise."[67]

Marico (India)

Marico is an innovative and highly purposeful Indian consumer products company. The company has a flat organizational structure, with just five levels between the CEO and frontline employees. Marico is focused on "transforming the lives of all stakeholders, be it our suppliers, farmers, distributors or shareholders, by helping them maximize their true potential."[68] A great example of their approach is the Saffola brand of cooking oil and other products, which are all based on the idea of "Heart Care" and have adopted the higher purpose of reducing the incidence of heart disease in India.

Novo Nordisk (Denmark)

Novo Nordisk is a 90-year-old global pharmaceutical company headquartered in Denmark whose overriding purpose is to "defeat diabetes," which includes preventing, treating, and ultimately curing the disease. It has offices in 76 countries and markets its products in more than 180 countries. The company is renowned for its commitment to ethics and quality, and a culture built on respect and accountability. Novo Nordisk was an early adopter of the "Triple Bottom Line" approach to business, and has striven to create value for all its stakeholders. The "Novo Nordisk Way" describes "who we are, where we want to go and how we work."[69] The company uses senior employees as "facilitators" who travel around the world looking at its operations to ensure that they adhere to the "Novo Nordisk Way" and to share best practices across the company.

POSCO (South Korea)

The most admired metals company in the world according to *Fortune* magazine, POSCO is one of the largest, most efficient, and most environmentally friendly steel companies in the world. The company has embraced the principles of stakeholder-based management, seeking to create value and being endearing with all of them. It is particularly noteworthy for the numerous ways in which it helps its suppliers become stronger over time. The company has created a significantly better method for producing steel that greatly lowers energy use and pollution and plans to share the technology with other companies in the global steel industry.

TCS (India)

Part of the highly admired Tata Group of India, Tata Consultancy Services is the largest Indian company by market capitalization. It has 285,000 employees and operates in 44 countries around the world, providing information technology services, solutions, and consulting. It has been recognized by *Forbes* as one of the World's Most Innovative Companies. Its values and culture derive from the legendary "Tata Way," which ensures a high level of integrity, respect for all individuals, and a strong commitment to the communities in which it operates.

Toyota (Japan)

The largest automobile manufacturer in the world, Toyota is renowned for its manufacturing methods and for producing efficient, reliable, and durable cars. Its Prius model has taken the lead in popularizing highly efficient hybrid cars. The company's sterling reputation for quality slipped somewhat in recent years as it started to chase market share goals, but by all indications it has corrected those problems and is now back to its values-driven way of operating.

Unilever (UK)

On any given day, two billion people worldwide use Unilever products. The company recognizes that customers are inviting it into their homes and lives when choosing Unilever brands. Unilever has always believed in the power of its brands to improve the quality of people's lives and in doing the right thing. Under the leadership of CEO Paul Polman, Unilever recognizes that global challenges such as poverty, access to water, and environmental degradation concern us all and is taking tangible steps to address each. Considering the wider impact of its actions is embedded in its values and is a fundamental part of the company's identity.

Endnotes

1. Kesmodel, David. "Revolutionizing American Beer." *The Wall Street Journal*, Apr. 19, 2010.

2. The Boston Beer Company, Investor Relations; About Us, http://www.bostonbeer.com/phoenix.zhtml?c=69432&p=irol-homeprofile (accessed April 19, 2013).

3. "On the Record: FedEx CEO Frederick W. Smith." *SFGate*. San Francisco Chronicle, Feb. 22, 2009.

4. Ibid.

5. Ibid.

6. Dumaine, Brian. "FedEx CEO Fred Smith on... everything." *CNNMoney*. CNN, May 11, 2012.

7. Google.com, "Our culture."

8. Company website.

9. Marriott company website.

10. Schawbel, Dan. "J. W. Marriott Jr.: From Root Beer Stand to Global Hotel Company." *Forbes*, Feb. 4, 2013.

11. retailindustry.about.com.

12. Panera.com: Our History.

13. "Schlumberger on the Forbes World's Most Innovative Companies List." *Forbes*, May 2013.

14. Sreekumar, Arjun. "Why Schlumberger's Profits Soared." *Fool.com*. The Motley Fool, 22 Oct. 2013.

15. Ibid.

16. Gallo, Carmine. "Customer Service the Disney Way." *Forbes*, 14 Apr. 2011.

17. Lipp, Doug. "The Four Circumstances Driving Disney's Organizational Culture." *CommPRO.biz*. N.p., 10 Apr. 2013.

18. Barry-Wehmiller company website.

19. Ibid.

20. Marchwinski, Chet. "Robert Chapman, Chairman and CEO of Barry-Wehmiller Companies, Inc: "Guiding Principles of Leadership"" *Lean.org*. Lean Enterprise Institute, n.d.

21. We would like to thank Frank Polleti for assistance with this profile.

22. Driscoll's company website.

23. Ibid.

24. Ibid.

25. "Driscoll Announces Organizational Changes." *The Produce News*. N.p., n.d.

26. Company website.

27. Company website.

28. Company website.

29. Company website.

30. Adler, Carlye. "Method Home Cleans Up With Style and (Toxic-Free) Substance." *Time*, May 3, 2011.

31. Company website.

32. White, Martha. "Eric Ryan, Co-Founder of Method." *Slate Magazine*, July 18, 2011.

33. Company website.

34. Yahoo Finance Company profile.

35. Company website.

36. Company website.

37. We would like to thank Frank Polleti for assistance with this profile.

38. Company website.

39. Company website.

40. Company website.

41. Kaplan, Melanie D.G. "Stonyfield Farm CEO: How an Organic Yogurt Business Can Scale." *SmartPlanet*. CBS Interactive, 17 May 2010.

42. Company website.

43. *Fortune*, "Best Companies to Work For 2011."

44. Company website.

45. Company website.

46. Company website.

47. Bonamici, Kate. "TIMBERLAND: THE SHOE-IN." *CNNMoney*, 23 Jan. 2006.

48. Bryant, Adam. "What Makes You Roar? Jeffrey Swartz Wants to Know." *The New York Times*, Dec. 19, 2009.

49. Company website.

50. Bates, Karen Grigsby. "'Soul Mates': Shoe Entrepreneur Finds Love in Giving." *NPR*, Nov. 26, 2010.

51. Company website.

52. Kowitt, Beth. "Inside the Secret World of Trader Joe's." *CNNMoney*, Aug. 23, 2010.

53. Llopis, Glenn. "Why Trader Joe's Stands Out From All the Rest in the Grocery Business." *Forbes*, Sept. 5, 2011.

54. Kowitt, Beth. "Inside the Secret World of Trader Joe's." *CNNMoney*, Aug. 23, 2010.

55. Lewis, Len. "Fostering a Loyal Workforce at Trader Joe's." *Workforce*, June 2, 2005.

56. Cardwell, Diane. "Spreading His Gospel of Warm and Fuzzy." *The New York Times*, Apr. 23, 2010.

57. *Op. cit.*

58. Company website.

59. Company website.

60. Company website.

61. *Fortune*, "100 Best Companies to Work For 2012."

62. Company website.

63. Smith, Jacquelyn. "The World's Most Reputable Companies." Forbes.com, June 7, 2012.

64. Company website.

65. Company website.

66. Company website.

67. Company website.

68. Company website.

69. http://www.novonordisk.com/about_us/novo_nordisk_way/nnway_about.asp.

Appendix B————

Interview with Rick Frazier

Acknowledging the contributions and support received from friends and colleagues was one of the most satisfying writing tasks for the authors of *Firms of Endearment*. At about the time the book was published, three of those contributors, Rick Frazier, Jeff Cherry, and Peter Derby, decided to devote themselves to the idea of creating investment portfolios composed of firms guided by a multi-stakeholder operating system, or "firms of endearment." In this interview with Raj Sisodia, Rick Frazier, founding partner of Concinnity Advisors, LP, provides an update on the status of their journey.

You have been at this for quite some time, Rick, so your commitment can hardly be questioned. Are you also being fueled by a higher purpose?

It's been about six years now, and along the way we faced a good number of challenges. So it probably would have been impossible to stay the course if we didn't feel purposeful in creating this business. A good deal of our staying power came from our belief that capitalism is the bedrock for reducing poverty and increasing living standards. So we think it's critical for capitalism to be practiced in a way that makes it more attractive and more defendable. And companies guided by a multi-stakeholder operating system are setting the example. They're showing that you *can* create wealth for shareholders without neglecting other stakeholders. Our objective is to prove that these companies are worthy of greater investor support.

So you set out to create investment products that would allow investors to provide that support.

That's right. We've always envisioned the possibility of a virtuous cycle of sorts whereby companies realize lower capital costs as more investors reward them for operating this way, which in turn should influence more companies to practice capitalism in this manner. And when I say investors I mean institutional investors, since we think they have more capacity to change capitalism's reward system than any other stakeholder.

How confident are you that this type of virtuous cycle will materialize?

Well, on the corporate side of the equation we're convinced that a multi-stakeholder operating system is becoming less of an option. All the market forces that make this so, many of which were described in *Firms of Endearment*, are just too powerful to ignore. Clearly, what we expect from the companies we buy from, work for, and let operate in our communities is changing. So this new marketplace reality is requiring companies to adopt a multi-stakeholder operating system ahead of any widespread investor demand that they do so.

But obviously the pace of adoption would accelerate if investors provided more capital to firms that do and less to those that don't. And maybe there's cause for some optimism on this front in light of the whole socially responsible and better governance movement. But understandably, most institutional investors still need to care more about returns than anything else.

So at the end of the day investors need strong evidence that they'll be rewarded if they invest in companies guided by a multi-stakeholder operating system. Our job is to show they don't have to make a trade-off—that they can make the returns they need and also influence the way capitalism is practiced. If we do that, the virtuous cycle we envision has a chance.

How good do the returns need to be? Will you be held to a higher standard since you're trying something new?

I think we need to be among the top performing actively managed funds, to be taken seriously. I don't know if we'll be held to a higher standard. I suppose we might by those who view our investment approach as a bit unconventional.

How long have you actually been investing and what is your return performance?

We've been investing in U.S. companies for more than three years now and our performance is about where we think it needs to be. We've always felt confident that a multi-stakeholder operating system ultimately boosts bottom-line financial performance. We've seen it first hand in our previous work as consultants. So we didn't think it was a big leap to expect stock prices to eventually track with that performance. And of course the long-term returns of companies featured in *Firms of Endearment* provided more fodder for creating an investment strategy based on that assumption.

How many U.S. public companies do you think are truly guided by a multi-stakeholder operating system?

We don't know for sure since we haven't evaluated all U.S. companies—and probably never will. Your use of the word "truly" is the key, though. If you plucked a random sample of 50 names from the S&P 500 and read each of their websites, you might conclude that as many as half or more of them have adopted it. My guess is that only around five percent are really achieving the requisite concinnity, though.

We used the term *concinnity* in the book. Is that why you selected it as the name of your firm?

Yes, we shamelessly confiscated it. It's a great word, and I didn't know what it meant until I saw it defined in the book. We chose it because it reflects what multi-stakeholder-minded companies achieve and it's also descriptive of our integrative research process.

How does your approach differ from socially responsible investing?

Socially responsible investing comes in many forms. I think we line up well with most SRI-minded investors. Our basic premise is that regardless of how you define SRI, the likelihood that companies will meet the expectations embedded in that definition largely depends on whether they're guided by a multi-stakeholder operating system.

How much emphasis do you place on a company's philanthropic actions?

We take a neutral position. Philanthropy is grounded in the notion of giving something back, which implies you took something in the first place. We're more interested in companies that add value for all stakeholders as a matter of course. But as it turns out, it's rare to find a company operating with a multi-stakeholder mindset that doesn't also have a strong charitable bent. As I recall, you made a similar observation in *Firms of Endearment*.

We like the way Peter Drucker separated social responsibilities into social impacts, or what business *does* to society, and social problems, or what business can *do* for society. Addressing or eliminating negative social impacts is something all businesses should try to do. Our take is that companies guided by a multi-stakeholder operating system are simply more likely to do that. We don't penalize companies for choosing not to address a social problem, but we do penalize them for not addressing social impacts.

You mentioned that you faced a number of challenges on this journey. What was the greatest challenge you needed to overcome?

That's difficult to answer. Several choices come to mind, not the least of which was starting this venture just as the financial crisis was unfolding. But I'd have to say it was the development of the investment research process. It was an exercise in humility that spanned a couple of years.

I'm surprised to hear this was such a challenge. You're one of the most qualified people I know when it comes to assessing the multi-stakeholder model. What made it so difficult?

Well, our whole accounting and reporting apparatus is designed to give investors information about tangible assets. Which is really crazy when you think about it since intangible assets account for 80 percent of the market cap of S&P 500 companies. And nearly everything we needed to evaluate was an intangible asset. So we had to build an information system from scratch.

But at least you knew what you wanted to look for, right?

Yes, that's right. And that was also part of the problem. We knew precisely what to look for as a result of our prior consulting experiences when we could thoroughly assess on-the-ground realties within companies. How finely tuned the stakeholder listening systems were. What the culture was like. How employees felt about working there. The quality of relationships with customers and suppliers and so on. So that was our ideal benchmark, and it was a very high bar.

The challenge was how can we assess what's really happening inside these companies without actually being inside? We felt blind and ill equipped at first, but you're right. Since we were never confused about what to look for, we felt qualified to at least have a go at it. A couple years later we finally felt we had something that allowed us to select companies with some measure of confidence.

Can you describe that something without giving away too much of your secret sauce?

Our research process is basically a proxy for no longer being able to assess a company from the inside. But that doesn't mean every piece of information we use is a proxy in and of itself. For example, we don't use proxies for determining how customers feel about a company. We can still determine that directly as outsiders. On the other hand, our analysis of employee sentiment does require proxies, as does our analysis of corporate culture.

I'll quickly give you an outline of what we do. The first stage is a screen that produces a universe of companies that seem worthy of further investigation. We use about 40 different information sources that recognize companies for achieving certain outcomes that we expect from firms guided by a multi-stakeholder operating system. A couple of examples are firms recognized as being ethically sound or great places to work. The companies receiving the highest scores based on our weighting system are then evaluated in our composite analysis.

The composite analysis incorporates data, ratings, and insights from about 20 different specialists who provide assessments associated with specific stakeholders. It also integrates ESG (Environmental, Societal, Governance) ratings from multiple ESG ratings providers. In a nutshell, the main blocks of analysis are culture, supplier relationships, employee relationships, customer relationships, community relationships, intangible asset management, management integrity, and fundamental analysis. I'm skipping over a lot of detail here. It would be too much territory to cover if I started diving in.

So the composite analysis views each company through a number of lenses, and a company needs to look pretty good across all those areas to make it into the portfolio. The finalists are then poured into a quantitative model for portfolio construction and risk management. And then the whole process is repeated every year.

Since you use a quantitative model, does that mean you're offering a quantitative investment product?

I think David [Wolfe] said it best when he described it as more of a whole-brained investment strategy. About 70 percent of our performance is attributable to the names selected by the research process and about 30 percent is due to quantitative portfolio management techniques. David always cautioned us to not let the quantitative drive out the qualitative—especially the pesky human-driven intangibles. He kept urging us to hold on to a more holistic view, and I think we have.

But it wasn't easy. Wall Street overall has a decidedly left-brained bent—quant jocks especially. So when you start talking about intangible investment criteria like culture, customer loyalty, employee commitment, corporate reputation, let alone values and trust, you don't exactly ooze with credibility in their eyes. But I think this is changing.

Are you suggesting Wall Street is becoming more right-brained? I must have missed that development.

Not by leaps and bounds and certainly not quickly, but there are some telltale signs of a subtle shift. To some degree I think it's happening out of necessity. I think the credit crisis exposed the limitations of overreliance on quantitative techniques. Corporate risk managers are now starting to explore how they can combine qualitative components with quantitative techniques to better manage risk. They may even be starting to wonder whether organizational culture is important to the mix. One could argue they're a little late to that party, right?

Another sign is that more quantitative investment analysts are looking at how to integrate intangible indicators with quantitative investment techniques. Again, I think this is born from necessity. They've all been slicing and dicing the same 20 percent pile of tangible asset information for a very long time. At this point it seems like they're all trying to squeeze alpha blood from the same information rock ("alpha" in investing terms simply means the performance of an investment relative to a benchmark, such as the S&P 500). Meanwhile, the intangible asset information pile that makes up about 80 percent of corporate value is still largely virgin soil.

So your analysis is mostly focused on the 80 percent?

Yes, mostly, and that's because a multi-stakeholder operating system is by its very nature an intangible asset. And it's also because we recognize that corporate financial performance and economic prosperity increasingly come from intangible assets.

But by no means do we claim to have completely cracked the intangible asset code. The most we dare say is that we're at least seeing shapes and shadows in areas that most analysts overlook entirely. We look at financial information as well, but only after a company has been qualified as multi-stakeholder proficient.

What sets us apart, I think, is that regardless of how attractive a company's financial metrics or ratios might be, it won't necessarily make our cut because it also matters to us how they achieve it. Is it at the expense of other stakeholders? Is it based more on becoming expert at the quarterly earnings game? Are they sacrificing long-term performance on the altar of short-term earnings?

We've never really understood why qualitative factors aren't considered part and parcel of fundamental analysis. I mean, what could be more fundamental to a company's ability to create future cash flow than customers who keep buying or employees who give their best effort? This is the upstream stuff that has more leading indicator potential. The financials are always laggards by comparison.

You mentioned that the research process begins anew or is refreshed every year. I assume this means some companies could be dropped from your portfolio after a year. Does this mean in some cases you're a short-term investor?

Keep in mind that hanging on to a stock for a year these days means you're a long-term investor. The bulk of our names have been in the portfolio from the very beginning. But they all need to qualify again each year.

We're a long-term investor so long as a company continues to demonstrate a commitment to the multi-stakeholder operating system. We do have some annual turnover, mostly because every year we increase the number of names that get put through the composite analysis. This means we're capturing some new names that score better in the composite analysis than previous years' names. And some names keep getting better each year to the point where one year they might leap past some names currently in our portfolio.

How much does executive compensation influence your view of whether management will safeguard the long-term health of the business?

We do incorporate opinions from specialists who evaluate executive compensation. But in our view, once you get past the likes of Whole Foods, Costco, and a handful of other exemplars on this issue, there's a big gap and then everybody else pretty much lands in the same bucket.

Most of the calls to fix executive compensation seem like tweaking at the margins to me. Until we get serious about ditching compensation systems that are mostly driven by short-term earnings and stock prices, we shouldn't expect much to change. I agree with those who think there's a fundamental flaw with the theory that underlies today's compensation systems. I know former IBM CEO Sam Palmisano recently argued as much in an interview he did with Michael Useem at Wharton. And Roger Martin (Dean, Rotman School of Management, University of Toronto) has been making this case for at least a decade. And Sumantra Ghoshal soundly discredited corporate governance based on agency theory in a paper you sent to me several years ago.

That paper was "Bad Management Theories Are Destroying Good Management Practices."

That's right. The point is that some very smart people have weighed in on this, but chances are we'll be living with what's now in place for quite some time. We'll see. But let's face it, everybody knows something is way out of whack when a CEO makes more in a day than the average worker makes in a year.

In *Firms of Endearment* we made an effort to profile companies that find a way to avoid layoffs during downturns. In one of our previous phone discussions you mentioned the impressive record of SAS Institute for avoiding layoffs. Do you evaluate a company's layoff history or policies in your analysis?

I loved the Southwest Airlines example in the book, where you describe how it was the only major airline that didn't lay people off immediately after 9-11. Let's go back to that virtuous cycle we discussed earlier. What if institutional investors started gobbling up Southwest stock after learning the company was determined not to lay people off. That was a great opportunity to send a message that if you take a long-term view, you'll be rewarded with lower capital costs. If Southwest's stock price held up while all other airlines announcing layoffs slid lower, that would have sent a powerful message. Usually, the opposite happens; the market bids up companies that announce large layoffs. And here's the thing: The more workers an airline laid off, the longer it took for their customers to return. But even now you can find analysts grumbling that Southwest pays people too much... that their labor unit costs are too high.

So, look, on the one hand we do seek out executives who appear to take a long-term, holistic view of the enterprise and its place in society. But if we only invested in companies that never lay people off, we wouldn't have much to choose from. We realize there are times when survival depends on cutting back. But when customers are temporarily unable to pay during a downturn, we might view a layoff as shortsighted and not worth the price of the pain it inflicts. But above all, the main thing we look for is whether leaders share in the hardship of layoffs.

I remember being in Pittsburgh about 15 or 20 years ago and reading a newspaper article about the CEO of Heinz paying millions for a diamond ring that he bought for his wife. In another section of the paper was an announcement of layoffs at one of the Heinz plants. I'll never forget that. I mean 19- and 20-year-old corporals implicitly understand that no one will respect them unless they lead by sharing in the hardship. Why is this simple truth so difficult to understand for a 50-year-old executive with above-average intelligence, a couple of degrees, and years of experience?

Index

Numbers

3M, 223

20 percent time, Google, 72

A

Adidas, 93
  Rule Makers, 192
Adobe Systems, 223-224
Age of Empowerment, xxiv-xxv
Age of Knowledge, xxv-xxvii
Age of Transcendence, xxii, xxvii-xxx,
  3, 62, 220
aging populations, 30-31
airline industry, 127-128
alchemy, 193
aligning stakeholders' interests,
  193-195
  Honda Motor Co., 196
alignment, 216
Allen, George, 126
Altria, 15
Amazon.com, 224
  culture of fun, 185-186
American Airlines, 183
American Messenger Company
  (AMC), 205
Amul Dairy Products, 22
Argroindustrias Unidas de Mexico
  S.A. (AMSA), 119
Austin, James, 147
Autodesk, 224
Autry, James, 5

B

balance, 71-74
Barrett, Colleen, 77, 183
  caring culture, 185
Barrett, Richard, 30
Barry-Wehmiller, 77, 235
Bean, Leon Leonwood, 99, 205
Beckham, David, 93
Bell, Alexander Graham, xxv
belonging, culture, 184
Benioff, Marc, 30
Berry, Len, 71
Best Partner (BP) program, Honda
  Motor Co., 134
beta, 115
Bezos, Jeff, 185-186
blending work and play,
  characteristics of FoEs, 199-201
BLICC (Business Leaders' Initiative
  on Climate Change), 150
BMW, 247
  connecting top to bottom, 79
  self-organizing systems, 52
  sustainability, 151
  trust culture, 180
Body Shop, 57
Bon Appetit Management Co., 235
bonding, investors, employees, and
  customers, 112-113
borderline personality disorder
  (BPD), 125
Boston Beer Company, 225

BP (Best Partner), Honda Motor Co., 196
BPD (borderline personality disorder), 125
breaking traditional trade-offs, 195-197
Bright Smiles, Bright Futures program (Colgate-Palmolive), 227
Brin, Sergey, 77
Brown, Tim, 237
Buffet, Warren, 109
Burke, James, 54
business, 27-28
    culture, 28-29
Business Leaders' Initiative on Climate Change (BLICC), 150
business values, versus human values, 142-144

C

C.A.F.E. (Coffee and Farmer Equity) Practices, 120-121
calculating, returns, 114
callings, 62
Campbell's Soup, 97
Canon, kyosei, 158-160
capitalism, 3, 33, 42, 138
    Conscious Capitalism, 33
    natural capitalism, 52
    self-actualization, 29-34
    social transformation, 4
career ladders, 65
Caregivers, 200
caring culture, 184-185
CarMax, 225
    career ladders, 65
Carmeron, Kim, 127
Carnegie, Andrew, 207
Casey, James, 205
CAT (Community Action Team), Honda Motor Co., 147
celebrations, 77
certainties, 132

Chapman, Bob, 77, 235
characteristics of
    culture, 179
        belonging and oneness, 184
        caring, 184-185
        fun, 185-186
        interconnectedness and interdependence culture, 181-183
        learning, 179-180
        loyalty, 183
        respect, 183-184
        trust, 180-181
    FoEs, 191
        aligning stakeholders' interests, 193-195
        blending work and play, 199-201
        breaking traditional trade-offs, 195-197
        challenging industry dogma, 192-193
        long-term perspectives, 198
        organic growth, 199
        rejecting traditional marketing models, 201
Cherry, Jeff, 16
childcare, 74
Chipotle, 225-226
Chouinard, Yvon, 240
Chubb, Hendon, 226
Chubb, Percy, 226
Chubb Corporation, 226
Churchill, Winston, 28
Cipla, 144-146, 248
Cipla Palliative Care Center, 145
citizenship, organizational vision, 176
Clean Air Act, Honda Motor Co., 151
Clean Air-Cool Planet, 153
Clement, Ronald W., 1
Clif Bar, 236
Cluetrain Manifesto, 54
Cognizant, 226-227
Colgate-Palmolive, 227

collaboration, partnerships, 132-134

Collins, Jim, 35

committed employees yield committed customers, 96-98

communication, 52-54

transparency

conduct conversations with genuine reciprocity, 57

establishing positive relationships, 54-55

foster reciprocal empathy, 55-56

showing a willingness to be vulnerable, 55

communities, nurturing local communities, 148-149

companies, selecting, 16-20

competition, concinnity, 124

competitiveness, enhancing, moral responsibilities, 149-150

complex adaptive systems, 50

complexity, 208-210

far side of complexity, 217-219

simplicity on the other side of complexity, 219

Conant, Doug, 97

Conceptual Age, xxix, 55, 102

concinnity, 8, 122-126

between competitors, 124

versus exploitation, stakeholders, 126-127

Concinnity Advisors, LP, 17

connecting top to bottom, employees, 79

Conscious Capitalism, 33

consciousness

Dove, 95-96

New Balance, 94-95

The Container Store, 243-244

fun, 71

learning culture, 179

training, 9, 76

transparency, 53, 68, 183

trust, 67-68

contracts, 21

honoring, 21-22

unspoken contracts, 21-22

Coolidge, President Calvin, 27

cooperating, with governments, moral responsibilities, 154-156

corporate alchemy, 193

corporate culture, 163

SAS Institute, 163-164

employees understand significance of their work, 166

to give is to get, 165

trust, 165-166

value people, 164-165

Southwest Airlines, 167

corporate mortality, 21

corporate nature versus human nature, 215

corporate social responsibility, 63

corporate vision, 169-170

broader purpose, 170-171

citizenship, 176

emotional intelligence (EI), 174-175

servant leadership, 172-174

corporations, history of, 154

Costco, 35-36, 227

concinnity between competitors, 124

connecting top to bottom, 79

employee compensation, 35

executive salaries, 8

human resources (HR), 81

Kirkland brand, 100

nurturing local communities, 148

organizations as living organisms, 177

rejecting traditional marketing models, 201

trust, 100

values, 179

co-ventures, 137

CRM (customer relationship management), 7

Csikszentmihalyi, Mihaly, 30
CTO (chief transformational
    officer), 218
cultivating, global community, 149
culture, 10, 166-168, 218. *See also*
    corporate culture
    business and, 28-29
    characteristics of, 179
        belonging and oneness, 184
        caring, 184-185
        fun, 185-186
        integrity and transparency,
            182-183
        interconnectedness and
            interdependence, 181
        learning, 179-180
        loyalty, 183
        respect, 183-184
        trust, 180-181
    as DNA, 186-187
    far side of complexity, 218
    nurturing organization values,
        178-179
    organizational energy, 169
    organizational vision, 169-170
        broader purpose, 170-171
        citizenship, 176
        emotional intelligence (EI),
            174-175
        servant leadership, 172-174
Culture Committee, Southwest
    Airlines, 71, 167
customer relationship management
    (CRM), 7
customer satisfaction, 9
customer service, 10
customer-centered business, 216
customers, 11
    bonding, 112-113
    committed employees yield
        committed customers, 96-98
    how not to build trust, 99-100
    loyalty, 87
Cypress Semiconductor, 135

D

Damasio, Antonio, 42
Dangi, Ajit, 146
Darwinism, 211-212
Davis, Anne, 90
Davis, Jim, 53, 82, 90-91, 130
Davis, Melinda, 88
Declaration of Interdependence,
    Whole Foods, 106-107, 213
Derby, Peter, 16
Descartes, Rene, xxx
development, 75-76
disorder, 49-50
DNA, culture, 186-187
Dobbs, Richard, 110
Dove, healing, 95-96
Dreher, Bill, 36
Driscoll's, 236
Drucker, Peter, 172, 260
Drucker Remuneration Test, 174
Dunlap, Al, 143
Dylan, Bob, 138

E

Earn and Learn, UPS, 76
Earth Watch Sabbaticals,
    Timberland, 148
East India Company, 154
Easterbrook, Gregg, xxvii
Eastman Kodak, 159
Edison, Thomas, 186
EI (emotional intelligence), 38-39,
    76, 98
    leadership, 174-175
Einstein, Albert, 5, 41, 44
emotional contracts, 21
emotional factors, 210
emotional intelligence (EI), 38-39, 76,
    98, 174-175
emotions, 7, 42-43
empathy fostering reciprocal empathy
    transparency, 55-56

employee compensation
Costco, 36
Trader Joe's, 9
employee engagement, 62
employee equity, 82
employee involvement, encouraging, 146-148
employee recruitment, selectivity, 63
employees, 11
bonding, 112-113
committed employees yield committed customers, 96-98
connecting top to bottom, 79
part-time employees, 78
passion, 65
psychological ownership, 65
understanding significance of their work, SAS Institute, 166
Employer of Choice Index, 81
empowerment, 69
encouraging, employee involvement, 146-148
environmental imbalances, 159
Environmental Internship Program, Patagonia, 63, 148
environmental standards, IKEA, 137
Erikson, Erik, 31
Eriksson, King Magnus, 154
ESG (Environmental, Societal, Governance) ratings, 261
Eskew, Michael, 183
ESOPs (employee stock ownership programs), 112
Esteve, Eduardo "Teddy", 119
Euripides, 52
executive compensation, 264
exploitation versus concinnity, stakeholders, 126-127

F

FabIndia, 248
far side of complexity, 217-219
FedEx, 228

Femina, Jerry Della, 53
FEMSA, 248
Feuerstein, Aaron, 220
financial performance, FoEs, 20
Finnegan, John, 226
Fiori, Pamela, 5
Firms of Endearment. *See* FoEs
flexibility, 71-74
FoEs (firms of endearment), 23-24
characteristics of, 191
aligning stakeholders' interests, 193-195
blending work and play, 199-201
breaking traditional trade-offs, 195-197
challenging industry dogma, 192-193
long-term perspectives, 198
organic growth, 199
rejecting traditional marketing models, 201
defined, 6-11
financial performance, 20
versus Good to Great companies, 15-16
identifying, 12-14
selecting companies, 16-20
values, 8-10
Fogel, Robert William, 33
forward-thinking companies, 213
Foundation Week, Container Store, 67
Frazier, Rick, 16, 218
interview, 257-265
Freedom with Fences, Harley-Davidson, 79
Freeman, R. Edward, 1, 35
Friedman, Milton, 32, 122, 126, 150, 220
Fromm, Eric, 30
Fukuyama, Francis, xxi, 180
fun, 70-71
culture, 185-186

Fun Committee, The Container Store,71
Future Search, 126
   Whole Foods, 193

G

Gandhi, Mahatma, 145
Gardner, Howard, 38
GE (General Electric), 34
   culture, 186
   self-organizing systems, 50
Gemalto, 249
generativity, 31
Ghosn, Carlos, 63
Gillette, 15
Gilmore, Jim, 101
Gladwell, Malcolm, xxii
global community, cultivating, 149
Global Food Safety program,
   Driscoll's, 236
Goleman, Daniel, 38, 41, 175
Good to Great companies versus
   FoEs, 15-16
Goodnight, Dr. Jim, 164
Google, 228
   20 percent time, 72
   blending work and play, 200
   corporate culture, 165
   culture of fun, 185-186
   fun, 71
   gourmet meals, 9
   long-term perspectives, 198
   marketing, 50
   marketing costs, 10
   quality-of-life benefits, 74
   recognition, 77
   team building, 68-69
Gould, Jay, 207
governments, cooperating with,
   154-156
Green Factory program, Honda
   Motor Co., 152
Greider, William, 30

growth, organic growth, 199
GSD&M, 236-237
Gutenberg, Johannes, 52

H

Hamel, Gary, 192
Hamied, Dr. K.A., 145
Hamied, Dr. Yusif, 145
Handy, Charles, 170
Harley-Davidson, 228-229
   aligning stakeholders' interests, 193
   blending work and play, 199
   connecting top to bottom, 79
   learning culture, 180
   partnerships, 129-130
   partnerships with unions, 66
   rejecting traditional marketing
      models, 201
   respect for individuals, 68
Harley-Davidson Foundation, 63
   encouraging employee involvement,
      146
Hartman, Harvey, 101
   Age of Soul, 102
Hartman Group, 101
Hawken, Paul, 33, 52
healing, 89-90
   Dove, 95-96
Heinz, 265
Hewlett-Packard, 159
Hirshberg, Gary, 242-243
HOGs (Harley Owners Group), 130
holistic thinking, 215-216
Holmes, Oliver Wendell, 209, 219
   far side of complexity, 217
Home Depot, Hurricane Katrina, 156
Honda Community Action Team
   (CAT), 147
Honda Motor Co., 82, 249
   aligning stakeholders' interests, 196
   Best Partner (BP) program, 134
   collaboration, 133-134
   connecting top to bottom, 79

open door policies, 9
REACH (Recognizing Efforts of Associates Contributing at Honda), 196
suppliers, 10
sustainability, 151-152
vulnerability, 55
Honest Tea, 237
honoring contracts, 21-22
Horgan, John, xxi
HR (human resources), 80-81
Hucksterism, 88
human nature versus corporate nature, 215
human needs, 158-160
human resources (HR), 80-81
human values, 171
versus business values, 142-144
humanistic companies, 3
humanizing the company, 9
Hurricane Katrina, private companies, 156
hybrid relationships, 112-113
hyperlife, 177

I

IBM, 132, 229
identifying FoEs, 12-14
IDEO, 65, 237
blending work and play, 201
cultivating a global community, 149
empowerment, 69
enhancing competitiveness, 150
fun, 71
quality-of-life benefits, 74
sustainability, 152
team building, 68-69
training, 76
IFBWW (International Federation of Build and Wood Workers), 150
IKEA, 249
balance and flexibility, 72
belonging and oneness, 184

caring culture, 185
concinnity, 124
cultivating a global community, 149
enhancing competitiveness, 150
environmental standards, 137
human resources (HR), 81
spirit of laws, 10
sustainability, 151
imbalances, Canon, 159
Immetl, Jeff, 34
income, psychic income, 62
income imbalances, 159
Inditex, 249-250
industry dogma, characteristics of FoEs, 192-193
intangible assets, 170, 263
integrity and transparency culture, 182-183
intensity, organizational energy, 169
interconnectedness and interdependence culture, 181
International Federation of Building and Wood Workers (IFBWW), 150
Internet, 202
Interstate Batteries, 238
interview with Rick Frazier, 257-265
investing, socially responsible investing, 259-260
investors, 11. *See also* shareholders
bonding, 112-113
pursuit of profit, 109-111
who they are, 107-109
ironic management, partnerships, 134-138

J

Jackson, Ira, 33
James, LeBron, 93
Japanese culture, interdependency, 181
Jefferson, Thomas, 219
Jesters, 200

J.M. Smucker Company, 229-230
Johnson & Johnson, 53
    Tylenol crisis, transparency, 53-54
Jordan's Furniture, 238
    aligning stakeholders' interests,
        194-195
    caring culture, 185
    concinnity between
        competitors, 124
    empowerment, 69
    fun, 71
    human resources (HR), 81
    marketing costs, 10
    rejecting traditional marketing
        models, 201
    team building, 68-69
    trust culture, 181
    values, 178
joy of work, 69-70
    balance and flexibility, 71-74
    fun, 70-71
    quality-of-life benefits, 74-75
J-team, 68-69, 71

K

Kaiser Permanente, partnerships with
    unions, 66
Kaku, Ryuzaburo, 157-158
Kamata, Satoshi, 70
Kamprad, Ingvar, belonging and
    oneness, 184
Kay, John, 142
    SIN (selfish, instrumental, and
        narrow view of business), 144
Kaymen, Samuel, 242-243
Kelleher, Herb, 66, 128, 183
    culture, 178
    fun, 71
    Jesters, 200
    leadership philosophy, 129
Kellerman, Mary, 53
Kelly, David, 71
    blending work and play, 201

Kelly, Kevin, 177
    self-organizing systems, 51
key ratios, 115
Kirkland brand, 100
Knight, Phil, 93
Koch, Jim, 113, 225
Kramer, Mark, 150
Kruse, Kevin, 97
Kurien, Dr. Varghese, 22
Kyosei, 158-160

L

labor costs, Wegmans Food Markets,
    Inc., 61
Lafley, A. G., 49
Lakoff, George, 40-41
laws, spirit of, 10
leadership
    EI (emotional intelligence), 174-175
    primal leadership, 175
leadership philosophy (Kelleher,
    Herb), 129
learning culture, 179-180
legal contracts, 21
Levinson, Daniel, 90
Levy, Pierre, xxii
life, meaning of, 2-3
Lindley, David, xxi
L.L. Bean, 65, 205, 239
    connecting top to bottom, 79
    naturalist employees, 98
    respect for individuals, 68
    self-organizing systems, 51
    trust, 99
long-term perspectives, characteristics
    of FoEs, 198
love, 87-89
    power of, 4-6
love and belonging, 158
Love and Profit, 5
Lowry, Adam, 239
loyalty, 42-44, 87, 132
    culture, 183

Loyalty Effect, 132
Lynch, Lee, 199

M

Mackey, John, 67, 107, 136, 214-215
  customer-centered business, 216
  empathy, 56
  servant leadership, 172-173
Mahindra & Mahindra, 250
management, 6
managers, quarter-to-quarter
  pressures, 111
Manpower Limited, 185
Marico, 250
market capture rate, 88
marketing, 49-50
  consciousness, 93-96
  healing, 89-90
  love, 88-89
  twentieth century, 87-88
marketing costs, 10
marketing models, rejecting
  traditional marketing models, 201
Marriot, Jr., J.W., 230
Marriott International, 230
Marx, Karl, 42
Maslow, Abraham, 31, 91, 122, 144
Maslow's Hierarchy, 158
MasterCard Worldwide, 230
materialistic values, 30
Matsushita, Konosuke, 171
Mayer, John, 38
McCormick, Chris, 239
McIntosh, Steve, xxvii
meaning of life, 2-3
mental frames, 40
Meredith Corporation Magazine
  Group, 5
Method, 239
middle age populations, 30-31
midlife, 33-34, 90-91
  New Balance, 91-93

Mid-life Transition, 91
Millennium Oncology, 239-240
Mississippi, Nissan, 63
moral responsibilities, 142-144
  cooperating with governments,
    154-156
  cultivating a global community, 149
  encouraging employee involvement,
    146-148
  enhancing competitiveness, 149-150
  nurturing local communities,
    148-149
  sustainability, 150-153
morality, 29-30
Morgan, J. P., 207
The Motley Fool, 244
Mycoskie, Blake, 245

N

The Naked Corporation, 182, 208
natural capitalism, 52
The Natural Step, IDEO, 152
negative externalities, 142
New Balance, 82, 240
  consciousness, 94-95
  encouraging employee
    involvement, 147
  flexibility, 72
  healing, 89-90
  marketing, 94
  midlife, 91-93
  partnerships, 130-131
  Rule Makers, 192
  transparency, 53, 68
  values, 91
new consciousness, 93-96
Nike, 93, 131
  Rule Makers, 192
  values, 91
Nissan, 63
Nordstrom, 230-231
  customer service, 10

Nordstrom Cares, 230-231
Northwest Airlines, 183
Novo Nordisk, 250-251
nurturing, organizational values
  through culture, 178-179
nurturing local communities, 148-149

O

Olds, Ransom E., xxvi
oneness, culture, 184
order, 158
O'Reilly, Prof. Charles, 65
Organic Exchange, Timberland, 153
organic growth, 199
organizational energy, 168-169
organizational values, 168
organizational vision, 168
  broader purpose, 170-171
  citizenship, 176
  emotional intelligence (EI), 174-175
  servant leadership, 172-174
organizations, as living organisms, 177
O'Toole, James, 209
outsourcing, 94

P

Panera, 141, 231
Panera Cares, 141, 231
Parker, James, 167
partners, 11
partnerships, 65-67
  collaboration, 132-134
  concinnity, 122-126
    stakeholders, 126-127
  Harley-Davidson, 129-130
  ironic management, 134-138
  New Balance, 130-131
  Southwest Airlines, 127-129
  with stakeholders, 127-132
  Starbucks, 121-122
part-time employees, 78
passion, employees, 65

passion zone, organizational
  energy, 169
passionate people, 9
Patagonia, 37, 65, 240
  climbing enthusiasts, 98
  Environmental Internship Program,
    63, 148
  flexibility, 72
  loyalty, 42
  passionate people, 9
  quality-of-life benefits, 74
  respect, 183-184
  respect for individuals, 68
  social responsibility, 137
  sustainability, 153
Path of Service, Timberland, 148
pay-what-you-can cafes, Panera
  Cares, 141
P/E ratios, 115
people, valuing (SAS Institute),
  164-165
People Department, Southwest
  Airlines, 80
Perry, John, 29
personality development, xxvii
Pfeffer, Prof. Jeffrey, 66
pharmaceutical companies, Cipla,
  144-146
philanthropy, 260
Pine, Joe, 101
Pink, Daniel, xxix, 2, 5, 33
  Conceptual Age, 102
  empathy, 55
Pohlenz, Erwin, 119-121
Pollard, C. William, 172
Pollution Prevention Pays, 3M, 223
Polman, Paul, 252
Port of Portland (Oregon), 149
Porter, Michael, 150
POSCO, 251
positive sum thinking, 212
power of love, 4-6
prAna, 241
Prigogine, Ilya, xxi

primal leadership, 175
Primal Leadership: Realizing the
  Power of Emotional Intelligence, 39
Prime Tanning Co., 131
private companies
  cooperating with governments, 155
  Hurricane Katrina, 156
profit, 209
  investors, 109-111
psychic income, 62
psychological contracts, 21
psychological ownership,
  employees, 65
Purdy, Kenneth, 131
Purple Promise, FedEx, 228
purpose, organizational vision,
  170-171
The Purpose Driven Life, 29
pursuit of profit, investors, 109-111

Q

Qualcomm, 231
quality, organizational energy, 169
quality-of-life benefits, 74-75
quantitative investment products, 262
quarter-to-quarter pressures, 111

R

ratios, key ratios, 115
REACH (Recognizing Efforts of
  Associates Contributing at Honda),
  Honda Motor Co., 196
Rebels, 199-200
reciprocity, conducting conversations
  with, 57
recognition, 77
REI, 63, 65, 241
  connecting top to bottom, 79
  respect for individuals, 68
Reichheld, Frederick, 43, 109, 183
Reiter, J. Miles, 236

rejecting traditional marketing
  models, 201
relationships
  establishing positive relationships,
    transparency, 54-55
  hybrid relationships, 112-113
relaxed concentration, 70
resonance, 175
respect, culture, 183-184
respect for individuals, 68
returns
  calculating, 114
  shareholder returns, 113-114
  U.S. FoE Returns, 116
Riley, William J., 89
robber barons, 207
Roberts, Kevin, 6, 22, 124
Rockefeller, John D., 207
Roddick, Anita, 57
Rodgers, T.J., 135-136, 213-214
Rule Breakers, 192
Rule Makers, 192
Rule Takers, 192
Ryan, Claude, 205
Ryan, Eric, 239

S

Saatchi & Saatchi, 6
safety and security, 158
salaries, Costco, 8
Salovey, Peter, 38
Samuel Adams, Boston Beer
  Company, 225
Sanders, Tim, 6, 124
Santa Teresa, 119-121
SAS Institute, 163-164, 241-242
  employees understand significance
    of their work, 166
  to give is to get, 165
  human resources (HR), 81
  trust, 165-166
  value people, 164-165

SC Johnson, 242
Schaefer, Bill, 132
Schein, Edgar H., 21
Schlumberger, 232
Schueth, Steven J., 108
Schultz, Howard, 122
    belonging and oneness, 184
Secretan, Lance, 185
selecting companies, 16-20
selectivity, employee recruitment, 63
self-actualization, 31-32, 34, 90-91,
    122, 128, 159
    capitalism, 29-34
self-assessment, 218
self-awareness, 38
self-interest, 122
self-organizing systems, 50-51
Semco, balance and flexibility, 72-74
Semler, Ricardo, 72-74, 218
Senegal, Jim, 8
Senge, Peter, 52
servant leadership, corporate vision,
    172-174
Service Sabbaticals, Timberland, 148
Shadders, Karen, 60
Shaich, Ron, 141
share of wallet, 7
shareholder returns, 113-114
    U.S. FoE Returns, 116
shareholders, 8, 143. *See also*
    investors
        bonding, 112-113
        versus stakeholders, 34-37
        Whole Foods, 106-107
simplicity on the other side of
    complexity, 219
Simpson, David, xxi
SIN (selfish, instrumental, and narrow
    view of business), 144
Sinegal, Jim, 100
Sloan, Alfred P., xxvi
Smith, Adam, xxiv, 33, 42, 214-215
Smith, Fred, 228

social actualization, 90
social agenda, 208
social benevolence, 206-207
social responsibility, 63
    Patagonia, 137
social transformation, capitalism, 4
social welfare, 156
socially responsible investing, 259-260
society, 11
soulfulness, 101-102
Southwest Airlines, 232, 265
    aligning stakeholders' interests, 193
    balance and flexibility, 72
    blending work and play, 200
    caring culture, 185
    challenging industry dogma, 193
    culture, 10, 178
    Culture Committee, 167
    empowerment, 69
    fun, 71, 185-186
    loyalty, 183
    partnerships, 127-129
    partnerships with unions, 66
    People Department, 80
    recognition, 77
    self-organizing systems, 51
    training, 76
    turnover, 9
Southwick, Karen, 30
SpeakUp, L.L. Bean, 79
SPICE stakeholders, 11-12
Spiers-Lopez, Pernille, 72, 124
    human resources (HR), 81
spirit of laws, 10
spirituality, xxiii
SRM (stakeholder relationship
    management), 2, 35, 37, 106
stakeholder-based business models, 2
stakeholders, 11-12, 143
    aligning interests, 193-195
        Honda Motor Co., 196
    concinnity versus exploitation,
        126-127
    holistic thinking, 216

partnerships with, 127-132
versus shareholders, 34-37
Starbucks, 120, 232-233
belonging and oneness, 184
C.A.F.E. (Coffee and Farmer
Equity) Practices, 120-121
marketing, 50
partnerships, 121-122
sustainability, 153
Stark, Myra, 2
Steinem, Gloria, 126
Stonyfield Yogurt, 242-243
culture, 10
Stoppard, Tom, xxi, 49
Stora Kopparberg mining
community, 154
suppliers, 10
Surace, Lee, 99
sustainability, moral responsibilities,
150-153
Swartz, Jeffery, xxiii, 72, 207-208,
218, 244

T

T. Rowe Price, 233
Taj Mahal hotel, 206
Tapscott, Don, 182, 208, 213
Tata, Jamshedji, 206
Tata Group, 206
Taylor, Frederick Winslow, xxvi
TCS (Tata Consultancy Services), 251
TDIndustries, 243
team building, 68-69
Teerlink, Richard, 129
Texas Instruments, 159
The Theory of Moral Sentiments, 42
Ticoll, David, 182, 208, 213
Timberland, 72, 244
Path of Service, 148
quality-of-life benefits, 74
social benevolence, 207
sustainability, 153

to give is to get, SAS Institute, 165
TOMS, 245
Toro, emotional contracts, 22
Toyota, 70, 251
belonging and oneness, 184
cooperating with governments, 155
corporate vision, 171
culture, 186
human resources (HR), 81
nurturing local communities, 149
quality-of-life benefits, 74
respect, 183-184
social benevolence, 207
training, 76
trust culture, 180
Toyota Production System,
interconnectedness and
interdependence culture, 181
trade imbalances, 159
trade-offs, breaking traditional
trade-offs, 195-197
Trader Joe's, 65, 245
breaking traditional trade-offs, 197
career ladders, 65
empathy, 56
employee compensation, 9
team building, 68-69
values, 178
Trafford, Abigail, 91
training, 75-76
The Container Store, 9
transparency, 53
communication, 52-54
*conduct conversations with
genuine reciprocity, 57
foster reciprocal empathy,
55-56
showing a willingness to be
vulnerable, 55*
culture, 182-183
establishing positive relationships,
54-55
trust, 68

Triggers: 30 Sales Tools You Can Use to Control the Mind of Your Prospect to Motivate, Influence and Persuade, 88
triple bottom line, 32
Truly Human Leadership, 77
trust
    building, 67-68
        empowerment, 69
        respect for individuals, 68
        team building, 68-69
        transparency, 68
    culture, 180-181
    how not to build trust, 99-100
    SAS Institute, 165-166
turnover, 9, 82
Tylenol crisis, 53

U

Unilever, 252
Union Square Hospitality Group, 246
unions, 128
    Harley-Davidson, 129-130
    partnerships, 65-67
University for People, Southwest Airlines, 76
unspoken contracts, 21-22
UPS, 37, 205, 233
    aligning stakeholders' interests, 194
    belonging and oneness, 184
    human resources (HR), 81
    part-time employees, 78
    training, 76
U.S. Airways, 183
U.S. FoE Returns, 116
USAA, 246
    empathy, 56

V

Valero, Hurricane Katrina, 156
values
    FoEs, 8-10
    nurturing organization values, through culture, 178-179
valuing, people, SAS Institute, 164-165
Vanderbilt, Cornelius, 207
Vanderbilt, William Henry, 143, 207
Virelli, Christine, 78
virtuous cycle, 258
vision. *See* corporate vision
vulnerability, transparency, 55

W

Waigaya, Honda Motor Co., 55
waigaya, Honda, 79
Wall Street analysts, perspective, 198
Wallace, Mike, 54
Walmart, Hurricane Katrina, 156
Walt Disney, 234
Warren, Rick, 29
Watson, John, xxvi
Wegman, Danny, 60
    challenging industry dogma, 193
Wegman, Robert, 61
Wegman, Walter, 61
Wegmans Food Markets, Inc., 37, 59-61, 65, 246-247
    challenging industry dogma, 193
    customer satisfaction, 9
    labor costs, 61
    loyalty, 183
    organic growth, 199
    part-time employees, 78
    partnerships, 68
    passion, 98

Welch, Jack, 32
Whole Foods Market, 30, 66, 136
  aligning interests, 8, 193
  Declaration of Interdependence,
  106-107, 213
  economic ecosystem, 51
  employee enthusiasm, 98
  servant leadership, 172-173
  organic products, 102
  partnership, 66-67
  respect, 184
  shareholders, 106-107
  stakeholder collaboration, 126
WL Gore, 247
Woods, Tiger, 93
worldviews, 40-41
Wright, Robert, 212

X-Y-Z

Zen, investing, 109-111
zero sum mindset, 211-212